A PRACTITIONER'S GUIDE TO THE AIM RULES

A PRACTITIONER'S GUIDE TO THE AIM RULES

Consultant Editor
Hugh Maule
Lawrence Graham LLP

Fourth Edition

City & Financial Publishing

City & Financial Publishing
8 Westminster Court, Hipley Street
Old Woking
Surrey GU22 9LG
United Kingdom
Tel: 00 44 (0)1483 720707 Fax: 00 44 (0)1483 727928
Web: www.cityandfinancial.com

This book has been compiled from the contributions of the named authors. The views expressed herein do not necessarily reflect the views of their respective firms. Further, since this book is intended as a general guide only, its application to specific situations will depend upon the particular circumstances involved and it should not be relied upon as a substitute for obtaining appropriate professional advice.

This book is current as at 1 November 2005. Whilst all reasonable care has been taken in the preparation of this book, City & Financial Publishing and the authors do not accept responsibility for any errors it may contain or for any loss sustained by any person placing reliance on its contents.

ISBN 1 905121 024
© 2006 City & Financial Publishing and the authors.

British Library Cataloguing-in-Publication Data. A catalogue record for this book is available from the British Library.

*Typeset by Cambrian Typesetters, Camberley
and printed and bound in Great Britain by Biddles Limited, King's Lynn.*

Biographies

Martin Graham is the Director of Market Services at the London Stock Exchange and Head of AIM, the Exchange's global market for smaller, growing companies. Martin is responsible for the market-facing functions within the Exchange, as well as the development of domestic and international markets services including client relationships, market operations, market regulation and RNS, the Exchange's regulatory news service. This division comprises approximately 250 staff and accounts for more than half of the Exchange's turnover. Martin is a Board member of FTSE International and the Indo-British Partnership.

Nick Williams is a Corporate Partner based in the London office of the international law firm, Hammonds. He acts for issuers and their advisers on IPOs and secondary offerings on AIM and the Official List. He has substantial experience of public and private M&A transactions and advises companies on their corporate affairs, including corporate governance. Nick also has experience of corporate reorganisations and joint ventures and establishing fund structures.

Tim Davis is the Head of Marketing for Charles Stanley's Corporate Finance & Broking Division. He is responsible for all aspects of marketing and a range of business development activities, all focused upon smaller quoted companies. Prior to this, he was Marketing Director of stockbrokers Teather & Greenwood; and managing director of the financial services division of an investor and public relations consultancy.

Linda Main is a Partner in KPMG LLP. She joined KPMG in 1984. She has specialised in IPOs since 1997 and she also has wide experience of other types of transactions. Linda spent two years on secondment to the Listing Group of the London Stock Exchange (now the UK Listing Authority) advising on the application of Listing Rules.

Hugh Maule is a Partner at Lawrence Graham LLP where he specialises in corporate finance. Hugh did a law degree at Cambridge University before joining Lawrence Graham as a trainee in 1989. Shortly after qualifying he spent 18 months at Credit Suisse in

London working as part of the bank's debt recovery team. Hugh's experience covers a wide area from acting for a number of entrepreneurs on public and private company work through to buying and selling companies and flotation and secondary issue work, although his principal focus is AIM.

John Bennett is a Departmental Managing Partner at Berwin Leighton Paisner. John is Head of the firm's Corporate department which was ranked in the top tier for domestic flotations, including AIM work, in the 2005 edition of *Legal 500* and was ranked first for mid-market deals in the 2006 edition of *Chambers UK, A Client's Guide to the Legal Profession*. He specialises in corporate finance and mergers and acquisitions. John is named as a leading corporate lawyer in *Chambers UK* and is a member of the City of London Law Society Company Law Committee.

Emma Bulleyment is an Associate in the corporate department of Memery Crystal. She has been involved in a number of domestic and international corporate transactions, including flotations, secondary fundraisings, and both public and private mergers, acquisitions and disposals.

Andrew Titmas is a Partner in the corporate department of Memery Crystal. He advises investors, companies and brokers on a wide range of domestic and international corporate transactions, including flotations, equity issues, public take-overs, joint ventures and private acquisitions and disposals. He qualified as a solicitor in 1996, joining Memery Crystal in 1998, before becoming a Partner in 2003.

Richard Collins is one of the founding directors of the Deloitte Corporate Finance real estate team. He has worked in corporate finance for over nine years having started at BZW after qualifying as an A.C.A.

Whilst at Deloitte, Richard has completed many transactions in the real estate sector, including fundraisings, restructurings and acquisitions, and is currently involved in two disposal mandates in the sector. Richard is also currently advising on the establishment of a UK commercial property fund.

Richard is a member of the London First Housing Committee.

Anthony Gordon is a Partner at Faegre & Benson LLP, the international law firm, in London and specialises in corporate finance. He joined the firm as a trainee in 1989 and qualified in 1991. Anthony has substantial experience advising international companies joining AIM having been involved with flotations of Australian, US, Canadian and Israeli companies. He advises companies, nominated advisers and brokers in relation to admissions to AIM and secondary issues.

Melanie Wadsworth is a Senior Associate in the corporate department of Faegre & Benson LLP. She has wide experience of M&A transactions, acting for domestic and international clients, but a significant part of her practice comprises public company work, including flotations, secondary fundraisings and public-to-private takeovers for clients of all sizes and in a variety of sectors and domiciles. The principal focus of Melanie's public company practice is AIM and she is particularly interested in the growing importance of corporate governance issues and how these are best addressed by AIM companies. Melanie is a member of the Corporate Governance Committee of the Quoted Companies Alliance.

Chilton Taylor is a Corporate Finance Partner and Head of Capital Markets at Baker Tilly who have been voted AIM Accountants of the Year for the three successive years 2003–2005 in the Growth Company Awards. He is a graduate of Cambridge University and qualified at KPMG in 1977. He has over 25 years of corporate finance experience specialising in flotations, due diligence and fund raising. He has acted on over 80 flotations. He is a specialist on AIM IPOs and is the only accountant invited to the AIM Advisory Group of the London Stock Exchange. Although a corporate finance partner, he is an acknowledged specialist in the VCT and EIS legislation and is the author of *"A Guide to AIM Tax Benefits"* a joint publication of Baker Tilly and the London Stock Exchange.

John Wakefield is a Director and Head of Corporate Finance at Rowan Dartington & Co. Limited.

John was educated at Oxford University, following which he became a university lecturer and subsequently qualified and practised for five years as a solicitor with McKenna & Co., (now CMS Cameron McKenna) specialising in company and corporate work. In 1985 he joined stockbrokers Williams de Broe, in London and was instrumental in establishing their newly formed corporate finance department. He has considerable experience of sourcing capital for companies and has been involved in over 50 company flotations. He joined Rowan Dartington as a director in 1991, participating as a founder shareholder in its subsequent buy-out in 1992.

He was a member of the London Stock Exchange AIM Advisory Group from 2000–2004 and is the author of chapters on the Trading Rules of AIM and the Official List in two Practitioners' Manuals.

Andrew Whalley is a Senior Solicitor specialising in corporate finance with the international law firm, Hammonds. He is based in the London office and has broad experience of acting for listed and private companies on flotations, fundraising and public and private M&A transactions. He also advises on joint ventures, corporate reorganisations and corporate governance.

Jane Tuckley has been a Partner in Travers Smith's Financial Services and Markets Group since 1997. She advises on a broad range of financial services and regulatory matters, both to authorised firms and market infrastructure providers. Jane is a member of the team at Travers Smith which advises CRESTCo, with particular responsibility for CRESTCo's international service and the CREST corporate actions framework. She also worked with CRESTCo in developing a settlement solution for overseas AIM traded companies whose securities are ineligible for the CREST international service.

Contents

Biographies   v

1 AIM   1
Martin Graham
Head of AIM
London Stock Exchange Plc

1.1 Introduction   1
1.2 A successful market for smaller growth
     companies   1
1.3 A change of status   2
1.4 The role of the Nomad   2
1.5 Checking whether companies are appropriate for
     AIM   3
1.6 Ongoing role of a Nomad after admission   4
1.7 The AIM Rules   4
1.8 Expedited admission: companies traded on other
     major markets   5
1.9 Further information   5

**2 An Overview of The AIM Rules, Eligible Companies,
   their Directors and the Role of the Exchange**   7
Nick Williams
Partner
Hammonds

2.1 Introduction   7
2.2 Eligible companies   11
2.3 Directors and employees   18
2.4 Provision and disclosure of information   22
2.5 Sanctions   23
2.6 Cancellation of admission at the request of the
     AIM company   25
2.7 Conclusion   27

3   The Role of the Nominated Adviser   29
.   Tim Davis
Head of Marketing
Charles Stanley Corporate Finance & Broking

3.1   Introduction   29
3.2   Nominated advisers' responsibilities to the
       Exchange   30
3.3   Approval of nominated advisers   31
3.4   The identity of nominated advisers   32
3.5   Retention of a nominated adviser   32
3.6   Minimum criteria for approval as a nominated
       adviser   32
3.7   Nominated adviser's agreement   38
3.8   Nominated adviser's responsibilities on admission
       of securities   42
3.9   Sanctions and appeals (Rules 42–45)   43
3.10 Conclusion   44

4   The Role of the Accountant   45
Linda Main
Partner
KPMG LLP

4.1   Introduction   45
4.2   Accountants' long form report   45
4.3   Presentation of financial information in the
       admission document   46
4.4   Pro forma financial information   49
4.5   Working capital   50
4.6   Financial reporting procedures   51
4.7   Other comfort letters   51
4.8   Other requirements of the Prospectus Directive   52
4.9   Conclusion   52

5   The Role of the Solicitor   53
Hugh Maule
Partner
Lawrence Graham LLP

5.1   Introduction   53
5.2   Solicitors to the company   53

5.3	Pre-flotation legal due diligence	54
5.4	Pre-flotation corporate matters	59
5.5	The admission document and the verification of its contents	60
5.6	Placing/underwriting or introduction agreement	62
5.7	Directors' service contracts	65
5.8	Employee share participation	65
5.9	Directors' duties and responsibilities on flotation and afterwards	66
5.10	Nominated adviser agreement and broker agreement	67
5.11	General advice on the flotation given by the solicitors to the company	68
5.12	Solicitors to the issue	69
5.13	Conclusion	70

6 The Statutory Framework 71

John Bennett
Partner
Berwin Leighton Paisner LLP

6.1	Introduction	71
6.2	Legislation	73
6.3	The new prospectus regime and AIM companies	78
6.4	Format of an admission document	81
6.5	Content requirements for an admission document	81
6.6	Filing and publication requirements	83
6.7	Supplementary admission documents and withdrawal rights	84
6.8	Further admission documents and secondary issues	84
6.9	Responsibility for admission document	85
6.10	Liability	85
6.11	Financial promotion	86
6.12	The future	87

**7   The Admission Document and the Application
     Procedure**   **89**
     Andrew Titmas
     Partner
     Emma Bulleyment
     Associate
     Memery Crystal

7.1   Introduction   89
7.2   AIM Rules   89
7.3   The nominated adviser and broker   90
7.4   Initial steps   91
7.5   Admission document   92
7.6   Legal considerations   97
7.7   Verification   99
7.8   Due diligence   100
7.9   Financial and accounting procedures   102
7.10   Legal restructuring   104
7.11   Shareholder resolutions   105
7.12   Employee share schemes   106
7.13   The board and corporate governance   106
7.14   Placing agreement   107
7.15   Directors' documents   109
7.16   Financial public relations   111
7.17   Application   112
7.18   Costs and timing   113
7.19   Conclusion   113

8   Continuing Obligations and Transactions   **115**
     Richard Collins
     Director
     Deloitte & Touche LLP

8.1   Introduction   115
8.2   Announcements   115
8.3   General disclosure obligations   116
8.4   Financial reporting   122
8.5   Transactions   124
8.6   Further share issues   129
8.7   The City Code on Takeovers and Mergers   130
8.8   Other eligibility requirements and restrictions   130

8.9	Sanctions and appeals	134
8.10	Conclusion	134

9 Directors' Dealings and Corporate Governance   **135**
Anthony Gordon
Partner
Melanie Wadsworth
Associate
Faegre & Benson LLP

9.1	Directors' dealings	135
9.2	Corporate governance	145
9.3	AIM companies and the Code	152
9.4	Conclusion	159

10 The Tax Regime   **161**
Chilton Taylor
Partner
Head of Capital Markets
Baker Tilly

10.1	Introduction	161
10.2	Enterprise Investment Scheme and Venture Capital Trusts	162
10.3	Common problems	170
10.4	Location of trade	176
10.5	Obtaining clearance	177
10.6	Capital gains tax ("CGT")	179
10.7	Corporate Venturing Scheme	185
10.8	Loss relief	188

11 The Broker and the Trading Rules   **191**
John Wakefield
Director and Head of Corporate Finance
Rowan Dartington & Co Limited

11.1	Introduction	191
11.2	The trading system	191
11.3	Information requirements	193
11.4	The market practitioners	196
11.5	Liquidity	199

11.6	The after-market	201
11.7	Relations with investors	202
11.8	Reporting and settlement	202
11.9	Market regulation	203
11.10	Information about AIM companies	210
11.11	Conclusion	210

12 Overseas Companies and the Fast-track Route   **213**
Nick Williams
Partner
Andrew Whalley
Senior Solicitor
Hammonds

12.1	Introduction	213
12.2	Why might an overseas company choose AIM?	213
12.3	How successful has AIM been in attracting overseas companies?	214
12.4	Legal and regulatory considerations for overseas companies	216
12.5	The fast-track route for certain companies quoted on AIM Designated Markets	218

13 Settlement Arrangements – CREST   **225**
Jane Tuckley
Partner
Travers Smith

13.1	Introduction	225
13.2	What is CREST?	225
13.3	The CREST legal framework	226
13.4	Admitting domestic securities to CREST	227
13.5	The relationship between the AIM company and CREST	230
13.6	Overseas securities – depository interests	232
13.7	Conclusion	241

Appendices		**243**
Appendix 1	AIM Admission Document	245
Appendix 2	Specimen AIM Documents List	305

Appendix 3   AIM Admission Timetable   311
Appendix 4   Specimen AIM Completion Board Minutes   321
Appendix 5   Application to be signed by the Company   341
Appendix 6   Declaration by the Nominated Adviser   347

Index   **351**

Chapter 1

AIM

Martin Graham
Head of AIM
London Stock Exchange Plc

1.1 Introduction

AIM, the London Stock Exchange's international market for smaller, growing companies, was launched in June 1995. Designed to be as flexible as possible to meet the needs of its companies, AIM has no minimum requirement relating to a company's track record, there is no minimum size and no minimum number of shareholders. AIM is open to companies from many different sectors and countries around the world.

1.2 A successful market for smaller growth companies

At the time of writing, more than 1,300 companies were quoted on AIM, and since its launch in 1995 companies on the market have raised €28 billion through a combination of new and further issues. More companies trade on AIM than all of the other European growth markets put together and it is the most international of all growth markets with more than 160 overseas companies.

The continued growth in trading of AIM securities was boosted by the introduction in May 2005 of a new FTSE AIM Index Series comprising the FTSE AIM UK 50 Index, the FTSE AIM 100 Index and the FTSE AIM All-Share Index. The objective of these indices is to provide greater transparency to investors, to attract additional investment in AIM and to improve the liquidity of underlying AIM companies.

1.3 A change of status

In October 2004, AIM changed its regulatory status to become an exchange-regulated market. This change was designed to preserve the current regulatory structure and maintain the market's flexibility whilst retaining the high standards of regulation that have played such an important part in AIM's development.

1.4 The role of the Nomad

All prospective and existing AIM companies must appoint and retain an approved nominated adviser ("Nomad"). These Nomads are responsible for warranting to the Exchange that a company is appropriate for AIM, and for advising the company to ensure it complies with its obligations under the AIM Rules. A company must retain a Nomad at all times.

The AIM admission process is very straightforward and probably the least bureaucratic of any global market. Ordinarily, when a Nomad declares to the Exchange that a company is appropriate for AIM, that company will be admitted to AIM by the Exchange three days later. It is hard to conceive of a more streamlined system. During the three-day period, the Exchange will set up all the necessary trading systems and notify various interested internal and external parties (such as market makers and index compilers) about a company's imminent admission.

In effect, Nomads act as the principal quality controllers for the market and put their reputations on the line when declaring companies suitable for the market. Consequently, as outlined below, they will carry out exhaustive due diligence checks alongside other advisers on companies before they agree to sign such a declaration, and as such are crucial to the success of AIM.

Given the importance of the role and the level of trust imparted to Nomads, the Exchange is very selective about who it will allow to act in this capacity. Only those advisers approved by the Exchange and placed on the Register of Nominated Advisers may act as Nomads. A copy of this register is available on the AIM section of the Exchange's website, www.londonstockexchange.com.

The background of the Nomads varies and they include:

(a) investment banks;
(b) the corporate finance arm of small and mid cap specialists or accountancy firms; and
(c) corporate finance boutiques.

The Exchange welcomes applications from suitable advisers from around the world.

However, in order to be approved all Nomads must meet the Exchange's "Nominated Adviser Eligibility Criteria". These are set out in full on the Exchange's website. Broadly, the minimum criteria require that a prospective Nomad must have undertaken, as a named principal corporate finance adviser, at least three major transactions on major Stock Exchanges and retain at least four similarly qualified full-time executives. Most importantly, the adviser must be able to demonstrate that it has a sound reputation for corporate finance.

Nomads have a number of specific responsibilities under the eligibility criteria. Above all, they have a duty to protect the reputation and integrity of the market. In short, this means that in addition to discharging their obligations under any specific rules, the adviser should use all reasonable endeavours to seek to ensure that the companies for which it acts conduct themselves in ways which befit companies that have their securities traded on a respected public market.

Nomads are subject to regular reviews by the Exchange and those who have failed to act with proper skill and care may be subject to one of the sanctions available to the Exchange.

1.5 Checking whether companies are appropriate for AIM

Nomads are responsible for coordinating the due diligence work of other advisers including the accountants and lawyers involved in the transaction. This due diligence covers areas such as the background and qualifications of the company's directors, the company's financial position and the statements which the directors make about the company's prospects and future strategy.

Financial due diligence will be carried out by suitably qualified accountants, and legal due diligence by appropriate lawyers. Should the company operate in a specific sector, such as mining, a specialist report may be commissioned to support the assertions and strategy which the company proposes to include in its admission document.

1.6   Ongoing role of a Nomad after admission

The second and in some ways most important responsibility of the Nomad is the role it plays in advising companies on the interpretation of the AIM Rules following admission. In nearly all cases, companies admitted to AIM will have no experience of public markets and will need help to understand what their obligations are as a public entity. Nomads will normally charge a flat fee for this ongoing service and it is in the interests of directors and their shareholders to ensure that they make full use of their Nomad once on the market.

1.7   The AIM Rules

The AIM Rules do not use legal or technical jargon and they are designed to be accessible to all types of companies including those from overseas. The AIM Rules are available on the Exchange's website with definitions and guidance notes to assist in the understanding of individual rules.

Generally, a company seeking admission to AIM will be required to produce an admission document, which will contain disclosures about areas such as background on the company's directors, the company's strategy, its financial position and its working capital. The contents required for an AIM admission document are based on a standard known as "AIM-PD" which is itself based on the Prospectus Directive, the standard applied to companies seeking admission of their securities to an EU Regulated Market and the standard applied to any company carrying out a public offer above certain thresholds. AIM-PD was introduced by the Exchange in July 2005 and is based on the contents of the Prospectus Directive with certain sections "carved out" as they were deemed unnecessary or too onerous for smaller companies.

Once admitted to AIM, a company will be required to disclose certain matters on an ongoing basis, such as major contracts, the appointment of directors and any matter which may be price sensitive.

Both the admission rules and the continuing obligations for AIM companies are based upon the principle of timely disclosure. Any failure to disclose material changes to a company's circumstances will be treated very seriously by the Exchange.

1.8 Expedited admission: companies traded on other major markets

In May 2003, the Exchange introduced a streamlined admission route for companies that have been admitted to certain overseas markets. These are NYSE, NASDAQ, Toronto Stock Exchange, Euronext, Deutsche Börse, Australian Stock Exchange, JSE Securities Exchange South Africa, the London Stock Exchange Main Market, the Swiss Exchange and Stockholmbörsen.

Provided that companies are admitted to the main boards of these markets and have been admitted for at least 18 months, they may be exempted from the need to publish an AIM admission document. Instead, prior to admission they will be required to make a substantive announcement to the market about their working capital position, their strategy and certain other matters. In addition, they will require a Nomad to warrant their appropriateness for AIM. Several companies have availed themselves of this facility and the Exchange believes that it provides a cost-effective route for qualifying companies to obtain a complementary quotation on AIM.

1.9 Further information

Updated information on recent and forthcoming admissions, trading statistics, company announcements, Nomads, conferences and events is available on the Exchange's website.

As AIM begins another 10 years, it does so in good health with a regulatory regime that continues to provide the flexibility and simplicity desired by smaller companies. The Exchange is committed to ensuring that the AIM Rules remain as concise and clear as possible, helping to reinforce AIM's reputation as the most attractive market anywhere in the world for smaller, growing companies.

Chapter 2

An Overview of The AIM Rules, Eligible Companies, their Directors and the Role of the Exchange

Nick Williams

Partner
Hammonds

2.1 Introduction

The rules applying to companies wishing to obtain and maintain a listing for their shares on AIM ("the AIM Rules") are published by the London Stock Exchange plc ("the Exchange"). As a result of widespread consultation prior to AIM's launch regarding the needs of growing companies, the Exchange has set accessible entry requirements and relatively relaxed continuing obligations. This is evidenced by the brevity of the AIM Rules as compared to the Listing Rules for companies listed (or applying to be listed) on the Official List. The current version of the AIM Rules and other relevant information are available on the Exchange's website at www.londonstockexchange.com.

Also relevant are the Rules of the London Stock Exchange which regulate trading in AIM securities. These are considered in Chapter 11.

The relatively relaxed regulatory regime is made possible by the requirement that each company applying and admitted to AIM appoints a nominated adviser. The nominated adviser is a professional firm that complies with the eligibility criteria published by the Exchange, and the adviser is responsible to the Exchange. It is the nominated adviser's obligation to take appropriate steps to ensure that the directors of a company applying for the first time to have a class of its securities admitted to AIM ("applicant company") or of a company with a class of its securities admitted to AIM ("AIM company") are aware of their responsibilities and obligations under the AIM Rules and that each such company complies with those Rules. In turn, the directors are required to seek advice from the nominated adviser and to take that advice into account. The nominated adviser is also required to confirm to the Exchange that it considers an applicant company and its securities to be "appropriate" for admission when that applicant company and its securities are first admitted to trading on AIM ("admission"). The Exchange has the power to impose sanctions on the company and the nominated adviser.

The AIM Rules comprise the following:

- Eligibility for AIM (Rule 1): the requirement for an applicant company to appoint a nominated adviser.
- Applicants for AIM (Rules 2–6): a description of the information (the "pre-admission announcement") and documents, including the principal document published at the time of admission (the "admission document"), which must be provided to the Exchange prior to admission, and an explanation of when admission becomes effective.
- Special conditions for certain applicants (Rules 7–9): a requirement for the related parties and applicable employees as at the date of admission of an applicant company whose main activity is a business which has not been independent and earning revenue for at least two years to retain any of that company's AIM securities they hold for one year from admission; a condition that investing companies raise a minimum of £3 million in cash; and provision for the Exchange to make admission subject to a special condition and to delay or refuse admission in certain circumstances.
- Principles of disclosure (Rule 10): the procedures for announcing information through a regulatory information service to the market.
- General disclosure of price-sensitive information (Rule 11): a requirement for an AIM company to announce price-sensitive information (information which, if made public, would be likely

8

to lead to a substantial movement in the price of its AIM securities) through a regulatory information service.

- Disclosure of corporate transactions (Rules 12–16): a description of the requirements for disclosure and approval of significant and related party transactions.
- Disclosure of miscellaneous information (Rule 17): matters that must be announced through a regulatory information service without delay.
- Half-yearly reports (Rule 18): an AIM company has to prepare half-yearly financial reports.
- Annual accounts (Rule 19): the requirements for audited annual accounts of an AIM company.
- Publication of documents sent to shareholders (Rule 20): rules for publication and availability of documents provided to holders of AIM securities.
- Restriction on deals (Rule 21): restrictions on dealing by directors and applicable employees in AIM securities, or the sale of any AIM securities held as treasury shares, and on the purchase or early redemption of AIM securities, or sale of AIM securities held as treasury shares by an AIM company.
- Provision and disclosure of information (Rules 22 and 23): the ability of the Exchange to require or disclose information.
- Corporate action timetables (Rules 24 and 25): the procedures whereby an AIM company must inform the Exchange in advance of any announcement of a timetable for proposed action affecting the rights of shareholders.
- Further issues of securities following admission (Rules 26 and 28–29): requirements where further securities are issued by an AIM company following its admission.
- Language (Rule 30): all relevant documents to be in English.
- Directors' responsibility for compliance (Rule 31): the directors of an AIM company are responsible for compliance with the AIM Rules, disclosing relevant information and seeking advice from the nominated adviser.
- Ongoing eligibility requirements (Rules 32–38): requirements to be met by an AIM company on and following admission.
- Nominated advisers (Rule 39): responsibilities of nominated advisers.
- Maintenance of orderly markets (Rules 40 and 41): circumstances in which the Exchange may suspend trading or cancel

the admission of AIM securities and in which an AIM company may cancel admission of its AIM securities.

- Sanctions and appeals (Rules 42–45): disciplinary action that the Exchange may take against an AIM company or a nominated adviser.
- Schedule 1: information which an applicant company or quoted applicant (*see* 2.2 below) must provide to the Exchange pursuant to Rule 2.
- Schedule 2: information that must be disclosed in an admission document.
- Schedules 3 and 4: the "class tests" for determining the size of a transaction pursuant to Rules 12, 13, 14, 15 and 19, and information which must be announced through a regulatory information service pursuant to Rules 12, 13, 14 and 15.
- Schedule 5: information on deals by directors (and relevant changes to significant shareholders) which must be announced through a regulatory information service pursuant to Rule 17.
- Schedules 6 and 7: confirmations required in relation to applicant companies, AIM companies and quoted applicants from a nominated adviser pursuant to Rule 39.
- Schedule 8: information that an AIM company must announce through a regulatory information service in relation to a block admission.
- Schedule 9: the information in respect of shares taken in and out of treasury which is required to be notified under Rule 17.
- Glossary: containing meanings of defined terms used in the AIM Rules.

Guidance Notes are also published by the Exchange and these do not form part of the Rules but are intended to assist in their interpretation.

Where an AIM company has concerns about the interpretation of the Rules it should consult its nominated adviser.

The term "AIM securities", as used in the AIM Rules, encompasses the different types and classes of shares and other securities which are admitted to trading on AIM.

2.2   Eligible companies

In contrast to the Official List's requirements (with certain exceptions) for a company to have a three-year trading record, a minimum market capitalisation of £700,000 and 25 per cent of its shares publicly held, AIM's admission requirements permit young and growing companies from around the world with limited or no trading records to join the market. In addition, the Exchange is not involved in considering whether a company is suitable for admission to AIM. This responsibility is placed on the nominated adviser. A company whose securities have been traded for at least 18 months prior to applying to AIM ("quoted applicant") on one of the major international markets designated by the Exchange, including the UKLA Official List ("AIM Designated Markets"), may follow an expedited procedure whereby it is exempted under Rule 3 from producing an admission document. Such companies are required instead to give a detailed pre-admission announcement at least 20 business days (i.e. days upon which the Exchange is open for business) before their expected date of admission to AIM. The current AIM Designated Markets are listed in the Exchange's publication of that name which can be downloaded from www.londonstockexchange.com.

2.2.1   Basic requirements

The basic requirements for eligibility, which must be satisfied on admission and at all times thereafter, are as follows.

2.2.1.1   *Nominated adviser (Rules 1, 34 and 39)*
An applicant for admission to AIM and an AIM company must appoint and have a nominated adviser at all times. A nominated adviser is a financial advisory firm which has been approved by the Exchange to act in that capacity, that is, to advise AIM companies. The register of approved nominated advisers is available on the Exchange's website at www.londonstockexchange.com. It is the obligation of the nominated adviser to take appropriate steps to make sure that the directors of an applicant company or AIM company are aware of their obligations to ensure compliance by the company with the Rules. The resignation, dismissal or appointment of a nominated adviser must be announced by its AIM company through a regulatory information service without delay. The Guidance Notes to Rules

11

1 and 34 provide that an AIM company can only retain the services of one nominated adviser at any one time.

2.2.1.2 *Investing companies (Rule 8)*

An investing company is defined in the Glossary as any AIM company which, in the opinion of the Exchange, has as a primary business the investing of its funds in the securities of other companies or the acquisition of a particular business. Under Rule 8, whether it is an applicant company or quoted applicant, an investing company is required to raise as a condition to admission a minimum of £3 million in cash via an equity fundraising on, or immediately before, admission. An investing company is also required to have an investing strategy which must conform to certain criteria (described in paragraph (j) of Schedule 2 of the Rules) and be published in its admission document or, if a quoted applicant, in its pre-admission announcement, and in any announcement and circular produced pursuant to Rule 15. The continuing obligations of investing companies (Guidance Notes to Rules 8 and 15) are described in Chapter 8.

2.2.1.3 *Published accounts (Rule 19)*

An AIM company must publish annual audited accounts prepared in accordance with UK or US generally accepted accounting practice or International Accounting Standards.

2.2.1.4 *Securities freely transferable (Rule 32)*

Securities admitted to trading on AIM must be free from restrictions on transferability. It is suggested, for instance, that the constitutional documents of a company should not provide for any minimum or maximum holdings of shares or restrict shareholders to, say, nationals of the country of incorporation.

However, there are limited exceptions to this requirement for free transferability:

(a) where, in any jurisdiction in which the AIM company operates, statute or regulation place restrictions upon transferability; or
(b) where the AIM company is seeking to limit the number of shareholders domiciled in a particular country to ensure that it does not become subject to statute or regulation.

2.2.1.5   Securities to be admitted to trading (Rule 33)

A company must ensure that application is made to admit all securities of the same class to trading on AIM. Only securities which have been unconditionally allotted can be admitted. In fact securities are usually allotted in advance "subject to admission". The Guidance Note to Rule 5 provides that the Exchange may require proof of allotment for any securities which are being issued on admission. A copy of the applicant company's board minutes allotting such securities or confirmation from its nominated adviser will suffice in most cases. "Allotted" includes provisionally allotted securities where such provisional allotments are unconditional. For example, nil paid rights must be allotted without condition, even if further action is required by the holders of provisional allotments to transform them into another class of securities such as fully paid shares. The Exchange has stated that all types and classes of securities, including ordinary shares, preference shares and debt securities, can be admitted to AIM.

2.2.1.6 Retention of a broker (Rule 35)

An AIM company must retain a broker at all times and its nominated adviser may assume this role as well. The broker's role is to support trading in the company's AIM securities generally. In particular, the Guidance Notes provide that an AIM company's broker will use its best endeavours to find matching business (i.e. match buy and sell orders for the AIM securities) if there is no market maker registered for the AIM securities of an AIM company for which it acts. A market maker is an Exchange member firm which offers to buy and sell the securities for which it is registered.

Any member firm of the Exchange may act as a broker, subject to obtaining any requisite authorisation by any other regulator. Applicants for membership will need to satisfy the Exchange that they have sufficient knowledge, experience and resources to carry out their proposed functions. A list of current member firms is available on the Exchange's website, www.londonstockexchange.com. There is also a separate list of brokers who have already been appointed by AIM companies and this is available from the Exchange's website. The resignation, dismissal or appointment of an AIM company's broker must be announced without delay through a regulatory information service (Rule 17).

2.2.1.7 Settlement arrangements (Rule 36)

An AIM company must ensure that appropriate settlement arrangements for its securities are in place. This is the mechanism by which a buyer's money is exchanged for the securities and the new owner is registered. In particular, except where the Exchange otherwise agrees, AIM securities must be eligible for electronic settlement. UK registered companies may be participants in the CREST settlement system. CREST was introduced in July 1996 and is an electronic, paperless form of settlement system operated by CRESTCo Limited. A company which joins CREST enables its shareholders to hold their shares without share certificates, although shares may still be held in certificated form if preferred.

A shareholder may hold shares within CREST in one of three ways:

(a) as a "full" member of CREST, provided the shareholder has the technological capacity to be linked with CRESTCo Limited. In this case the member's name will appear in the company's register of members;

(b) as a "sponsored" member. The member's name will appear in the register but the member is not required to be linked to CRESTCo Limited, since the sponsor, who is likely to be a broker or fund manager, will charge a fee to provide this link; or

(c) as a client of a member or sponsored member (the "nominee"). In this case the nominee's name will appear in the company's register.

A UK company may join CREST by passing a board resolution by virtue of the enabling legislation provided by the Uncertificated Securities Regulations 2001 (SI 2001/3755). The company's shareholders must be notified of the resolution, in accordance with its articles of association, either before or within 60 days of its being passed.

The CREST contact details are: CRESTCo Limited, 33 Cannon Street, London, EC4M 5SB, www.crestco.co.uk (Tel: +44 (0)20 7849 0000). Application is normally made by the nominated adviser in advance of the application for admission.

The Exchange will grant derogations from the requirement to be eligible for electronic settlement in only the most exceptional circumstances, such as where none of the current electronic systems can cope with settling the AIM company's securities, or where the local law to which the AIM company is subject prohibits such settlement.

Further details regarding CREST can be found in Chapter 13.

2.2.1.8   Fees (Rule 37)

An AIM company must pay AIM fees as set by the Exchange as soon as such payment becomes due. An admission fee is payable by all applicants for admission to AIM in accordance with Rule 5. The fee is payable no later than three business days (i.e. days upon which the Exchange is open for business) prior to the expected date of admission of the applicant company's securities to trading on AIM. A further admission fee is payable where an enlarged entity seeks admission to AIM following a reverse takeover under Rule 14 of the AIM Rules. No admission fee is payable by AIM companies for further issues.

An annual fee is also payable by all AIM companies. Annual fees are billed in the first week of April for the 12 months commencing 1 April and must be paid within 30 days of the invoice date.

Details of admission fees and annual fees are contained in *Fees for Companies and Nominated Advisers* which can be downloaded from the Exchange's website at www.londonstockexchange.com. These fees are reviewed with effect from the beginning of April each year, and the current version of *Fees for Companies and Nominated Advisers* should always be referred to.

The current tariffs, effective from 1 April 2005, are a fixed amount of £4,180 for both the admission and annual fee. A pro-rata annual fee is payable by applicant companies no later than three business days prior to admission to trading. The fee is calculated by taking the number of calendar days, including the date of admission to trading, up to and including 31 March, and dividing the resultant number by 365 and multiplying the result by the annual fee. No pro-rata annual fee is payable by the enlarged entity admitted to AIM following a reverse takeover under Rule 14 of the AIM Rules. Also, no pro-rata annual fee is payable by companies transferring to AIM from the Official List. The annual fee is not refundable, including where securities are suspended or cancelled.

Further information on the calculation and payment of fees is available in *Fees for Companies and Nominated Advisers* as above.

Interest may be added to overdue payments at HSBC Bank plc base rate (as varied from time to time) plus 3 per cent. AIM fee queries, including any requests for repayment of admission fees resulting from incorrect fee calculations, will only be considered where less than six months have elapsed since the date of the invoice for the relevant charge. UK Value Added Tax (VAT), currently at 17.5 per cent, must be added to the fee if the relevant AIM company is subject to UK VAT.

Payment of admission fees should be sent to Issuer Implementation, London Stock Exchange plc, 10 Paternoster Square, London EC4M 7LS. Payment of the annual fees should be made via direct debit. A direct debit mandate can be obtained from Sales Invoicing, London Stock Exchange plc, 10 Paternoster Square, London EC4M 7LS, Tel: +44 (0)207 797 4355. Instructions for cheques and BACS payments are contained in *Fees for Companies and Nominated Advisers*.

Queries relating to AIM fees can be referred to the Issuer Implementation team on +44 (0)20 7797 1473.

2.2.1.9   Contact details (Rule 38)
Details of an AIM company contact, including an e-mail address, must be provided to the Exchange at the time of the application for admission and the Exchange must be informed immediately of any changes thereafter.

2.2.2   Suitability for admission

The nominated adviser must be satisfied that, in its opinion, an applicant company and its securities are appropriate to be admitted to AIM (Rule 39 and Schedules 6 and 7).

The nominated adviser is likely to require that:

(a)   the company has reached a stage of development where a substantial market for its products is demonstrable;
(b)   the core management team of the company has been with it for some time and built an infrastructure for growth; and

(c)   substantial profitability is in prospect in the short term (say, within a year of joining the market).

Occasionally, new companies with exceptional prospects, often in the field of technology, will be admitted on the basis of projected earnings and profitability.

2.2.3   Reorganisation and rationalisation of share structure

To comply with the above requirements, and to meet market expectations, a company is likely to undertake certain preparatory steps in the months prior to admission. For instance, a review is likely to be undertaken of the company's corporate structure, including any other members of its group. A UK company which is not already a public company will have to re-register as one, which requires shareholder approval and an allotted share capital with a minimum nominal value of £50,000. It is also likely that, prior to admission, there will need to be some corporate reorganisation, which may involve moving assets or businesses around within the group and/or a rationalisation of the share structure of the company whose shares are being admitted to AIM. Some companies, particularly those which have obtained venture capital finance, have different securities in issue, such as preference shares, warrants and loan stock. The different classes of shares are almost invariably reorganised into one class of ordinary shares, with the aim of ensuring that there is a single class of shares trading on AIM, that the share price on admission is appropriate, and that there are sufficient numbers of shares in issue to allow future liquidity. A firm of registrars will be appointed to maintain the company's share register.

The reorganisation of the company's share capital will require shareholders' consent which, depending on what is being done, is likely to involve the passing of special or extraordinary resolutions at shareholders' meetings or class meetings. Lack of harmony between shareholders or different classes of shareholders may hinder the admission process.

Where an overseas company intends to apply for admission, local legal and regulatory issues will have to be addressed. For instance, the method of transferring shares in the overseas company may not be compatible with the AIM market, and there have been instances of UK holding companies being set up and their shares admitted to trading on AIM to address this.

2.2.4 Additional pre-admission arrangements

A company coming to AIM will often adopt one or more employee share schemes, such as share option schemes. The executive directors should have service contracts, and companies often need to adopt new articles of association in a form appropriate for a company whose shares are publicly traded.

It will also be necessary to carry out a due diligence review, under which lawyers acting for the company, together with its accountants, will investigate its legal arrangements and financial information and procedures with a view to satisfying the nominated adviser that the affairs of the company and its group are in order. The process will also elicit information to be incorporated into the admission document – the document which is required to be produced on admission and which is used to market shares to investors (*see* Appendix 1 of this Guide for a model admission document). This work will also assist the verification exercise carried out on the information contained in the admission document.

2.3   Directors and employees

2.3.1   Role of directors

A director of an AIM company has an important role in ensuring that the company operates in a proper manner and complies with its obligations under the AIM Rules. As the onus is on the company under the AIM Rules to ensure that the directors fulfil their obligations, the board of a company coming to or on AIM should consider whether its directors' service contracts should contain provisions requiring compliance with those obligations. In particular, it would be good practice for such service contracts to be terminable and to provide for a director to leave the board if the director materially breaches or causes the company materially to breach the AIM Rules. However, the company would need to consider carefully whether or not to exercise the right to terminate if the situation arose.

In interpreting the AIM Rules, it should be borne in mind that the Glossary defines a "director" as a person who acts as a director, whether or not officially appointed to such position.

2.3.2   Lock-ins (Rule 7)

An applicant company (including a quoted applicant) must, where it has as its main activity a business which has not been independent and earning revenue for at least two years, ensure that all persons who are, at the time of its admission, its related parties and applicable employees, agree not to dispose of any interest in the applicant company's AIM securities for a period of one year from the date of admission. Such agreement will be evidenced by a written undertaking by each person affected. The purpose of this restriction is to protect investors by ensuring that a company's management do not simply use admission as a means of realising their investment in the company, and nominated advisers may seek to impose a longer lock-in period and require other significant shareholders to retain their shares. The meaning of the terms "related party" and "applicable employee" are described in the Glossary attached to the AIM Rules.

A related party is:

(a)   a director of any member of an AIM company's group (defined by reference to parent/subsidiary undertakings); or

(b)   a substantial shareholder (a person who holds any legal or beneficial interest directly or indirectly in 10 per cent or more of any class of AIM security (excluding treasury shares) of the AIM company or 10 per cent or more of the voting rights (excluding treasury shares) of the AIM company); or

(c)   an "associate" (as defined in the Glossary definition of "related party") of any of those.

For the purposes of Rule 7, the definition of a "substantial shareholder" excludes any authorised person (a person who under European Union directive or UK domestic legislation is authorised to conduct investment business in the UK) or any company with securities quoted upon the Exchange's markets, unless the company is an investing company.

Also, the Exchange will not require a substantial shareholder to be the subject of a lock-in under Rule 7 where that shareholder became a substantial shareholder at the time of the relevant AIM company's admission and at a price which was more widely available.

An applicable employee means any employee of an AIM company, or its subsidiary or parent undertaking, who (for the purposes of Rule 7) together with that employee's family has any legal or beneficial interest, whether direct or indirect, in 0.5 per cent or more of a class of AIM securities (excluding treasury shares). The following are treated as family members: the employee's spouse, any child under 18 and any trust in which the employee or such individuals are trustees or beneficiaries and any company over which they have control or more than 20 per cent of its equity or voting rights (excluding treasury shares) in a general meeting. Any employee share or pension scheme where such employee or such individuals are beneficiaries rather than trustees is not taken into account.

The restrictions contained in Rule 7 are intended to apply to the interests of such family members as well as those of the relevant applicable employee.

Rule 7 will not apply:

(a) in the event of an intervening court order;
(b) if a party subject to the Rule dies; or
(c) in respect of an acceptance of a takeover offer for the AIM company which is open to all shareholders.

If lock-in agreements are not properly drafted a concert party may arise for the purposes of the City Code on Takeovers and Mergers. The Guidance Notes recommend that to minimise the risk of parties to lock-in arrangements subsequently being deemed to constitute concert parties under the City Code on Takeovers and Mergers, applicant companies or their advisers may wish to consult the Panel on Takeovers and Mergers, 10 Paternoster Square, London EC4M 7DY (Tel: +44 (0)20 7382 9026) prior to drafting any lock-in agreement.

2.3.3 Notifying deals and changes in directors (Rule 17)

An AIM company must announce through a regulatory information service and without delay any deals by directors disclosing, insofar as it has such information, the information specified by Schedule 5 to the AIM Rules. It must similarly announce the resignation or dismissal of any director or the appointment of any new director, giving the date of such occurrence and, in the case of an appointment, the details required by paragraph (g) of Schedule 2 to the AIM Rules and any shareholding in the AIM company.

2.3.4 Restrictions on dealings in AIM securities (Rule 21)

Rule 21 provides that an AIM company must ensure that its directors and applicable employees (as defined in the Glossary for the purposes of Rule 21) do not deal in any of its AIM securities (i.e. securities of a class which has been admitted to dealing on AIM) during a close period. This Rule is considered in more detail in Chapter 9.

2.3.5 Directors' responsibilities (Rule 31)

An AIM company must ensure that each of its directors accepts full responsibility, collectively and individually, for the AIM company's compliance with the AIM Rules.

2.3.6 Directors' disclosure (Rule 31)

In addition, an AIM company must ensure that each of its directors discloses without delay all information which the AIM company needs in order to comply with Rule 17 (disclosure of miscellaneous information), so far as that information is known to the director or could with reasonable diligence be ascertained by the director.

2.3.7 Advice from the nominated adviser (Rule 31)

An AIM company must ensure that each of its directors seeks advice from its nominated adviser regarding the AIM company's compliance with the AIM Rules whenever appropriate and takes that advice into account. As the directors are under a positive obligation to continue to seek advice and guidance from the nominated adviser, they should consider whether the company's agreement with the nominated adviser should include specific obligations on the nominated adviser to update and meet with the directors on a regular basis. The nominated adviser, in turn, is likely to want to establish in the agreement who is the appropriate recipient of information at the company and to have the right to receive management information and attend board meetings. But the nominated adviser should bear in mind that it may receive unpublished price-sensitive information and should take care to ensure that neither it nor any of its representatives becomes a "shadow director". A shadow director is defined in the Companies Act 1985 as a person in accordance with whose directions or instructions the directors of a company are accustomed to act, although a person is not deemed to be a shadow director by reason only that the directors act on advice given by that person in a professional capacity. A shadow director incurs many of the statutory responsibilities of an appointed director.

2.3.8 Obligations of the AIM company

The Guidance Notes to Rule 31 state that an AIM company must ensure that it has in place sufficient procedures, resources and controls to enable compliance with the AIM Rules. An AIM company must provide its nominated adviser with any information the adviser requests in order to carry out its duties under the AIM Rules.

2.4 Provision and disclosure of information

2.4.1 Wide powers to require publication (Rule 22)

The Exchange has wide powers to require an AIM company to provide information, and may at any time require an AIM company to:

(a) provide to the Exchange such information in such form and within such time limit as the Exchange considers appropriate; and

(b) publish such information.

2.4.2 The Exchange's power to make disclosure (Rule 23)

The Exchange may disclose any information in its possession:

(a) to cooperate with any person responsible for supervision or regulation of financial services or for law enforcement;

(b) to enable it to discharge its legal or regulatory functions, including instituting, carrying on or defending proceedings; or

(c) for any other purpose where it has the consent of the person from whom the information was obtained and, if different, the person to whom it relates.

2.5 Sanctions

The Exchange considers it important that the AIM Rules are carefully observed, not only to build investor confidence in the companies on AIM, but also for the protection of investors and the credibility of the market as a whole.

2.5.1 Failure to have a nominated adviser (Rule 34)

If an AIM company ceases to have a nominated adviser, this must be announced without delay through a regulatory information service (Rule 17) and the Exchange will suspend trading in its AIM securities. If within one month the AIM company has failed to appoint a replacement nominated adviser, the admission of its AIM securities to trading will be cancelled. Where an AIM company needs to announce the loss of its nominated adviser, it should first liaise with AIM Regulation (Tel: +44 (0)20 7797 4154) so that where no replacement has been appointed the necessary suspension may be put in place to coincide with the announcement. Where a new nominated adviser is appointed, an announcement will be required under Rule 17 and a new nominated adviser's declaration should be submitted to the Exchange under Rule 39.

Although an AIM company must retain a broker at all times (Rule 35) and announce its resignation or dismissal without delay (Rule 17) there is no equivalent provision whereby trading in an AIM company's securities is suspended immediately upon the loss of its broker. This is to allow the Exchange to take account of the particular circumstances of each case in deciding appropriate action. As with a nominated adviser's agreement, an AIM company's agreement with its broker should still have a suitable notice period.

2.5.2   Investor protection (Rules 40 and 41)

The Exchange may suspend the trading on AIM of AIM securities where:

(a)   trading in those securities is not being conducted in an orderly manner;
(b)   the Exchange considers that an AIM company has failed to comply with the AIM Rules;
(c)   it is required for the protection of investors; or
(d)   the integrity and reputation of the market has been or may be impaired by dealings in those securities.

Suspensions are effected by a dealing notice involving an announcement being disseminated to the public through RNS (the regulatory information service operated by the Exchange).

The Exchange will cancel the admission of AIM securities to trading on AIM where those securities have been suspended from trading for six months. Cancellations are also effected in the same way by a dealing notice.

2.5.3   Disciplinary action against an AIM company (Rule 42)

If the Exchange considers that an AIM company has contravened the AIM Rules, it may take the following measures:

(a)   fine it;
(b)   censure it;
(c)   publish the fact that it has been fined or censured; and/or
(d)   cancel the admission of its AIM securities.

2.5.4   Disciplinary action against a nominated adviser (Rule 43)

If the Exchange considers that a nominated adviser is in breach of its responsibilities under Rule 39, or that the integrity and reputation of

AIM has been or may be impaired as a result of the conduct or judgement of the nominated adviser, the Exchange may:

(a)   fine it;
(b)   censure the nominated adviser;
(c)   remove the nominated adviser from the register of approved nominated advisers maintained by the Exchange; and/or
(d)   publish what action it has taken and the reasons for that action.

If action is taken against a nominated adviser by the Exchange, it may also result in disciplinary proceedings being brought by the nominated adviser's regulator.

2.5.5   Disciplinary process (Rule 44)

Where the Exchange proposes to take any of the steps described in Rules 42 and 43 it will follow the procedures set out in its *Disciplinary Procedures and Appeals Handbook* which is available from the Exchange's website, www.londonstockexchange.com.

2.5.6   Appeals (Rule 45)

Any decision of the Exchange in relation to the AIM Rules may be appealed to an appeals committee in accordance with the procedures set out in the Exchange's *Disciplinary Procedures and Appeals Handbook*.

2.6   Cancellation of admission at the request of the AIM company

2.6.1   Requirement for announcement

If the board of an AIM company wishes the Exchange to cancel the admission of its AIM securities to trading on AIM it must announce, through a regulatory information service, the preferred date of cancellation at least 20 business days prior to such date (Rule 41).

2.6.2   Requirement for shareholder consent

Rule 41 also provides that, unless the Exchange agrees otherwise, cancellation of admission shall be conditional upon the consent of not less than 75 per cent of the votes cast by the relevant AIM company's shareholders given in general meeting. The Guidance Notes make it clear that the threshold of 75 per cent refers to the percentage of votes cast (rather than 75 per cent of the class) for each class of AIM security. Notice of the relevant shareholder meeting or meetings will have to be given in accordance with the constitutional documents of the AIM company and the legal regime to which it is subject. Consent may be granted through shareholders voting in person or by proxy at the general meeting. The Guidance Notes also make it clear that the requirement for an announcement to be made at least 20 business days before the preferred cancellation date is a minimum, and if earlier notice is sent to the shareholders of an AIM company convening a general meeting to approve the intended cancellation, the announcement that such meeting has been convened must be made through a regulatory information service without delay.

2.6.3　Contents of announcement

The announcement of intended cancellation should set out the preferred date of cancellation, the reasons for seeking the cancellation, a description of how shareholders will be able to effect transactions in the AIM securities once admission has been cancelled, and any other matter relevant to shareholders reaching an informed decision upon the issue of the intended cancellation.

2.6.4　Where shareholder consent is not required

Circumstances where the Exchange might otherwise agree that shareholder consent in general meeting is not required would be:

(a) where comparable dealing facilities such as upon an EU regulated market or AIM Designated Market are or will be put in place to enable shareholders to trade their AIM securities in the future; or

(b) where, pursuant to a takeover which has become wholly unconditional, an offeror has received valid acceptances in excess of 75 per cent of each class of AIM securities.

2.6.5   Cancellation by dealing notice

Cancellations are effected by a dealing notice involving an announcement being made to the public through the regulatory information service operated by the Exchange. Cancellation will not take effect until at least five business days (any day upon which the Exchange is open for business) have passed since shareholder approval has been obtained and a dealing notice has been issued.

2.7   Conclusion

As will be gathered from this Chapter, the accessible entry requirements for AIM, and the relatively relaxed continuing obligations, each of which are considered in more detail in the following Chapters, are made possible to a great extent by the supervisory responsibilities of nominated advisers for their AIM companies. The role of the nominated adviser is also considered in more detail in Chapter 3. It should be borne in mind, however, that notwithstanding the supervisory role of nominated advisers, the Exchange retains significant powers to sanction AIM participants.

Chapter 3

The Role of the Nominated Adviser

Tim Davis
Head of Marketing
Charles Stanley Corporate Finance & Broking

3.1 Introduction

A nominated adviser is a firm or company which has been approved by the London Stock Exchange ("the Exchange") as a nominated adviser ("Nomad") for AIM and whose name has been placed on the register of Nomads published by the Exchange.

It is the responsibility of the Nomad to ensure that companies whose shares are admitted to trading on AIM, or those in the process of seeking admission for their shares to be traded on AIM, are "appropriate" at the point of admission and that the company and its management are fully aware of their obligations under the AIM Rules.

When a company seeks to float on AIM, it has to produce an admission document, unless it is transferring from the Official List or from another AIM Designated Market. The AIM Rules specify the contents of the admission document and require the Nomad to submit a Nomad declaration form, confirming that the directors of the company have received satisfactory advice as to their obligations under the AIM Rules and that, to the best of the Nomad's knowledge and belief, having made due and careful enquiry, all relevant requirements of the AIM Rules have been complied with. Furthermore, the Nomad is required to confirm that, in its opinion, the company and its securities, which are the subject of the application, are appropriate to be admitted to AIM.

Accordingly, there is a high degree of responsibility on the Nomad to undertake extensive due diligence on the applicant company. The

Exchange does not itself seek to screen applicant companies for appropriateness, instead relying upon the Nomad to act as a gate-keeper to the market. Once the applicant company has gained admission to AIM, it is the company's directors who are responsible for ensuring the company's ongoing compliance with the AIM Rules. The Nomad is required, under Rule 39, to be on hand at all times to advise and guide the company and its directors on their continuing obligations under the AIM Rules, whilst the directors are each required, under Rule 31, to seek advice from the Nomad regarding the company's compliance with the AIM Rules whenever appropriate, taking that advice into account.

Consequently, the relationship between company and Nomad will be close, to the extent that the Nomad is always available both to advise and guide the company's board and senior management, and also to act as an adjunct to the board, liaising with the Exchange on the company's behalf and endeavouring to ensure that strategic and price-sensitive developments at the company are properly announced to the investment community in a timely and orderly fashion, as required by the AIM Rules.

This Chapter examines the role of the Nomad as set out in the AIM Rules (last published in July 2005) and *Nominated adviser eligibility criteria* published by the Exchange in April 2005.

3.2 Nominated advisers' responsibilities to the Exchange

AIM is operated, regulated and promoted by the London Stock Exchange and it is an overriding consideration that all Nomads should act so as to preserve the reputation and integrity of AIM. The Nomad's relationship with its corporate client will be set out in a contract, usually referred to as the "nominated adviser agreement".

However, a Nomad will also have responsibilities to the Exchange. The Exchange expects the Nomad:

(a)   to be available at all times to advise and guide the board of its AIM-quoted clients;

(b) to ensure that directors of those companies remain aware of changes to the AIM Rules; and

(c) to ensure that the board remains aware of its continuing obligations.

The obligations of the board relate principally to timely disclosure to the market of material information regarding the company's activities, performance and prospects.

In general, the Exchange also expects the Nomads:

(a) at the time of an application by a client to be admitted to AIM, or upon an appointment to act as Nomad to a company already admitted, to submit a nominated adviser's declaration form;

(b) to provide the Exchange with any other information, in such form and within such time limits as it may reasonably require;

(c) to liaise with the Exchange where requested to do so by the Exchange or an AIM company for which it acts;

(d) to review regularly an AIM company's actual trading performance and financial condition against any published forecasts available to the stock market at large, or any estimate or projection included in the original admission document (or otherwise made public on behalf of the AIM company) in order to assist it in determining whether a notification is necessary under Rule 17;

(e) to inform the Exchange when it ceases to be the Nomad to an AIM company;

(f) to abide by the eligibility criteria for Nomads at all times; and

(g) to act with due skill and care at all times.

3.3 Approval of nominated advisers

All Nomads are approved by the Exchange, which determines the eligibility criteria set out at 3.6 below. A complete list of approved advisers is maintained and published by the Exchange on its website, www.londonstockexchange.com. Only those whose names are included on that list may act as Nomads.

3.4 The identity of nominated advisers

The Exchange approves companies, rather than individuals, as Nomads. Nomads are typically investment banks, stockbroking firms or accountants.

3.5 Retention of a nominated adviser

An AIM company must retain a Nomad at all times (Rule 34). If a company ceases to have a Nomad, the Exchange will suspend trading in its shares. If within one month of that suspension the company has failed to appoint a replacement Nomad, the admission of the company's shares to trading on AIM will be cancelled.

Similarly, an AIM company must retain a broker at all times (Rule 35). The broker liaises with shareholders, promotes awareness of the company in the marketplace, assists in the raising of finance and attempts to ensure that there is a market for the shares.

There is no requirement for companies to retain separate Nomads and brokers; indeed the majority of financial advisory firms also have broking arms. Attitudes vary, and some companies choose to retain two sets of advisers while others prefer to reduce management time, administration and the financial costs associated with such an arrangement. This is particularly relevant to smaller companies.

3.6 Minimum criteria for approval as a nominated adviser

The Exchange's minimum criteria for approval as a Nomad are published in an April 2005 document entitled "Nominated adviser eligibility criteria".

The criteria are that an applicant seeking approval as a Nomad must:

(a)   be a firm or company (individuals are not eligible);
(b)   have practised corporate finance for two years;

(c) have acted as the principal corporate finance adviser in three "relevant transactions" during that two-year period; and

(d) employ at least four "qualified executives" (*see* 3.6.1 below).

The Exchange may waive its requirement for a two-year track record where the applicant has highly experienced qualified executives. Typically, this occurs when a team of qualified executives transfers from one existing Nomad to another.

3.6.1 Qualified executives

The Exchange stipulates that a qualified executive should be a full-time employee of an applicant who is involved in giving corporate finance advice and who has acted in a corporate finance advisory role, which includes the regulation of corporate finance, for at least three years and in at least three "relevant transactions" (*see* 3.6.2 below).

The exceptions to this are:

(a) where an employee has been subject to disciplinary action relating to corporate finance or financial services related work by a regulator or law enforcement agency in the context of corporate finance or financial services; or

(b) if in, or as a result of, an interview which it conducts, the Exchange considers the individual has an inadequate understanding of corporate finance, market practice, or the prevailing legal or regulatory framework for corporate finance.

Where an individual who is a qualified executive of a Nomad leaves the full-time employment of that Nomad, that executive will be taken off the register of qualified executives.

In addition, the Exchange may remove an employee as a qualified executive for a Nomad where that employee is subject to bankruptcy or disciplinary action by another regulator, is mentally incapacitated, or has been shown by formal review of the Nomad by the Exchange to have failed to act with due skill and care in relation to his employer's role as a Nomad.

Either a Nomad or qualified executive may appeal against a decision to disqualify that executive in accordance with the procedures set out in the latest published version of the Exchange's *Disciplinary Procedures and Appeals Handbook.*

3.6.2 Relevant transactions

The Exchange describes qualifying transactions as:

(a) those requiring listing particulars or a prospectus (under European Directives 80/390/EEC and 89/298/EEC) in any Member State of the European Union; and

(b) takeovers of public companies within the European Union or on AIM.

It adds that at least two of these transactions must be in respect of shares quoted on a regulated market (as defined by European Directive 93/22/EEC).

In addition, the Exchange will consider similar initial public offerings and major corporate transactions for publicly quoted companies including mergers and acquisitions whether within the EU or elsewhere in the world. It will also decide whether a transaction is relevant for the purpose of these eligibility criteria. In assessing whether a transaction is relevant, however, the Exchange will ensure that only transactions on the world's major Stock Exchanges are included.

The Exchange will not allow an adviser to claim a transaction as relevant unless that applicant acted as a principal corporate finance adviser and was named prominently and unequivocally in the public documentation pertaining to that transaction. Copies of this publicly available documentation must be included with the application to become a Nomad.

3.6.3 Preservation of the reputation and integrity of AIM

The Exchange reserves the right to reject an application where it considers that the approval of the applicant might endanger the reputation or integrity of AIM. It reserves the right to reject an applicant on these grounds alone, even if the applicant otherwise meets the criteria stated at 3.1, 3.2 and 3.6 above. In considering whether an applicant might endanger AIM's reputation and integrity, the Exchange will examine:

(a) whether the applicant is adequately regulated;
(b) the applicant's standing with its regulators;
(c) the applicant's general reputation;
(d) whether the applicant or its executives have been the subject of adverse disciplinary action by any legal, financial or regulatory authority;
(e) whether the applicant is facing such disciplinary action; and
(f) insofar as is relevant, the commercial and regulatory performance of its clients to whom it has given corporate finance advice.

3.6.4 Independence

A Nomad must be able to demonstrate that both it and its executives are independent from AIM companies for which it acts such that there is no reasonable basis for impugning its independence, typically as a result of conflicts of interest.

Where the Exchange requires a Nomad to demonstrate clearly that neither its independence nor that of any of its executives has, or could be, compromised by any potential conflict, the burden of proof will be upon the Nomad.

If at any time a Nomad is in any doubt about its independence, it should consult the Exchange immediately and certainly before entering into any commercial arrangement. In practical terms, a Nomad will usually identify any potential conflict of interest at the outset and, if appropriate, decline to act for the applicant company.

Whilst it is acceptable for Nomads with stockbroking branches to fulfil both roles for one company, the following points should be noted:

(a) a Nomad may not act as both reporting accountant and Nomad to an AIM company unless it has satisfied the Exchange that appropriate safeguards are in place;

(b)   no partner, director or employee of a Nomad nor an associate of any such partner, director or employee may hold the position of a director of an AIM company for which the firm acts as Nomad;

(c)   neither a Nomad nor a partner, director or employee of a Nomad nor an associate of any such partner, director or employee either individually or collectively may be a substantial shareholder (i.e. hold 10 per cent or more) of an AIM company for which the firm acts as Nomad;

(d)   a Nomad or partner, director or employee of a Nomad or an associate of any such partner, director or employee may be a significant shareholder (i.e. hold 3 per cent or more, but not a substantial shareholder) of an AIM company for which the firm acts as Nomad provided adequate safeguards are in place to prevent any conflict of interest;

(e)   during any closed period for an AIM company, no partner, director or employee in a Nomad, nor an associate of any such partner, director or employee may deal in the securities of that company for which the firm acts as Nomad;

(f)   when calculating an interest in a client company, a Nomad is permitted to disregard any interest in shares pursuant to Companies Act 1985, Section 209; and

(g)   where a Nomad breaches any of the above limits as a result of its underwriting activities, it must make best endeavours to sell down its holding to within the guidelines as soon as reasonably practicable.

3.6.5   Wider conflicts of interest

A Nomad must not have and must take care to avoid the semblance of a conflict between the interests of the AIM companies for which it acts and those of any other party. In particular, a Nomad must not act for any other party to a transaction or takeover other than its client company.

3.6.6   Obligations under the AIM rules

At all times, a Nomad must abide by its responsibilities under the latest edition of the AIM Rules for companies, as published by the Exchange. It is also incumbent upon the Nomad to ensure that the directors of its client are apprised of changes to the AIM Rules in a timely fashion.

3.6.7 Proper procedures

A Nomad must ensure that at all times it maintains procedures which are sufficient for it to discharge its ongoing obligations under these criteria. In particular, it must ensure that any members of staff who are not approved as qualified executives are properly supervised by those who are.

3.6.8 Adequacy of staff

A Nomad must ensure that it has sufficient corporate finance staff to discharge its obligations as a Nomad under these rules at all times. In determining what constitutes a sufficient level of staffing, a Nomad must have regard to the number and type of AIM companies for which it acts. As a minimum, the Exchange states that the Nomad must retain at least four qualified executives who would have sufficient experience for that Nomad to be approved by the Exchange were it a new applicant.

3.6.9 Ongoing experience of corporate finance

A Nomad must ensure that it continues to meet the minimum approval criteria for Nomads. In particular, a Nomad must have been involved in sufficient recent relevant transactions to allow it to qualify were it a new applicant at any time.

The Exchange reserves the right to conduct further tests to ensure that qualified executives maintain an understanding of corporate finance and the responsibilities of being a Nomad.

It is the responsibility of the Nomad to ensure that qualified executives receive appropriate levels of training to ensure they are fully equipped to fulfil their roles.

3.6.10 Maintenance of records

A Nomad must retain sufficient records to maintain an audit trail of the advice which it has given to those AIM companies for which it acts. It is also obliged to retain these records for a minimum of three years.

3.6.11 Annual fees

A Nomad must pay the annual fees as set by the Exchange from time to time in respect of each year it wishes its name to be maintained on the register of approved Nomads.

3.6.12 Additional qualified executives

Application to have further employees registered as qualified executives may be made to the Exchange at any time. The Exchange must also be notified without delay of any qualified executives leaving the Nomad's full-time employment.

3.6.13 Performance review of nominated advisers

A Nomad may be subject to formal review by the Exchange to ensure that it has fully discharged its responsibilities under these criteria. A Nomad must ensure that its qualified executives cooperate fully with the Exchange and that the appropriate partner or director for a transaction is available to answer any questions by the Exchange about those transactions.

A Nomad must allow Exchange officers access to its records and business premises when so requested by the Exchange.

3.6.14 Moratorium on acting for further AIM companies

Where, in the opinion of the Exchange, a Nomad has insufficient staff and/or is appealing against disciplinary action taken by the Exchange, the Exchange may prevent that Nomad from acting as a Nomad for any additional AIM companies until that situation is resolved to the Exchange's satisfaction.

3.7 Nominated adviser's agreement

An agreement setting out the terms of engagement will be entered into between the Nomad and the applicant company or existing AIM company. It will usually address the following.

3.7.1 Admission: responsibilities of the nominated adviser

The Nomad will usually be responsible for some if not all of the following with respect to admission:

(a) assisting with the appointment and coordination of the company's advisers, including solicitors, reporting accountants, public relations advisers and registrars (and, if a separate company or firm, its brokers);

(b) evaluating the company's suitability for admission, including its management, strategy, financial and trading positions and valuation range. In practical terms, this involves the Nomad and broker developing a thorough understanding of the company and the business in the context of its industry, usually through working very closely and intensively with the senior executive management and, where appropriate, any non-executive directors;

(c) evaluating fund-raising options;

(d) managing the entire admission process, to include setting and controlling the timetable, as well as guiding the company through the necessary paperwork and documentation, including the 10 business-day announcement (or 20 business-day pre-admission announcement in the case of companies moving to AIM from the Official List);

(e) coordinating the drafting of the admission document, to include overall responsibility for content and the distribution of revised versions;

(f) liaising with the company's legal advisers, reporting accountants and auditors, particularly in terms of the working capital review, long form report, legal due diligence, the overall verification process, and the placing agreement (if there is to be one);

(g) in parallel with the development of the admission document, assuming overall responsibility for the development and verification of the marketing presentation to be used in any fund-raising; and

(h) in the event of fund-raising, advising the company on the pricing of shares on admission (in conjunction with the broker).

3.7.2 Ongoing responsibilities of nominated advisers

Nomads will usually agree to act on a continuing basis. Responsibilities, which are encapsulated in the AIM Rules, usually include:

(a) advising the company's board of changes to the AIM Rules and their interpretation as they may affect that company relative to the investment community;

(b) maintaining close contact with the company's board to ensure that at all times the Nomad has a clear understanding of the company's financial and trading positions, especially as they may affect any published stock market estimates;

(c) advising the company in relation to the requirement for, and management of, any price-sensitive information, the production and timing of regulatory announcements, circulars, full and half-year accounts and any other financial information required to be released or published under the AIM Rules; and

(d) liaising with the London Stock Exchange or any appropriate regulatory body (e.g. the Panel on Takeovers and Mergers) on behalf of the company.

3.7.3 Nominated adviser also acting as broker

The same responsibilities as those outlined above will apply in the event of the Nomad also acting as broker to the company. Additionally, the broker will:

(a) undertake to provide equity research coverage and institutional sales support for that company;

(b) act as the point of contact between the investment community and the company and use its reasonable endeavours to generate investor interest in the securities of the company;

(c) advise the company on investment conditions and assist in the pricing of securities during a fund-raising exercise;

(d) use its best endeavours to match buyers and sellers of the company's shares if there is no registered market maker.

3.7.4 Provision of information

The company should undertake to provide the Nomad with all relevant material information and documents (such as management accounts) in a timely manner, and to keep the Nomad fully informed of all developments relevant to its engagement.

3.7.5 Compliance with law and regulation

The company should also undertake to procure that its directors will comply with all relevant legal and regulatory requirements, in particular the AIM Rules, and will do whatever else the Nomad reasonably requires to allow the Nomad properly to discharge its responsibilities.

3.7.6 Announcements

The company and the Nomad are likely to agree that no public announcements or public documents relating to the company will be issued by either of them without consulting with, or obtaining the authorisation of, the other.

3.7.7 Confidentiality

The Nomad will undertake to maintain the confidentiality of any information which it receives with respect to the company. The company will also usually agree to keep confidential any information provided, advice given and views expressed by the Nomad in connection with its appointment.

3.7.8 Indemnities

The company will indemnify the Nomad and its associates from any liability incurred in connection with its appointment. However, this will be subject to certain exceptions which will invariably include liability arising out of negligence; fraud or wilful default of the Nomad; or the Nomad's breach of contract or breach of its regulatory duties.

3.7.9 Conflicts of interest

The agreement should set out how the Nomad proposes to avoid or manage any actual or potential conflicts of interest between itself and the company.

3.7.10   Fees

The agreement will usually provide for the Nomad to be entitled to:

(a)   a fee for assisting with the preparations for admission;

(b)   a separate fee and commission based upon funds raised for arranging for the placing of the company's shares on admission (if applicable); and

(c)   reimbursement of the Nomad's expenses, including legal fees and other expenses with respect to admission.

In addition, the Nomad will also charge an annual fee (usually a retainer, payable quarterly in advance) with respect to its continuing role as Nomad.

3.7.11   Termination

Given the consequences of a company ceasing to have a Nomad, it will usually want the Nomad to give at least one to three months' notice of termination. The Nomad is likely to require the company to give similar notice.

Typically, this will come after an initial fixed term (usually one year), although both parties will retain the right to terminate the relationship with immediate effect if either side (including any director in the case of the company) is in material breach of any legal or regulatory requirements or standard, or, in the case of the Nomad, if it is removed from the register of Nomads maintained by the Exchange.

3.7.12   Warranties

The Nomad may obtain short-form warranties from the company.

3.8   Nominated adviser's responsibilities on admission of securities

The overriding responsibility of the Nomad at admission is to ensure that the company is compliant with the AIM Rules.

The Nomad is required to confirm to the Exchange that, in relation to any application for admission of securities to AIM which requires the production of an admission document, the company has satisfied the following criteria (as set out in Schedule 6 of the AIM Rules):

(a) the directors of the company have received satisfactory advice and guidance from the Nomad as to the nature of their responsibilities and obligations to ensure compliance by the company with the AIM Rules;

(b) to the best knowledge and belief of the Nomad, having made due and careful enquiry, all relevant requirements of the AIM Rules have been complied with; and

(c) in the Nomad's opinion, it is satisfied that the company and the securities, which are the subject of the application, are appropriate to be admitted to AIM.

The Nomad must lodge its declaration at least three business days before the expected date of admission of the securities to trading on AIM (Rule 5). (Business days are days on which the Exchange is open for business.)

The Exchange has also stated that for the purpose of fulfilling the obligations owed to the Exchange, it expects Nomads to satisfy themselves that an appropriate due diligence/verification exercise has been completed on the applicant company.

Where a company is transferring to AIM from the Official List or another AIM Designated Market where it has had a quotation for at least 18 months, no admission document is required. Instead, the company must submit to the London Stock Exchange three copies of its latest report and accounts. The company will still require a Nomad, however, both to submit the Nomad declaration form and to continue to act for it on an ongoing basis. For further details of the AIM designated market provisions in the AIM Rules *see* Chapter 12.

3.9 Sanctions and appeals (Rules 42–45)

The Exchange considers it important that the AIM Rules are carefully observed, not only to build investor confidence in the companies on

AIM, but also for the protection of investors and the credibility of the market as a whole.

3.9.1 Disciplinary action against a nominated adviser (Rule 43)

If the Exchange considers that a Nomad is in breach of its responsibilities under these criteria or under the AIM Rules, or has failed to act with due skill and care, or that the integrity and reputation of AIM has been or may be impaired as a result of its conduct or judgement, the Exchange may:

(a)   fine the Nomad;
(b)   censure the Nomad;
(c)   remove the Nomad from the register; and/or
(d)   publish the action it has taken and the reasons for that action.

3.9.2 Disciplinary process

Where the Exchange proposes to take such steps, it will follow the procedures set out in the *Disciplinary Procedures and Appeals Handbook*.

3.9.3 Appeals by nominated advisers

In the event of the Exchange taking steps against a Nomad, that Nomad may appeal against the Exchange's decision in accordance with the procedures in the Exchange's *Disciplinary Procedures and Appeals Handbook*.

3.10   Conclusion

In summary, the Nomad has clearly defined responsibilities and obligations, both to the Exchange (based upon preserving the integrity and reputation of AIM) and to its client (to ensure compliance with the AIM Rules). The relationship between Nomad and client is typically a very close one, vitally so with young, growing businesses usually going through their first incarnation as a publicly quoted company.

Chapter 4

The Role of the Accountant

Linda Main

Partner
KPMG LLP

4.1 Introduction

This Chapter deals with the role of the reporting accountant and the financial reporting requirements for listing on AIM. It also touches on practical points covering:

(a) the accountants' long form report;
(b) presentation of financial information in the admission document;
(c) the working capital statement;
(d) financial reporting procedures.

The reporting accountant is involved throughout the AIM admission process. The role encompasses the review of financial information in the admission document and related due diligence on the company. Some aspects of the role are driven by the AIM Rules whereas others are designed to assist the nominated adviser in carrying out his role. The precise scope of the work to be carried out by the reporting accountant is agreed at the outset between the accountant and the nominated adviser and set out in a detailed engagement letter.

4.2 Accountants' long form report

There is no regulatory requirement for a company to commission a long form report prior to listing on AIM. However, this type of due diligence is typically requested by the nominated adviser to help discharge his responsibilities to the Stock Exchange.

The long form report is a detailed due diligence report covering all aspects of the business and usually incorporates a review of the company's operations including its products and markets as well as a detailed analysis of its recent financial performance. The company's management structure and system of internal control are also key areas covered as part of the exercise.

The due diligence process is time consuming and requires input from the directors and management team. It is important that sufficient attention is given to this process as the long form provides much of the information which is subsequently used to draft the admission document itself.

4.3 Presentation of financial information in the admission document

A company wishing to join AIM must produce an admission document unless it is already quoted on one of the AIM Designated Markets. The admission document must contain the financial information specified by the AIM Rules which require the presentation of information consistent with that set out in Annex 1 of the Prospectus Directive Regulations. If an offer is being made to the public requiring a prospectus there are some additional requirements and these are discussed below.

Annex 1 of the Prospectus Directive Regulations requires the inclusion of the financial statements for each of the last three years which must have been independently audited or reported upon.

In practice this means that either the financial statements will be reproduced in full including each of the auditors' reports which were issued at the time, or a new "accountants' report" will be prepared, with a new report from the reporting accountant covering all three years.

No guidance is given as to which approach is preferred, although an accountants' report is usually prepared where there have been changes in the accounting policies or group structure during the period under review.

The reproduction of the previously published annual accounts is generally a less costly option but can also be more cumbersome, as the three years comprising the track record are presented sequentially rather than in a single document as with an accountants' report.

The format of an accountants' report is not dissimilar to an audit opinion on a set of financial statements. New Standards for Investment Reporting ("SIR") guidance issued by the Auditing Practices Board in 2005 in SIR 2000 clarifies that the underlying financial information on which the accountants' report is based is the responsibility of the directors of the company, and the accountants' responsibility is to form an opinion as to whether the information gives a true and fair view of the state of affairs and profit or loss of the company.

The financial information in the document should contain all the information typically found in a set of annual accounts (including the income statement, balance sheet, cash flow statement and notes).

Paragraph 20.1 of Annex 1 to the AIM Rules requires the financial information to be prepared in accordance with Regulation (EC) No. 1606/2002 (in other words in accordance with International Accounting Standards) or, if this is not applicable, in accordance with a Member State's national accounting standards. In practice, for a UK company, this means that either UK GAAP or IFRS would be acceptable.

For issuers from outside the EU, IFRS is the obvious choice, although the Committee of European Securities Regulators ("CESR") has issued guidance on additional disclosures which are required to enable US, Canadian or Japanese GAAP to be treated as equivalent to IFRS.

Since Rule 19 of the AIM Rules states that once admitted to AIM annual accounts must be prepared and filed using UK GAAP, US GAAP or IFRS, in practice most companies choose to use one of these for their admission document in order to avoid confusing investors when the first set of accounts after admission are published. As mentioned above, if US GAAP is used in the admission document the additional disclosures recommended by CESR must also be included.

If the admission document is to be published more than nine months after the end of the company's financial year, the AIM Rules require the inclusion of interim accounts covering at least six months of the new financial year.

These interim accounts can either be included in the accountants' report referred to above or in a separate section of the admission document.

The interim accounts need not be audited, but must otherwise be prepared to the standard applicable to the accounts for a financial year. In practice, it is relatively unusual for unaudited interims to be included in an admission document; most companies and their nominated advisers choose to have the interims audited. Where an accountants' report is presented, it is possible in some circumstances to adjust the previously published financial information.

Some examples of the circumstances where adjustments can be made are:

(a) to ensure that the same accounting policies have been applied throughout the period covered by the report (e.g., if new accounting standards have been introduced during the period);
(b) to enable the reporting accountant to eliminate audit qualifications which arose because the company had not complied with an accounting standard;
(c) to correct fundamental errors which have come to light since the original accounts were produced.

The overriding objective is to arrive at a set of figures which presents a fair picture of the results of the business in which people are asked to invest.

The application of the same accounting policies throughout the period is, in theory, a relatively simple matter, but it can give rise to practical complications if the information necessary to enable the accounts of previous years to be restated on the current policies is not easily available. The important issue is the question of materiality. What the accountant may have to do is decide whether he believes that, whilst the figures cannot be computed precisely, reasonable estimates can nevertheless be arrived at which are acceptable and which enable a true and fair opinion to be given.

The issue of considering fundamental errors is more difficult. There can well be circumstances in which the reporting accountant will say that the figures he is looking at are clearly wrong and in his view were clearly wrong at the time. This is important. The accountant always has to avoid the excessive use of hindsight and has to put himself in the position of judging whether or not the view taken on a particular issue was reasonable at the time even though subsequent events may cause a different view to be taken.

It is an unavoidable part of accounts preparation that estimates have to be made. Each year's accounts contain the adjustments made to the previous years' estimates as well as the estimates made at that year end. Subject to the overriding need to present a true and fair view, it is not the purpose of the accountants' report to substitute more accurate information subsequently ascertained in place of reasonable estimates made at the time. A useful maxim in these circumstances might be, "if in doubt, do not adjust".

Where a company applying to join AIM is already quoted on another exchange (one of the AIM Designated Markets), an admission document may not be required. In this case, the AIM Rules require the publication of a website address where the latest published annual report and accounts (and interims if it is more than nine months since the year end) can be viewed. These accounts should be prepared using UK or US GAAP or International Accounting Standards. Although this route dispenses with the need for an accountant's report, the nominated adviser may still require the preparation of a working capital report and in some cases a long form report.

4.4   Pro forma financial information

Pro forma financial information is not required by the AIM Rules but is often included to satisfy the requirement to illustrate the effect of a transaction on the assets and liabilities and earnings of a company. Examples of circumstances where pro formas are typically included are where a group is coming together for the first time or an issuer is making a significant acquisition or disposal. Pro forma statements of net assets may also be included to show the effect of funds raised on flotation on the gearing of the company.

The Institute of Chartered Accountants has published a technical release which gives detailed guidance on the preparation of pro forma financial information. This guidance is particularly useful in determining when it is appropriate to make adjustments.

If the admission document also constitutes a prospectus pursuant to the Prospectus Directive Regulations, pro forma financial information must be included in compliance with Annex II of the Regulations. Further, a letter from the Reporting Accountants must be published in the admission document stating whether in their opinion the pro forma financial information has been properly compiled on the basis of preparation stated therein and whether, in their opinion, such basis is consistent with the accounting policies of the company. Where the document is not a prospectus the accountant typically provides a private comfort letter to the nominated adviser.

4.5   Working capital

The AIM Rules require the issuer to make a statement in the admission document that, in the opinion of its directors, having made due and careful enquiry, the working capital available to it and to the group is sufficient for its present requirements (i.e., 12 months from admission). The nominated adviser typically asks the reporting accountant to review the underlying projections and prepare a comfort letter.

This comfort will take the form of a private letter from the accountants to the company and the nominated adviser. In order to give such comfort, it is necessary for the company to prepare a board memorandum setting out the cash flow projections and the assumptions which underlie them. The board memorandum will be reviewed by the reporting accountants. The level of detailed work that has to be done in carrying out a working capital review will vary, to a certain extent, depending upon the margin between the working capital resources available (cash at bank, overdraft facilities and other facilities) and the requirements shown by the forecast. Although the period has to be a minimum of the next 12 months, in practice a longer period may need to be covered and it is particularly necessary to consider any known circumstances beyond that time.

Confirmations of available facilities should be obtained from banks. Typically, these will expire during the period covered by the review. In these circumstances, the banks should be asked to confirm that they would expect in normal circumstances to renew the facilities at the review date.

4.6 Financial reporting procedures

The directors of new applicants to AIM are required to confirm that they have established procedures which provide a reasonable basis for them to make proper judgement as to the financial position and prospects of the issuer. The reporting accountants are usually asked to provide comfort to the nominated adviser in this area. Whilst it will be possible to provide a commentary on the company's financial reporting procedures, it will be for the directors of the company to form a conclusion on whether the procedures are a reasonable basis for their judgements about the financial position and prospects. In particular, it will not be possible to give any assurance on the day-to-day effectiveness of the procedures. The reporting accountant will therefore restrict any specific comfort to the process which the directors have gone through to give their confirmation, and will deal with the question of whether it has been given after due and careful enquiry.

4.7 Other comfort letters

There are a number of other areas where the nominated adviser may request comfort letters from the reporting accountant. The most common are:

(a) a request for the accountant to review the disclosures in the admission document relating to the tax effects of the transaction on UK shareholders; and

51

(b) confirmation that the financial information included in the document has been properly extracted from the various source documents.

A letter may also be provided confirming to the nominated adviser that the accountant has reported all the matters which came to his attention during his work which he thought were material in the context of the proposed transaction.

4.8   Other requirements of the Prospectus Directive

In addition to the points mentioned above there are two other areas where additional information must be included if the admission document also constitutes a prospectus. The first is the need to include a statement of indebtedness showing the total indebtedness of the group as at a date not more than 90 days before the date of publication of the admission document.

The second is the formalisation of the requirement to include an "operating and financial review" setting out in narrative form the key factors influencing the performance of the company during the period covered by the financial statements. In practice this requirement is simply formalising what had already become common practice. There is no standard format for an operating and financial review, but it typically takes the form of a discussion of the reasons for the movements in turnover, profits and net assets in each year compared to the one before, as well as discussion of the key accounting policies adopted by the group and how these have been applied.

4.9   Conclusion

Overall, as can be seen from the above, the accountant's role is wide-ranging and goes far beyond the presentation of the basic financial information in the admission document. It is important not to underestimate the amount of time the various tasks will take. Although the detailed rules governing the work have been substantially altered by the Prospectus Directive in July 2005, the underlying requirements have not changed materially, particularly where a prospectus is not required.

Chapter 5

The Role of the Solicitor

Hugh Maule
Partner
Lawrence Graham LLP

5.1 Introduction

The role of the solicitor in an AIM flotation or in any secondary issue will vary depending on whether the solicitor is acting for the company or the nominated adviser and/or broker. These roles are typically known as "solicitor to the company" and "solicitor to the issue" respectively. The solicitor to the company normally has a wider role which will include the initial advice on all structuring issues and advice on all aspects of the documentation involved. The solicitor to the issue usually concentrates on the drafting of and advice to the nominated adviser/broker on any placing or underwriting agreement and otherwise generally has a secondary role overseeing the whole process from the nominated adviser/broker perspective.

5.2 Solicitors to the company

5.2.1 Principal functions of solicitor to the company

The responsibility of the solicitor to the company is to work as part of the team advising the company and its directors, liaising with the company's auditors and other advisers including the nominated adviser, broker and reporting accountants.

The principal functions include:

(a) handling the pre-flotation legal due diligence;
(b) reviewing and advising on any necessary corporate restructuring;

53

(c)   advising on the drafting of the admission document (which may also comprise a prospectus under the new Prospectus Regulations) which will be required to be published, with principal responsibility for the statutory sections of that document and managing the process of the verification of the contents of the admission document;

(d)   negotiating the terms of any placing, underwriting or introduction agreement between the company, the directors, the nominated adviser/broker and any other relevant party;

(e)   preparing directors' service contracts, if required;

(f)   preparing employees' share participation schemes, if required;

(g)   advising the directors of the company on their responsibilities as directors of a company whose securities are traded on AIM, particularly in relation to the flotation arrangements and including advice on corporate governance;

(h)   negotiating the terms of the ongoing advisory agreements between the nominated adviser and the company and the broker and the company; and

(i)   giving general advice which may be required in relation to matters arising out of the flotation.

5.3   Pre-flotation legal due diligence

5.3.1   Reasons for the legal due diligence

It is common for the professional team to insist that a comprehensive legal due diligence exercise is conducted by the solicitors to the company in respect of the business of the company prior to flotation. They will generally be expected to address the due diligence report to the nominated adviser and broker as well as to the company. Together with the reporting accountant's long-form report, the legal due diligence report is particularly relevant to the nominated adviser, who owes certain duties to the London Stock Exchange in its capacity as a nominated adviser, not least confirming that it is satisfied that the company and its shares are appropriate to be admitted to AIM.

It is important to try not to overlap to any significant degree with the work that the reporting accountants will undertake in compiling the long-form report. Unnecessary duplication will waste the time of the directors charged with the task of collating information, who are often under considerable pressure in any event. For this purpose, it is vital that there is early dialogue between the reporting accountants, the solicitors to the company, the nominated adviser and the solicitors to the issue to coordinate the scope of the accounting and legal due diligence. The scope of the work to be undertaken by each for the company should be agreed at an early stage in engagement letters for the purpose.

At the outset, the solicitors to the company typically send a legal due diligence questionnaire to the company covering all aspects of its business. This questionnaire is similar in nature to a pre-acquisition due diligence enquiry form which a buyer (or its solicitors) would send to a seller. The questionnaire will contain questions designed to elicit the information which will be required to compile the statutory and general information to be included in the admission document. Inaccurate or incomplete responses to the legal due diligence questionnaire have a profound influence on the ability of the solicitors to the company to prepare and complete the statutory and general information in the admission document quickly, accurately and efficiently. The directors need to be made aware of this if cost and timing overruns are to be avoided. It is usually of great benefit if one person at the company (company secretary, financial controller, finance director or any other single director) is designated with and/or assumes direct and full-time responsibility for dealing with the due diligence issues. This serves to aid the consistency and flow of the information provided to the professional team.

5.3.2   What information is required for the due diligence?

The pre-flotation legal due diligence questionnaire will include questions on the following subjects:

(a)   Details of the basic corporate history and current corporate information on the company including its full name and company number, registered office, authorised share capital, details of its directors, company secretary, shareholders and subsidiaries and copies of its memorandum and articles of association, all of which will be checked against the public records of the company held at Companies House (as these will not necessarily be consistent).

(b) Details of the existing issued share capital and existing share-holders, particularly director shareholders and details of any existing shareholder agreement(s) or any other similar arrangements between shareholders (which will, most likely, need to be brought to an end immediately prior to or consequent upon admission of shares to trading on AIM).

(c) Details of principal customers of, and suppliers to, the company together with copy contracts in order that a review of such contracts can take place. This is not only to check if any such contracts have, for example, change of control provisions in them, unduly onerous terms or abnormally short notice provisions, all of which would clearly have a potentially significant effect on the flotation, but also to check to see that such principal contracts are legally enforceable.

(d) Details of service contracts between the company or any subsidiary company and the directors, and employment details for all the employees and consultants in the business including entitlements under bonus schemes and pension schemes and other benefits in kind as well as details of share incentive schemes together with complete records of current share capital under option. Care should be taken in reporting details of employees, to avoid infringement of the Data Protection Act 1998 (normally by anonymising the information).

(e) In respect of each of the directors, details of his or her current directorships and former directorships in the previous five years, unspent convictions, bankruptcies or individual voluntary arrangements, public criticisms, details of any receiverships, compulsory liquidations, creditors' voluntary liquidations, administrations, company voluntary arrangements or any composition or arrangement with creditors of companies generally where such director was a director at the time of or within the 12 months preceding such events, as well as the information otherwise required by paragraph (g) of Schedule 2 to the AIM Rules. This of itself can be a very time consuming exercise if the directors have extensive current and former directorships to disclose, particularly where numbers of overseas companies are involved where the information will not be readily ascertainable through Companies House.

(f) Details of material contracts of the business entered into by the company or any group company in the two years immediately preceding the publication of the admission document. These do not need to include contracts entered into in the ordinary course of the business of the company. Acquisition or disposal documentation entered into by the company or financing documentation of significance to the company including any placing or underwriting agreement entered into by the company as part of the flotation would generally be considered as outside the ordinary course of business.

(g)   Details of any governmental, legal or arbitration proceedings being brought by or against the company or any subsidiary. Where any such matters are active, pending or threatened they must be disclosed in the admission document covering a period of up to one year if it is having or may have a significant effect on the company's financial position or profitability. An assessment as to whether any disclosures are required can be made based on the information given, if any, in answer to the due diligence enquiries.

(h)   Details of any person or entity, other than the professional advisers named in the admission document, who has received cash, shares or any other benefit with a value of £10,000 or more in the year prior to the application for admission or will or may receive any such benefit on or after admission, as required by paragraph (h) of Schedule 2 to the AIM Rules.

These are some of the standard areas of questioning in a pre-flotation due diligence exercise. Complete and accurate answers with all supporting documentation will ease the preparation of the due diligence report and, ultimately, the admission document.

5.3.3   Examples of actions consequent upon the legal due diligence

Inevitably, the results of the legal due diligence exercise may give rise to a number of other eventualities. For example, it may be that arrangements have to be put in place to terminate a shareholders agreement, which is not appropriate for a public company, or to restructure the share capital in order to convert different classes of share into one single class in readiness for flotation.

It may transpire that an important part of the company's business is not properly dealt with in the legal documentation that it uses. Whilst this may not preclude the flotation, the recommendation may be that the flaw needs immediate rectification. The solicitors to the company will need to draft appropriate documentation.

It may be that the legal due diligence reveals that documentation does not exist at all for part of the business of the company. This could be, for example, either that service agreements or terms of employment for directors and employees have never been prepared, or a part of the day-to-day means of doing business between the company and its customers have just not been committed to writing. This is not wholly unusual for young and growing companies. Once again, the solicitors to the company will need to create and agree the documentation with the company, as appropriate.

It is critical that the solicitors to the company have a very clear understanding of the business of the company and how it operates. It is equally important that the operation of the business is consistent with the underlying legal documentation. It is also worth noting here that specialist reports may also be commissioned in certain circumstances if the legal due diligence exercise uncovers some particular specialist issue or if the nature of the company requires it. If the business of the company is heavily reliant on, say, patents, then a patent agent's report may be required. Likewise, if the company has significant property interests, a valuation report may be required and/or a solicitor's report or certificate on title commissioned. A mining or exploration company will require an independent mining expert's report or a geological report.

5.3.4   Draft and final legal due diligence report

An interim or draft form of the legal due diligence report should be circulated to the professional team involved as soon as possible. This usually gives the nominated adviser an early indication of any problems or any areas which may require attention before the flotation process progresses any further. It also may assist the reporting accountants and inevitably helps with the task of verification.

At the end of the legal due diligence process, the report will be signed off by the solicitors to the company. This is usually immediately before publication of the admission document itself. As mentioned above, the report will be addressed to the company and to the nominated adviser. It will have covered the entire business, as summarised at the outset, and will highlight certain issues or problems as well as making recommendations.

5.4 Pre-flotation corporate matters

A number of changes may need to take place in the corporate structure of the company prior to its flotation. These may have been planned as part of the flotation agenda or they may only have become apparent because of the legal due diligence exercise. Corporate structural changes may include some or all of the following:

(a) the company may be required to be re-registered as a public limited company in accordance with the requisite provisions in Part II of the Companies Act 1985 (or if that is not possible, for example because the net assets of the company are less than its called up share capital and undistributable reserves, then a new public holding company will need to be formed and a share exchange agreement entered into between the shareholders of the limited liability company and the newly formed plc);

(b) there may need to be a reorganisation of the capital of the company, in order to comply with the public company share capital requirements in Part V of the Companies Act 1985 and/or to create a uniform share structure appropriate for flotation (i.e., to convert different classes of share into a single class of ordinary shares, all of which will be admitted to trading on AIM);

(c) the company's articles of association are likely to need to be amended so that they are in a form appropriate for a publicly quoted company, not least to include provisions stating that the shares and any other securities to be admitted to AIM are freely transferable (AIM Rule 32); and

(d) in order to be able to raise new money on flotation and subsequently, the authorised share capital of the company may need to be increased and power given to the directors to allot new shares, if necessary excluding the statutory pre-emption rights to give flexibility to issue new shares for cash in appropriate circumstances in the future.

Once the changes have all been identified and agreed, the solicitors to the company will prepare the necessary documentation. Normally this would then be signed and any filings to Companies House made in advance of publication of the admission document.

5.5 The admission document and the verification of its contents

5.5.1 Drafting the admission document

Once sufficient work has been undertaken on the long-form report by the reporting accountants and on the legal due diligence report by the solicitors to the company, work can commence on the drafting of the narrative section and the other parts of the admission document. The nominated adviser generally leads the drafting team, and the solicitors to the company are primarily responsible for the "statutory and general information" section of the admission document. In addition, the solicitors to the company review the main descriptive sections of the admission document, which are prepared by the nominated adviser together with the company.

The solicitors to the company will need to make sure that all applicable AIM Rules have been complied with. Completion of a tick list of these rules is essential to ensure full and proper compliance. A considerable number of these rules are satisfied by means of the information which is contained in the "statutory and general information" section. By way of contrast, it is interesting to note that this "tick list" exercise is something which would actually be agreed between the United Kingdom Listing Authority and the nominated adviser in the context of a prospectus required under the Prospectus Regulations, or the sponsor in the context of a flotation on the Official List. The AIM team at the London Stock Exchange have no such involvement in relation to an AIM admission document and the responsibility of the solicitors to the company is therefore more onerous.

5.5.2 Verification of the admission document

After a number of iterations of the draft of the admission document, it will eventually be possible to allow the verification process to begin. The solicitors to the company will prepare verification notes to check the accuracy of the admission document. These verification notes take the form of questions which the directors must answer to verify the relevant statements of fact and opinion and to provide supporting material.

The actual verification usually falls into two distinct areas within the admission document, although the process is a composite exercise.

(a) First the narrative sections describing the company and its business, which are typically agreed between the nominated adviser and the company, need to be verified. This is the sales pitch within the admission document and therefore, by its very nature, is likely to contain more subjective statements of opinion about the company, its business and the market in which it operates. Great care is needed to verify all subjective statements properly.

(b) Then the factual, more objective statements in the admission document also need to be verified. These are typically matters in the control of the solicitors to the company and the other professional members of the advisory team. This area could and should be capable of verification with relative ease. This is particularly so if sufficient attention has been paid to the preliminary due diligence enquiries and the responses to those enquiries as well as to the provision of full documentation by the company to its solicitors.

5.5.3 Relevance of the verification process

It is true to say that the verification process often receives bad press and *its reputation goes before it*. However, its importance cannot be stressed enough. The company and its directors are responsible for the admission document. The directors are personally responsible for the accuracy of the admission document and may be personally liable to pay compensation to investors in the company if the admission document is inaccurate, untrue or misleading. Each director must therefore be satisfied on reasonable grounds that each statement of fact or opinion is not only accurate but also is not misleading in its context. The verification process is designed to eradicate any statement incapable of substantiation by the company and its directors. It is also designed to factually test all significant statements. Together with the tick list, the verification process therefore represents a vital check that the admission document must pass, thus protecting the company, its directors and the nominated adviser. The verification process is not, in itself, a defence, but it is intended to provide the evidentiary basis for establishing that reasonable care has been taken by the persons responsible for the admission document.

5.5.4 When should verification have been completed?

The verification process should generally be substantially completed by the time the broker to the company sets up presentations to be made by the company to potential institutional investors or any other third party. Depending on the type of business, its maturity and the experience of its management, among other things, a so-called teaser or pathfinder admission document may be sent out to prospective investors early in the process before any formal presentations are made. Exactly the same concerns exist regarding the accuracy of the information in any teaser or pathfinder document, as well as in any presentational slides shown to prospective investors. The solicitors to the company will be responsible for making sure that this process is properly completed in respect of any pre-flotation material, ensuring that no additional information is contained in presentational materials which is not contained in the public admission document.

5.6 Placing/underwriting or introduction agreement

5.6.1 Parties to the placing agreement

If it is proposed to raise "new money" as part of the flotation process, the solicitors to the company will negotiate and advise the company and the directors in relation to the placing or underwriting agreement. Any such agreement is the prime responsibility of the solicitors to the issue. The parties to the placing or underwriting agreement will be the company, possibly also the directors, and the party which is carrying out the placing or underwriting (namely the nominated adviser and/or broker). It is not uncommon for there to be existing investors in the company who wish to exit the company as part of the flotation arrangements. Quite apart from director shareholders, private equity investors, venture capitalists or banks with part of their investment in equity may wish to sell shares upon the flotation. It is likely that the terms of any such arrangements will also need to be negotiated with such investors and their advisers subject to any lock-in requirement, as discussed at 5.6.4 below.

5.6.2 Contents of the placing agreement

Apart from the pure mechanics of the placing or underwriting, a number of other key issues will need to be negotiated by the parties. These may include some or all of the following:

(a) the conditions attaching to the obligations of the nominated adviser, including, ultimately, assisting the company in connection with the admission of its existing issued, and to be issued, shares to trading on AIM;

(b) the placing obligations of the broker and whether the broker is, for example, going to use its reasonable endeavours to find subscribers for new shares but not otherwise subscribe itself, or whether it will underwrite the issue and subscribe for new shares to the extent that it cannot find subscribers for some or all of the intended issue;

(c) the fees, commissions and expenses to be paid by the company to the nominated adviser and/or broker;

(d) the warranties, undertakings and indemnities to be given by the company and its directors to the nominated adviser and/or broker in respect of the admission document, the company and its business;

(e) the events which entitle the nominated adviser and/or broker to terminate the placing or underwriting agreement, including breach of agreement, breach of warranty and an event of *force majeure* which is outside the control of the company (11 September 2001 is often now cited as an example of event of *force majeure*);

(f) the limitations on future activities and the obligations imposed on the company to consult with the nominated adviser and broker;

(g) the lock-in provisions restricting directors and other parties from selling their shares (as to which *see* 5.6.4 below).

5.6.3   Negotiation of the placing agreement

Certain issues can become very emotive topics in the course of nego-
tiations, particularly on the subject of whether directors will be
required by the nominated adviser and/or broker to give warranties
and indemnities alongside the company. If directors are required to
do so, then there is the further issue of whether, and if so what, limitations on liability should apply to those warranties and indemnities
given by the directors. Common limitations on liabilities might
include a limitation on how long the directors remain liable and for
how much they are liable. Whilst practice does develop and change,
every flotation is different and it is the task of the solicitors to the
company to guide and advise the company and its directors according to the circumstances prevailing at the time.

If no "new money" is being raised then an introduction agreement
will be prepared by the solicitors to the issue. This will be similar to a
placing agreement with deletion of references to any placing of
shares!

5.6.4   Requirement for "lock-in" of shares in a placing agreement

The AIM Rules impose special conditions on companies where the
main activity of the company is a business that has not been independent and earning revenue for at least two years. In such a case, the
company must ensure that all directors, substantial shareholders
(owning 10 per cent or more of the voting share capital) and employees (owning a half per cent or more of the voting share capital) agree
not to dispose of any interest in their AIM shares for a year from
admission. Certain others may be required to lock in their shares if
they are associates of a director or substantial shareholders. This lock
in can sometimes be contained in the placing agreement.
Alternatively, a separate lock-in agreement will be prepared, typically
between the company, the nominated adviser and the shareholder in
question. This may occur, for example, where there are quite a
number of shareholders who fall within the ambit of the rule and
where, therefore, it is not necessarily appropriate for all of them to be
a party to the placing agreement. The solicitors to the company will
want to draft this document as the obligation in the AIM Rules is
primarily imposed on the company to ensure compliance by directors

and applicable employees. It will often be the case, even when a company has traded for two years, that the nominated adviser or broker will still require a form of lock in from the same group of people, albeit that the level of exceptions and carve-outs to the lock in may be greater than permitted in the AIM Rules. The exceptions or carve-outs for a mandatory lock in under the AIM Rules only include an intervening court order, death or a takeover offer.

5.7   Directors' service contracts

The AIM Rules, the Companies Acts and the requirements of the investor protection committees lay down certain criteria relating to directors' service contracts and certain matters which need to be disclosed in the admission document. These govern what is acceptable in such contracts and also the circumstances in which such contracts must be disclosed to shareholders and approved by them. The solicitors to the company will advise the company and draft the necessary contracts (and letters of appointment for non-executive directors) accordingly. The nominated adviser will want to ensure that key directors and employees are sensibly tied in to the business, as well as being sensibly remunerated.

5.8   Employee share participation

A flotation offers the company the opportunity of adopting one or more of the share incentive and share option schemes which are capable of approval by HM Revenue & Customs and which allow employees to obtain an equity participation in the company on a beneficial tax basis. The existence of share option packages can dovetail with the overall employment package to properly incentivise staff. There are three types of scheme that can be approved by the HM Revenue & Customs:

(a)   executive share option schemes (which may include Enterprise Management Incentives or employee share ownership plans, known as "ESOPs");
(b)   save-as-you-earn schemes; and
(c)   profit sharing schemes.

In addition to HM Revenue & Customs' approved schemes, it may be appropriate to set up particular share option schemes which are outside HM Revenue & Customs' rules. These would still need to conform to the guidelines laid down by the investment protection committees.

If management do have plans to grant options then it is highly advisable to give early consideration to drafting and implementing the appropriate scheme. In the context of approved schemes, HM Revenue & Customs are paying increased attention to those where a flotation is in the offing. The closer to flotation the less likely it is to be able to achieve a discount to the float price when valuing the options and therefore the option price and the tax consequences for the option holder are less advantageous.

5.9 Directors' duties and responsibilities on flotation and afterwards

The directors of the company already have significant responsibilities under the Companies Acts and the insolvency legislation. However, with the introduction of outside public shareholders and inevitable greater public scrutiny of the actions of the board of a company which has its shares traded on a public share market, these responsibilities are significantly increased.

The directors of the company will be accepting new responsibilities under:

(a) the Financial Services and Markets Act 2000 and, if the admission document constitutes a prospectus, the Prospectus Regulations 2005;

(b) the rules of the London Stock Exchange relating to the continuing obligations of AIM companies;

(c) the insider dealing legislation in the Criminal Justice Act 1993;

(d) the City Code on Takeovers and Mergers; and

(e) the reports upon corporate governance, including the constitution of the board of directors and the terms of reference of remuneration, audit and nominations committees.

As part of the flotation process the solicitors to the company will give formal advice to the directors on their new responsibilities and will prepare for them a detailed reference memorandum covering all these topics. The formal advice is usually given at a full board meeting of the company either by the solicitor to the company or the nominated adviser. The memorandum, together with the oral explanation, effectively allows the company to give the first of six declarations it has to make on the AIM application form signed by the company before flotation. (The form of the application is set out at Appendix 5.) This particular declaration states that the applicant has received advice and guidance "as to the nature of our rights and obligations under the AIM Rules and the Rules of the London Stock Exchange and fully understands and accepts these rights and obligations".

5.10 Nominated adviser agreement and broker agreement

The AIM Rules require that a company whose securities are traded on AIM must retain a nominated adviser and a broker at all times. Accordingly, part of the role of the solicitors to the company will be to negotiate and advise the company and the directors in relation to the nominated adviser agreement and broker agreement. These agreements may be combined into one agreement (particularly if the nominated adviser and broker is the same investment bank) or alternatively they may take the form of two separate agreements. A practice is developing to include the appropriate terms that would otherwise be contained in the nominated adviser and broker agreement in the original engagement letter with the company.

Whatever the form of agreement, the main provisions that will be included to govern the relationship between the company and the nominated adviser and broker are:

(a) the appointment of the nominated adviser and its obligations (such obligations typically include making the nominated adviser's declaration in accordance with Rule 39 of the AIM Rules, ensuring compliance by the company with the AIM Rules, liaising with the AIM team in relation to the continued trading of the company's shares on AIM, reviewing the trading performance and financial condition of the company against any profit forecast, estimate or projection included in the admission document and releasing to a regulatory information service all information received by the company which is required to be announced under the AIM Rules);

(b)   the appointment of the broker and its obligations (such obligations typically include advising and coordinating an appropriate investor liaison programme for the company, maintaining an orderly market in the company's shares and consequently coordinating transactions in the company's shares, advising the company on investment conditions, the pricing of its securities and significant movements in its share price, and providing advice to the company on anticipated market reactions to matters such as finance raising, acquisitions and disposals);

(c)   the obligations of the company and its directors (which will typically include complying with the AIM Rules on a timely basis, adhering to all statements of intent contained in the admission document, informing the nominated adviser and/or broker of any material changes affecting the financial or trading position or prospects of the company and providing the nominated adviser with the information that the company is required in accordance with the AIM Rules to notify to a regulatory information service);

(d)   the fees and expenses to be paid by the company to the nominated adviser and broker;

(e)   the undertakings and indemnities to be given by the company and, as appropriate, its directors to the nominated adviser and broker in respect of their appointments; and

(f)   the events which entitle a nominated adviser or broker to terminate their appointment.

5.11   General advice on the flotation given by the solicitors to the company

The solicitors to the company will also be responsible for providing general advice to the company, which may be required in relation to matters arising out of the flotation. Such general advice would include drafting and negotiating ancillary documentation. These documents will comprise:

(a) directors' responsibility statements (pursuant to which directors agree, amongst other things, to accept responsibility for the admission document);

(b) powers of attorney (pursuant to which each director of the company appoints any other director of the company to be his attorney to agree and execute any documents required for admission);

(c) comfort letters (these would usually include letters from the company and/or the directors addressed to the nominated adviser confirming the company's financial reporting procedures, confirming that the directors understand the nature of their responsibilities and obligations as a director of an AIM company and confirming that the admission document includes all information which the company reasonably considers necessary to enable investors to form a full understanding of the assets and liabilities, financial position, profits and losses and prospects of the company and of the rights attaching to its shares); and

(d) engagement letters to be entered into by the company with its registrar, printers and public relations firm.

5.12   Solicitors to the issue

The principal responsibility of the solicitors to the issue is to advise the nominated adviser and/or broker in relation to admission.

The principal functions include:

(a) reviewing and advising on the drafting of the admission document;

(b) reviewing the legal due diligence report;

(c) reviewing and advising on the verification notes which will be prepared by the solicitors to the company;

(d) reviewing, commenting on and (if necessary) negotiating the ancillary documentation; such documentation would include lock-in agreements, the directors' responsibility statements, powers of attorney and comfort letters;

(e) drafting and negotiating the placing, underwriting or introduction agreement;

(f) drafting and negotiating the nominated adviser agreement and broker agreement; and

(g) providing general advice to the nominated adviser regarding research notes, presentation slides, any "pathfinder" or teaser admission document, placing letters and any other communication by the nominated adviser and/or broker on behalf of the company with potential investors or any third party, particularly in respect of the financial promotion restrictions contained in the Financial Services and Markets Act 2000.

These functions have been discussed above in relation to the responsibilities of the solicitors to the company. However, obviously the solicitors to the issue will be looking at these documents from a different perspective to the solicitors to the company as they act for the nominated adviser and broker.

In similar fashion to the declaration given by the company in its application to AIM, the nominated adviser has to declare, among other things, that the directors of the applicant have been appropriate advice and guidance. (*See* the nominated adviser declaration form at Appendix 6.) Moreover, the nominated adviser has to confirm to the AIM team that the AIM Rules have been complied with and that it is satisfied that the company and its securities are appropriate to be admitted to AIM. These are serious declarations and ones on which the nominated adviser and broker need legal input and assistance from their solicitors.

5.13   Conclusion

The roles of solicitors to the company and to the issue are complex and far-reaching. They are central to the process of achieving admission to AIM. Fulfilling their roles properly requires great experience of the flotation process, an ability to display significant manpower and to understand the extensive teamwork required.

Chapter 6

The Statutory Framework

John Bennett
Partner
Berwin Leighton Paisner LLP

6.1 Introduction

6.1.1 The old regime

Up until 30 June 2005, the Public Offers of Securities Regulations 1995 ("POS Regulations") set out the prospectus regime for public offers in the UK of unlisted securities of UK and foreign issuers, including securities to be admitted to AIM.

AIM is owned and regulated by the London Stock Exchange plc ("LSE") and, subject to any other regulatory requirements, the rules for companies with a class of securities admitted or seeking admission to AIM are set out in the AIM Rules for companies ("AIM Rules"). Until 30 June 2005, the AIM Rules provided that an applicant to AIM had to produce an admission document which contained information equivalent to that which would be required by the POS Regulations, whether or not the applicant was making a public offer and would otherwise be required to produce a prospectus under the POS Regulations.

6.1.2 The new regime

In 2003 the new EC Prospectus Directive (2003/71/EC) ("Prospectus Directive") and the Market Abuse Directive (2003/6/EC) were published as part of the Financial Services Action Plan. These were required to be implemented by EU Member States by 1 July 2005.

In the UK, the new prospectus regime was implemented through the EU Prospectus Regulations 2005 (SI 2005/1433) ("the Regulations").

Section 85 of the Financial Services and Markets Act 2000 ("FSMA 2000") (as amended by the Regulations) introduced with effect from 1 July 2005 a requirement for a prospectus approved in advance by the Financial Services Authority ("FSA") to be published beforehand (unless an available exemption applies) in two distinct circumstances:

(a)   where a company offers its transferable securities to the public;
(b)   where a company requests the admission of its transferable securities to trading on a regulated market.

The Regulations also revoked the POS Regulations and authorised the FSA to make the Prospectus Rules (*see* 6.2.3).

At the same time the new market abuse regime was implemented in the UK through the Financial Services and Markets Act 2000 (Market Abuse) Regulations 2005 (SI 2005/381). Among other things these authorised the FSA to make disclosure rules relating to the publication and control of inside information for companies with securities admitted to trading on a regulated market in the UK.

The aim of the new regime was broadly to harmonise investor protection and the requirements relating to the issue of a prospectus when securities are offered to the public or are admitted to trading on a regulated market in any European Economic Area ("EEA") State. A regulated market for this purpose means a securities market recognised by a Member State for the purposes of the Investment Services Directive (93/22/EEC).

6.1.3   The implications for AIM

There was general concern that the implementation of the EU Directives which form part of the Financial Services Action Plan would damage AIM in view of the "one size fits all" requirements which would apply to all regulated markets. Accordingly, with effect from 12 October 2004, the AIM market of the LSE ceased to be a regulated market and instead became an exchange-regulated market. The goal was to preserve AIM's regulatory regime and market structure with continued regulatory oversight by the FSA whilst avoiding some of the more onerous requirements of the EU Directives.

As a consequence, AIM companies and prospective AIM companies are less affected by the new regulatory regime. In particular, an AIM company will not be required to issue a prospectus approved by the FSA just because its securities are trading, or are to be admitted to trading, on AIM. It will only have to issue an approved prospectus where any marketing of its securities constitutes an offer to the public under the Prospectus Directive and no relevant exemption applies. Most AIM companies are likely to seek to fall within one of the exemptions such as the exemptions for an offer made to or directed at:

(a) qualified investors; or
(b) fewer than 100 persons, other than qualified investors.

The LSE consulted on what standard of information should be required for an AIM admission document where a Prospectus Directive FSA approved prospectus was not required. The options were:

(a) to adopt the Prospectus Directive requirements with certain carve-outs to reflect the nature of AIM ("AIM-PD");
(b) to maintain the current POS standard by copying POS into the AIM Rules; or
(c) to await a possible POS 2 regime to replace the POS Regulations.

After consultation, the LSE adopted AIM-PD as the standard of information required for an admission document where an approved prospectus is not required. It recognised that the full Prospectus Directive was not appropriate in these circumstances but, whilst maintaining broadly equivalent standards to those which applied under the old regime, it wished to ensure consistency in the type and format of information seen by investors, adopt an up-to-date and well-recognised standard (albeit with carve-outs) and simplify the process for companies wishing to move across to an EU regulated market in due course.

6.2 Legislation

6.2.1 The Prospectus Directive and related EC measures

The aim of the Prospectus Directive is to harmonise the requirements for the drawing up, scrutiny and distribution of prospectuses to be published when transferable securities are:

(a)   offered to the public; or
(b)   admitted to trading on a regulated market situated or operating within an EU Member State.

The Prospectus Directive introduces the concept of a "single passport" for issuers, making it easier to raise capital throughout the EU. This means that once a prospectus has been approved by the competent authority of the home Member State, it must be accepted throughout the EU subject only (if the relevant host state authority requires) to translation of the summary into the official language of the host state and to certain notifications to the host state authority.

The Prospectus Directive, like many of the measures under the Financial Services Action Plan, was adopted and implemented through the so-called Lamfalussy approach. This introduced a new four-level legislative approach to the harmonisation of financial services regulation in the EU that deals with framework principles, implementing measures, regulatory cooperation and finally enforcement. The Prospectus Directive, as a piece of framework legislation, does not specify the form and content of prospectuses but instead these are prescribed in a detailed EU Level 2 implementing regulation known as Commission Regulation 809/2004 of 29 April 2004 ("EU Prospectus Regulation"). The EU Prospectus Regulation became directly applicable as law in Member States from 1 July 2005. Alongside the EU Prospectus Regulation, the Committee of European Securities Regulators ("CESR") has published recommendations ("the CESR Recommendations") setting out detailed guidance on how the provisions of the Prospectus Directive and the EU Prospectus Regulation should be interpreted.

6.2.2   The Financial Services and Markets Act 2000

The EU Prospectus Regulations 2005 (SI 2005/1433) implement the Prospectus Directive into domestic legislation in the UK under Section 2(2) of the European Communities Act 1972. The Regulations amend the FSMA 2000 by setting out, among other things, the basic circumstances in which an approved prospectus is required. Section 85 FSMA 2000 states the general rule that a person may not make an offer of securities to the public in the UK or seek admission to trading on a regulated market in the UK unless a prospectus approved by the FSA has first been published. The Regulations implement some of the important exemptions from the Prospectus Directive (the Prospectus Directive includes further exemptions which are incorporated into the Prospectus Rules), authorise the FSA to make the Prospectus Rules and revoke the POS Regulations and the Financial Services and Markets Act 2000 (Offers of Securities) Order 2001 (SI 2001/2958).

FSMA 2000 (as amended) also deals with the procedure for dealing with an application for approval of a prospectus. The period for consideration of an application is, except in the case of a new issuer, 10 working days starting with the first working day after the date on which the application and all required information is received by the FSA. In the case of a new issuer, the equivalent period is 20 working days.

6.2.3 The FSA's Prospectus Rules

The FSA's Prospectus Rules made in exercise of powers granted under FSMA 2000 set out further detailed requirements relating to prospectuses and incorporate some of the permitted exemptions from the prospectus requirements. The relevant provisions of FSMA 2000 must therefore be read in conjunction with the Prospectus Rules.

As the Prospectus Directive is a "maximum harmonisation" directive it does not permit Member States to require additional disclosure in a prospectus and there was therefore little scope for the UK to apply discretion in the way it was implemented. Section 84 FSMA 2000 sets out the matters that may be dealt with by the Prospectus Rules through rules (labelled "R" in the Prospectus Rules), including the form and content of a prospectus, the period of validity of a prospectus and the ways in which a prospectus may be published. Under Section 157 FSMA 2000, the FSA can also give guidance (which is labelled "G" in the Prospectus Rules) with respect to the operation of the Prospectus Rules. Paragraphs 1.1.6G and 1.1.8G of the Prospectus Rules state that, in determining whether the prospectus regime has been complied with, the FSA will take into account whether a person has complied with the CESR recommendations. As a result the Prospectus Rules will need to be read in conjunction with the CESR recommendations.

6.2.4 The Companies Act 1985 ("CA 1985")

A domestic private company limited by shares is prohibited by Sections 81 and 742A CA 1985 from offering its shares or debentures to the public or from allotting or agreeing to allot its shares or debentures with a view to all or any of them being offered for sale to the public. Under Section 742A CA 1985, an offer is not made to the public if it can properly be regarded, in all the circumstances, as either not being calculated to result in the shares or debentures becoming available for subscription or purchase by persons other than those receiving the offer, or as being a domestic concern of the people receiving and making it. This definition of an "offer to the public" differs from the definition of an "offer of transferable securities to the public" in FSMA 2000 (*see* 6.3.3 below). It will be necessary to consider each of these tests in context.

Various provisions of CA 1985 detailed below still apply to any offer of shares or debentures to the public by a domestic UK company whether or not it is required to publish a prospectus in accordance with Part VI FSMA 2000. These provisions have been repealed in relation to listed securities but not in relation to unlisted securities, including securities admitted or to be admitted to AIM. This hangover from the days of the Financial Services Act 1986 is to be addressed as part of the pending reform of company law. Although the Government stated that it was its objective to align, as far as possible, the CA 1985 meaning of "offer to the public" (and in particular the related exemptions) with the definition and exemptions which apply in relation to an offer to the public for the purposes of FSMA 2000, it does not appear that the relevant provisions of the Company Law Reform Bill which was published on 1 November 2005 achieve this objective.

In addition to Sections 81 and 742A CA 1985, the residual provisions which for the time being apply to offers by domestic companies of unlisted securities include the following:

(a) Section 82 CA 1985 requires that no shares or debentures be allotted by a company in pursuance of a prospectus issued generally until the beginning of the third business day after that on which the prospectus is first issued or such later time (if any) as may be specified in the prospectus.

(b) Section 83 CA 1985 provides that no allotment is to be made of any share capital of a company offered to the public for subscription unless a minimum subscription, which must be stated in the prospectus, is raised.

(c) Section 84 CA 1985 provides that no allotment can be made of any share capital of a public company offered for subscription unless the issue is fully subscribed or the offer states that, even if it is not fully subscribed, the actual amount of capital subscribed may be allotted in any event or in the event of specified conditions being satisfied.

(d) Section 97 CA 1985 requires that where a UK company offers shares to the public for subscription, any commissions to be paid by the company to any person in consideration for his subscribing or agreeing to subscribe for any shares in the company or procuring or agreeing to procure subscriptions are to be disclosed in the prospectus and where shares are not so offered any such commissions are to be disclosed in a statement in the required form delivered to Companies House for registration.

6.2.5 Financial promotion

The financial promotion regime contained in Section 21 FSMA 2000 prohibits "a person in the course of business, from communicating an invitation or inducement to engage in investment activity" unless he is an authorised person under FSMA 2000, or an authorised person approves the content of the communication, or the communication is exempt.

In order to avoid any regulatory overlap, the financial promotion regime does not apply to a prospectus or supplementary prospectus, any other document required or permitted to be published by the Prospectus Rules or any non-real time or solicited real-time communication required or permitted to be communicated by the rules of a relevant market or a body which regulates the market. For this purpose, AIM constitutes a relevant market and accordingly an AIM admission document which is not a prospectus but which is produced pursuant to the AIM Rules and any other document required or permitted to be communicated by the AIM Rules is exempt.

A pathfinder prospectus will not be covered by these exemptions but the distribution of the pathfinder by an AIM company will typically be designed to take advantage of the professional, sophisticated and high net worth investor exemptions. Any other advertisement which is used in conjunction with the marketing of an AIM company's securities but which is not an approved prospectus or an AIM-PD will generally need to comply with the financial promotion regime unless it can also take advantage of those exemptions.

6.3 The new prospectus regime and AIM companies

6.3.1 When is a prospectus required to be issued by AIM companies?

An AIM company will not be required to issue a prospectus approved by the FSA just because its securities are admitted to trading on AIM. However, it will have to issue an approved prospectus when any marketing of its securities constitutes an offer of tradeable securities to the public in the UK.

6.3.2 What if a prospectus is not required?

If the transaction does not involve an offer of transferable securities to the public in the UK or an exemption from the requirement for an approved prospectus applies, an applicant (whether or not its shares are already quoted) will be required under the AIM Rules to prepare an admission document (complying with the Prospectus Directive with carve-outs).

6.3.3 Is there an "offer of transferable securities to the public"?

This concept is significant because unless an exemption is available, an FSA approved fully compliant prospectus will have to be published by an AIM company if there is an offer of transferable securities to the public in the UK as defined in Section 102B FSMA 2000. In practice, many AIM companies are likely to seek to fall within one of the exemptions to the requirement to prepare a prospectus in order to avoid the obligation to have a prospectus approved by the FSA even if there is an offer of transferable securities to the public.

An "offer of transferable securities to the public" is defined widely as a communication to any person in any form and by any means which presents sufficient information on the transferable securities to be offered and the terms on which they are offered, to enable an investor to decide to buy or subscribe for the securities in question. It includes the placing of securities through a financial intermediary. To the extent that an offer of transferable securities is made to a person in the UK, it is an offer of transferable securities to the public in the UK unless an exemption applies. Transferable securities include shares, bonds or other forms of securitised debt which are transferable securities (for the purposes of the Investment Services Directive 93/22/EEC) other than money-market instruments which have a maturity of less than 12 months. An option granted under an employee share option scheme which is not transferable will not be caught by the new regime.

6.3.4   Does an exemption apply?

There are a number of exemptions from the requirement to publish a prospectus. Although most of these are similar to exemptions that were available under the old prospectus and listing particulars regimes, there are important differences. Exemptions are contained both in Section 86 FSMA 2000 and in the Prospectus Rules (PR 1.2.2R and 1.2.3R) and must be considered separately in relation to public offers and the admission of securities to trading. Where a transaction involves both a public offer and the admission of securities to trading on a regulated market, an exemption from both requirements would be needed to avoid a prospectus. For example, a rights issue of less than 10 per cent of an existing class of listed shares would benefit from the 10 per cent exemption from the requirement to produce a prospectus for admission to trading on a regulated market, but a prospectus would nevertheless be required because there is a public offer of the securities and the 10 per cent exemption does not apply to a public offer. In the context of the AIM market, only the exemptions which apply to a public offer will be relevant.

One of the most significant exemptions relates to offers to "qualified investors". This is a broader category than the "professionals only" exemption that was available under the old regime and includes small and medium-sized enterprises and individuals who satisfy certain criteria set out in the Directive and who are registered as qualified investors with the FSA. The FSA allows such investors to "self-certify" that they satisfy the relevant criteria.

There is also an exemption for offers made to or directed at fewer than 100 persons (other than qualified investors) per Member State and an exemption for offers where the minimum consideration per investor for, or the minimum denomination of, the securities is at least €50,000.

An offer to a qualified investor who can accept offers of securities without referring to the underlying clients (which would include a discretionary private client broker) will not be treated as an offer to those underlying clients when applying the qualifying investor or the 100 persons exemptions.

Prospectus Rule 1.2.2R(2) contains an exemption from the requirement to produce a prospectus where securities are offered in connection with a takeover made by means of an exchange offer, if a document is available containing information which is regarded by the FSA as being equivalent to that of a prospectus, taking into account the requirements of EU legislation. The FSA proposes to apply the full vetting process to any such takeover document to determine whether it is equivalent to a prospectus. There will be a degree of discretion about what will be acceptable as equivalent, but it will be limited.

Sub-paragraph (h) of Article 1(2) of the Prospectus Directive excludes from the scope of the Prospectus Directive securities included in an offer where the total consideration under the offer is less than €2.5 million, calculated over 12 months, and this is reflected in Section 85(5) and paragraph 9(1), Schedule 11A FSMA 2000.

Somewhat confusingly there is also an exemption from the requirement for an approved prospectus which applies to an offer of securities with a total consideration of less than €100,000, which limit is calculated over a 12-month period (Article 3(2) of the Prospectus Directive and Section 86(1)(e) and 86(4) FSMA 2000). The effect of the interaction of these provisions is that currently the higher limit applies but HM Treasury could, at a domestic level, implement a separate regime to cover public offers between €100,000 and €2.5 million. However, there are no current plans to introduce such a regime.

6.4   Format of an admission document

If a prospectus is required, it may be drawn up as a single document containing all the requisite information or as a three-part document consisting of a registration document (which is valid for 12 months and can be used for a number of issues of securities during that period), a securities note (containing information relating to the securities), and a non-technical summary not exceeding 2,500 words setting out the essential characteristics and risks relating to the issuer and the securities. The necessary information must be presented in a form which is comprehensible and easy to analyse. These format requirements do not apply if a prospectus is not required. In practice it is likely that a single document in a similar format will be used whether or not a prospectus is required.

6.5   Content requirements for an admission document

The Prospectus Rules introduced a number of changes to the content requirements for prospectuses. The principal changes are to require inclusion of a summary which must, briefly and in non-technical language, convey the essential characteristics of, and risks associated with, the issuer and the transferable securities to which the prospectus relates. Risk factors specific to the issuer or its industry must be disclosed prominently in a section headed "risk factors". An Operating and Financial Review of the issuer's business, including the causes of material changes from year to year in the financial information to the extent necessary for an understanding of the issuer's business as a whole, is required. A statement of board practices is also required.

Where a prospectus is being prepared, the relevant Annexes to the EU Prospectus Regulation (Annexes I–III) should be followed but supplemented with any additional or more stringent requirements set out in Schedule 2 to the AIM Rules.

Where a prospectus is not required, a new applicant to AIM will be required to produce an admission document containing the information specified in Schedule 2 to the AIM Rules. This essentially adopts the Prospectus Directive with carve-outs (AIM-PD). The AIM Rules refer to the information required by Annex I–III of the EU Prospectus Regulation. These have been reproduced and colour-coded in the AIM Rules to indicate the carve-outs relevant to AIM-PD.

As a result, the specific contents requirements under AIM-PD is broadly equivalent with the standard of information previously required by the POS Regulations but is based on the requirements of the Prospectus Rules for consistency. Carve-outs were chosen with the overall objective of preserving the previous admission process in terms of the level of detail required within admission documents whilst ensuring that AIM maintains high standards of regulation and transparency and keeps up to date with best practice. Some information required in Annex I–III of the EU Prospectus Regulation was deemed of a higher standard than the POS Regulations and was therefore carved out of the mandatory requirements of AIM-PD.

Some sections of Annex I–III represent areas which overlap with more rigorous disclosure requirements for an AIM admission document under Schedule 2 to the AIM Rules. In these cases, the LSE has maintained its existing higher standards. These relate to profit forecasts or estimates, directors' disclosures and working capital statements.

In addition, Schedule 2 to the AIM Rules requires that an admission document must include certain additional information including a standard risk statement regarding AIM, a statement of compulsory 12-month lock-ins for directors and certain employees where the issuer's main activity is a business which has not been independent and earning revenue for at least two years, and details of its investing strategy where it is an investing company.

Under the POS Regulations there was an overriding requirement, which is replicated under the new prospectus regime, that a prospectus must contain all information which is necessary to enable investors to make an informed assessment of the assets and liabilities, financial position, profits and losses, and prospects of the issuer and of the rights attaching to the securities. However, there is now arguably a more stringent general duty of disclosure under Schedule 2 to the AIM Rules requiring the inclusion in the admission document (whether or not it constitutes a prospectus) of all other information which the applicant reasonably considers necessary to enable investors to form a full understanding of:

(a) the assets and liabilities, financial position, profits and losses, and prospects of the applicant and its securities for which admission is being sought;

(b) the rights attaching to those securities; and

(c) any other matter contained in the admission document.

The FSA may authorise the omission of information from a prospectus on the grounds that its disclosure would be seriously detrimental to the issuer (provided that the omission would be unlikely to mislead the public with regard to any facts or circumstances which are essential for an informed assessment) or that the information is only of minor importance for a specific offer to the public or admission to trading and unlikely to influence an informed assessment. Where the admission document is not a prospectus, the LSE can, without FSA approval, authorise the omission of information in similar circumstances where the applicant's nominated adviser confirms that those circumstances exist.

6.6   Filing and publication requirements

At least three business days before the expected date of admission, an applicant must submit to the LSE a completed application form and an electronic version of its admission document accompanied by a nominated adviser's declaration. The admission document must be published by making copies available free of charge to the public for not less than one month from the date of admission.

If the admission document is a prospectus, the document must be approved by the FSA and then filed with the FSA and made available to the public (in the manner required by the Prospectus Rules) as soon as practicable, and in any case at a reasonable time in advance of, and at the latest at the beginning of, the offer or the admission to trading of the securities involved. In the case of an initial public offer of a class of shares not already admitted to trading that is to be admitted to trading for the first time, the prospectus must be made available to the public at least six working days before the end of the offer. A prospectus no longer needs to be filed at Companies House.

6.7 Supplementary admission documents and withdrawal rights

If between the date of publication of the admission document and the date of admission of the company's shares to AIM, any material new factor, mistake or inaccuracy arises or is noted relating to the information contained in the admission document, a supplementary admission document containing details of the new factor, mistake or inaccuracy must be published. If the admission document is a prospectus, any supplementary document must comply with the Prospectus Rules in the same way as the prospectus if any significant new factor, material mistake or inaccuracy arises or is identified.

If the admission document is a prospectus and a supplementary prospectus is published, a person who has agreed to buy or subscribe securities may withdraw his acceptance during the period ending two working days after publication of the supplementary prospectus. This was not the case under the old prospectus regime. It is worth noting that the FSA has indicated that it considers that once the contract resulting from the offer has been performed by way of allotment or transfer of the relevant securities, the withdrawal right of the investor in respect of those securities ceases (the FSA's "List!", publication Issue No. 11 – September 2005).

6.8 Further admission documents and secondary issues

A further admission document will be required for an AIM company only when it is:

(a)   required to issue a prospectus for a further issue of AIM quoted securities. An AIM company is no longer exempt from preparing a further admission document where less than 10 per cent of a class of AIM securities are being offered; or

(b)   seeking admission for a new class of securities; or

(c)   undertaking a reverse takeover.

There is an obligation on AIM companies to prepare and publish a prospectus (where an exemption is not available, which invariably it will not be) in relation to open offers, rights issues and takeover offers where AIM securities are used as consideration.

As noted above, there is an exemption in relation to takeovers where a document is available containing information that is regarded by the FSA as being equivalent to that of a prospectus, but this is unlikely to make any difference in practice.

6.9   Responsibility for admission document

The Prospectus Rules set out the persons responsible for an approved prospectus (Rule 5.5). The new regime is broadly similar to the old regime. Those responsible include the directors of the issuer. Where the prospectus relates to non-equity securities the Prospectus Rules do not expressly make the directors responsible. However, in practice they are likely to be responsible in their capacity as persons who have authorised the contents of the prospectus.

The Guidance Notes to the AIM Rules confirm that the persons responsible for the information provided in the admission document are the same persons that would be responsible for the information in a prospectus under the Prospectus Rules (Guidance Notes to Schedule 2 (a)). The admission document will also need to include a declaration of responsibility from those responsible for the document.

6.10   Liability

6.10.1   Criminal liability

Section 85(3) FSMA 2000 makes it a criminal offence for a person to offer transferable securities to the public in the UK unless an FSA approved prospectus has been made available before the offer is made or an exemption from the requirement to publish a prospective applies. Section 397(1) FSMA 2000 also imposes criminal liability on any person who makes a statement, promise or forecast which he knows to be misleading, false or deceptive, or dishonestly conceals any material facts for the purpose of inducing (or is reckless as to whether it may induce) another person to enter into or offer to enter into, a contract for the subscription or purchase of an investment.

6.10.2 Civil liability

Liability for the admission document can also arise under the civil offence of market abuse contained in Sections 118–131 FSMA 2000. One of the new categories of market abuse arising from the implementation of the EU Market Abuse Directive is behaviour involving the dissemination of information which gives, or is likely to give, a false or misleading impression as to a qualifying investment traded (or for which a request for admission to trading has been made) on a prescribed market (including AIM) by a person who knew or could be reasonably expected to have known that the information was false or misleading.

Where market abuse is committed, the FSA may impose sanctions, but the enforceability of any contract is not affected. The sanctions include the imposition of a financial penalty or the publication of a statement that the person concerned has engaged in market abuse.

Civil liability can also arise under common law in respect of untrue or misleading statements and omissions in an admission document. Those who suffer as a result of untrue or misleading statements and omissions in the admission document may be able either to claim damages or to rescind their contract. Directors and others who authorise the issue of the admission document may be liable at common law and under the Misrepresentation Act 1967 for a fraudulent or negligent misstatement made in the admission document.

6.11 Financial promotion

An admission document is exempt from the financial promotion regime whether or not it constitutes an approved prospectus. Any other communication which is published in conjunction with the marketing of an AIM company's securities but which is not an admission document or a prospectus and is not otherwise required or permitted to be communicated by the AIM Rules will need to comply with the financial promotion regime unless it is only issued to the categories of investor designated by the Financial Services and Markets Act 2000 (Financial Promotion) Order 2005 (e.g. sophisticated investors).

6.12   The future

AIM has now been in operation for over 10 years. Even before the Prospectus Directive, the number of companies moving from the Official List to AIM was growing. This is likely to increase further, particularly in light of the implementation of the Prospectus Directive and the Market Abuse Directive as AIM companies are more lightly regulated than listed companies. However, the raising of equity finance by open offers and rights issues is likely to be more costly for AIM companies now as they will almost always have to issue a full prospectus which will need to be approved by the FSA. There are two further practical implications of the recent developments:

(a)   a move to AIM from the Official List will now require the listed company to obtain a 75 per cent shareholder vote at a general meeting; and

(b)   a move to the Official List from AIM will trigger the requirement for a full approved prospectus. AIM companies can no longer seek an exemption from the UKLA.

Although AIM has secured its current flexible regulatory regime, it has decided to adopt International Accounting Standards for all AIM companies for financial years on or after 1 January 2007.

The Government is also in the process of modernising company law under the Company Law Reform Bill which will take into account a number of other developments currently under way including the implementation of further measures under the Financial Services Action Plan. AIM companies may find that they are still subject to new regulatory measures to be introduced pursuant to the Transparency Obligations Directive which must be implemented in Member States by 20 January 2007.

Chapter 7

The Admission Document and the Application Procedure

Andrew Titmas
Partner

Emma Bulleyment
Associate
Memery Crystal

7.1 Introduction

The process of applying for admission to AIM primarily seeks to ensure that the applicant company and its directors are prepared for life as a quoted company and that all material information about the company and its quoted securities are disclosed to the market.

This Chapter explains the legal, regulatory and other requirements and procedures which are involved in the admission process.

7.2 AIM Rules

The admission process is governed by the AIM Rules.

Under the AIM Rules, new applicants are required to publish an admission document which complies with the content requirements set out in Schedule 2 to the AIM Rules.

Schedule 2 to the AIM Rules requires an admission document to contain information equivalent to that required by Annexes I, II and III of Regulation 809/2004 of the European Commission (known as the Prospectus Directive) subject to certain carve-outs, some of which only apply if an admission document is issued prior to 1 January 2007. The Prospectus Directive came into force on 1 July 2005.

In addition, a company may be required by Section 85 of the Financial Services and Markets Act 2000 ("FSMA 2000") to produce a prospectus. A prospectus must be approved by the Financial Services Authority ("FSA") and comply with the Prospectus Rules issued by the FSA, which incorporate Annexes I, II and III of the Prospectus Directive in full. In practice, if a company is required to produce both an admission document and a prospectus, it would produce a document which complies with both the AIM Rules and the Prospectus Rules.

A prospectus is required if securities are offered to the public, although there are a number of circumstances set out in Section 86 FSMA 2000 where an offer will be an exempt offer and therefore no requirement to produce a prospectus will arise. These include where an offer is directed at qualified investors only or at fewer than 100 persons, other than qualified investors, per European Economic Area ("EEA") state. The Treasury has clarified that where an offer is made to a retail broker and then offered by the retail broker to his discretionary private clients, the offer is treated as having been made to one person for the purposes of establishing whether the offer is directed at more than 100 persons. It is therefore likely that few companies will be required to produce a prospectus in connection with an application for admission to AIM.

Applicants must also comply with the various administrative procedures set out in the AIM Rules, including the payment of a fee and the submission to the London Stock Exchange of certain application forms and other information.

7.3   The nominated adviser and broker

Under the AIM Rules, all new applicants must appoint a nominated adviser and broker.

Unlike applications for listing on the Official List, the London Stock Exchange does not itself generally seek to vet applicants for admission to AIM and will not comment on the admission document unless it is also a prospectus. Instead, it seeks the assurances it requires from the company's nominated adviser that the company and its directors have complied with the AIM Rules and that the company and its securities are suitable for admission to AIM.

Therefore, the nominated adviser will effectively be acting as the company's regulator as well as adviser in relation to the admission process. In order to be able to give the required assurances to the Exchange, the nominated adviser will need to seek its own assurances from the company and its directors and other professional advisers. It will often also impose a number of additional requirements on the company and its directors beyond those set out in the AIM Rules.

Where admission is accompanied by a fund-raising, the company's broker may also impose its own additional requirements for the protection of its investors and the after-market in the company's shares.

On top of the requirements of the AIM Rules, therefore, an applicant will need to comply with a number of additional requirements and procedures which have been developed, partly by reference to the requirements of the Listing Rules and partly by reference to general market practice, as a benchmark for ensuring best practice. Additional requirements and procedures may develop by reference to the Prospectus Directive.

7.4 Initial steps

7.4.1 Engagement letters

The first step in the admission process will normally be for the new applicant to appoint, and sign engagement letters with its professional advisers, including reporting accountants, lawyers, printers, financial public relations advisers and its nominated adviser and broker. The engagement letters should confirm the fact that such advisers are acting on behalf of the company (as well as, in the case of the reporting accountants, the nominated adviser and broker) and set out the scope of work that each party will undertake in the admission process and their estimated fees. Companies will usually seek to negotiate a reduced fee in the event that admission does not take place or any proposed fund-raising is not completed.

7.4.2 Administrative documents

Lists of parties and documents and a timetable will be produced at an early stage in the admission process, usually by the nominated adviser with input from the directors and other professional advisers. The timetable will act as a means of coordinating the activities of the various professional advisers and should assist the company's directors in prioritising their various commitments at different stages of the process.

7.5 Admission document

7.5.1 When is an admission document required?

An admission document is generally required for all new applicants, whether or not money is being raised on admission. However, unless a company is required to publish a prospectus under Section 85 FSMA 2000 or is carrying out a transaction classed as a reverse takeover under the AIM Rules, it will not need to publish an admission document if it already has securities of the same class quoted on AIM.

Exemptions are also available for new applicants transferring from the Official List or whose securities (of the same class) are already listed on one of the other AIM Designated Markets. This last relaxation was introduced with a view to attracting overseas companies to AIM. In practice, however, the nominated adviser or broker may, in any event, require some form of (modified) admission document or information memorandum for investors, particularly where there is to be a fund-raising on admission.

7.5.2 Content requirements – overview

Where an admission document is required, Rule 3 of the AIM Rules requires that it must disclose the information set out in Schedule 2 to the Rules. In practice, the document will typically be divided into sections relating broadly to:

(a) a description of the company and its group, including its share capital, its business, its directors, employees and organisational structure, its policies regarding corporate governance, its dividend policy, any fund-raising and how the proceeds are to be applied and the group's current trading and prospects;

(b) prominent disclosure of the risk factors which should be considered by investors when purchasing the company's securities;

(c) historical financial information relating to the group – usually the last three years' audited accounts and, often, a pro-forma statement of the group's net assets and liabilities; and

(d) an additional information section setting out, amongst other things, the rights attaching to the company's securities, summaries of material contracts, material litigation, details of the directors' terms of engagement and directors' and major shareholders' interests in the company's securities, and details of any option schemes or warrants.

7.5.3 General duty of disclosure

There is a general duty of disclosure set out in Schedule 2 which states that an admission document must contain all such information as the company considers reasonably necessary to enable investors to form a full understanding of:

(a) the assets and liabilities, financial position, profits and losses, and prospects of the issuer and its securities;

(b) the rights attaching to those securities; and

(c) any other matter contained in the admission document.

This catch-all provision means that, effectively, any information which might reasonably be considered to be material by a potential investor should be disclosed.

7.5.4 Equivalent information to the Prospectus Directive

The AIM Rules require an admission document to contain information equivalent to that which would be required by Annexes I–III (subject to certain carve-outs), unless a prospectus is required, in which case the document must comply fully with Annexes I–III. The admission document will need to be carefully checked against the content requirements of the three annexes to ensure compliance. Amongst other things, an admission document must include the following:

(a) relatively detailed risk factors specific to the group and its business or its industry;

(b) disclosure of any significant change in the financial or trading position of the group since the last financial period or a negative statement that, since the date to which the last published audited accounts have been prepared, there has been no material adverse change in the group's business or prospects;

(c) information on the most significant recent trends and any known trends, uncertainties, commitments or events which are reasonably likely to have a material effect on the issuer's prospects;

(d) detailed information regarding the company's share capital and the securities being offered and/or admitted to AIM along with any dilution effects if a fund-raising is being carried out.

7.5.5 Additional specific content requirements

Schedule 2 goes on to list a number of additional specific content requirements, including:

(a) A statement by the company's directors that, in their opinion, having made due and careful enquiry, the working capital available to the company and its group will be sufficient for its present requirements, that is for at least 12 months from the date of admission of its securities to AIM.

(b) Where the document contains a profit forecast, estimate or projection:

    (i) a statement from the directors that this has been made after due and careful enquiry;

    (ii) a statement of the principal assumptions for each factor which could have a material effect on its achievement; and

    (iii) confirmation from the nominated adviser that it has satisfied itself that such statement has been made after due and careful enquiry by the directors; and

    (iv) such profit forecast, estimate or projection must be prepared on a basis comparable with the historic financial information.

(c) Prominently on the first page, warnings to prospective investors that:

(i) AIM is a market designed primarily for emerging or smaller companies to which a higher investment risk tends to be attached than to larger or more established companies;

(ii) AIM securities are not admitted to the official list of the United Kingdom Listing Authority ("UKLA");

(iii) a prospective investor should be aware of the risks of investing in such companies and should make the decision to invest only after careful consideration and, if appropriate, consultation with an independent financial adviser; and

(iv) the London Stock Exchange Plc has not itself examined or approved the contents of the document.

(d) Where directors or other related parties or employees of a new or recently acquired company are required to be locked in under Rule 7 of the AIM Rules (for which *see* Chapter 2), a statement that the relevant persons agree not to dispose of their shares in the company for a period of at least 12 months from admission. In practice, this statement will usually set out the full extent of any lock-in required by the nominated adviser or broker in addition to the lock-in requirements of the AIM Rules.

(e) Information relating to each director (including shadow directors) and proposed director, including:

(i) their full name and age;

(ii) the names of all companies and partnerships of which each has been a director or partner at any time in the past five years;

(iii) any unspent convictions in relation to indictable offences;

(iv) details of all bankruptcies or individual voluntary arrangements;

(v) details of any receiverships, compulsory liquidations, creditors' voluntary liquidations, administrations, company voluntary arrangements or any composition or arrangements with its creditors generally or any class of its creditors of any company where such director was a director at the time of or within 12 months preceding such events;

(vi) details of any compulsory liquidations, administrations or partnership voluntary arrangements of any partnerships where such director was a partner at the time of, or within the 12 months preceding, such events; and

(vii)   details of any receiverships of any asset of such director or of a partnership of which the director was a partner at the time of or within the 12 months preceding such events;

(viii)   details of any public criticisms of such director by statutory or regulatory authorities (including recognised public bodies) and whether a director has ever been disqualified from acting as such.

(f)   The name of any person (except for professional advisers disclosed in the admission document and trade suppliers) who either has received within the 12 months preceding the application for admission, or has entered into contractual arrangements to receive on or after admission, directly or indirectly, fees, benefits or securities in the company having a total value of £10,000 or more.

(g)   The name of any director or member of a director's family who has a related financial product referenced to the company's AIM securities or securities being admitted, together with details of such financial product.

(h)   In the case of investment companies, details of their investment strategy.

The company's nominated adviser and broker may also require specific additional information to be included in the admission document, which is not expressly required under the AIM Rules.

So long as it does not also constitute a prospectus, the Exchange can authorise the omission of information from an admission document if the nominated adviser confirms that such information is minor and not likely to influence the assessment of the company by an investor or which could be seriously detrimental to the company if disclosed.

7.5.6 Public document

The admission document will, from the date of its publication, be a public document. An electronic version of the admission document must be sent to the Exchange along with the completed application form (for further details *see* 7.17.2), and copies must be made available to the public, free of charge, at an address in the UK for a period of not less than one month from the date of admission. However, there is no requirement under the AIM Rules to register a copy of the admission document with Companies House.

7.5.7   Display documents

The nominated adviser or broker will often require the company to make certain documents referred to in the admission document available for inspection by investors. This will normally include the company's memorandum and articles of association, the directors' service contracts and letters of appointment, the last three years' statutory accounts and material contracts. Sometimes, it will not be possible or desirable to display a material contract due to confidentiality clauses or for reasons of commercial sensitivity. There is no requirement under the AIM Rules to put any such document on display and the nominated adviser and broker may, therefore, agree to relax the requirement in appropriate cases, unless the admission document is a prospectus, in which case the company's memorandum and articles of association, historical financial information for the two preceding years and any documents prepared by an expert included or referred to in the admission document must be made available for inspection.

7.6   Legal considerations

7.6.1   General

It is the responsibility of the company and its directors to ensure that the admission document complies with all relevant legal and regulatory requirements, although the nominated adviser must itself confirm to the Exchange that to the best of its knowledge and belief, having made all due and careful enquiries, all requirements of the AIM Rules have been complied with. The AIM Rules also state that a company must ensure its directors accept full responsibility for its compliance with the AIM Rules and the disclosure of all relevant information. What these requirements are will, in part, depend upon:

(a) whether or not the company is using the admission document to raise new money; and

(b) the number and nature of the proposed investors.

The relevant requirements and the potential liability for the company and its directors are summarised below and more fully set out in Chapter 6.

7.6.2 Financial promotion

The admission document will normally constitute a financial promotion for the purposes of Section 21 FSMA 2000. This means that it will need to be issued or approved by an authorised person, such as the company's nominated adviser or broker, unless it constitutes an exempt communication. In practice, exemptions will normally be available under the Financial Services and Markets Act 2000 (Financial Promotion) Order 2005 (SI 2005/1529), either because the document is required to be published under the AIM Rules (Article 67), or because it is being published in connection with admission to AIM (Article 68), or because it comprises a prospectus (Article 72).

7.6.3 Prospectus liability

If the admission document also constitutes a prospectus under FSMA 2000, strict statutory liability (known as "prospectus liability") will apply where a person suffers loss as a result of any inaccuracy in, or omission from, a prospectus. Persons responsible for the prospectus (and so subject to such potential liability) include the company, its directors, the nominated adviser and broker, and any expert whose report is included in the prospectus.

7.6.4 Liability under general law

Even in the absence of prospectus liability, liability may still arise under general law. Claims may, for example, be brought for misrepresentation, negligence or deceit in circumstances where it can be demonstrated that an investor has suffered loss as a result of having relied upon an inaccurate or misleading statement in the admission document.

7.6.5 Directors' responsibility statement

The admission document must include a declaration by the directors taking responsibility for the information contained in the document (on a joint and several basis) that, to the best of their knowledge and belief (having taken all reasonable care to ensure such is the case) that information is in accordance with the facts and does not omit anything likely to affect the import of such information. Even in the absence of prospectus liability, therefore, it may be possible for investors to bring claims successfully against the directors in their personal capacity if the admission document is inaccurate or misleading.

7.6.6 Section 397 FSMA 2000

In all cases, the requirements of Section 397 FSMA 2000 will be relevant. Under this Section it is a criminal offence for a person (including a company and its directors) to make a statement, promise or forecast, which the person making it knows to be (or is reckless as to whether it will be) misleading, false or deceptive, or to dishonestly conceal any material fact for the purpose of inducing (or being reckless as to whether it will induce) another person to acquire or dispose of investments.

7.6.7 General

It is therefore crucial to ensure that, in all material respects, the admission document is fair, accurate and not misleading, whether or not it is being used in connection with a fund-raising. The usual ways of seeking to ensure this are for the company and its advisers to conduct comprehensive due diligence on the company and its subsidiaries and for the directors to satisfy themselves, again with the assistance of the company's advisers, that every statement in the admission document is capable of being independently verified and that they have not omitted information which ought to be disclosed.

7.7 Verification

In order to help ensure that the admission document is accurate and not misleading, the company's solicitors will assist the directors in an exercise of verifying the information contained in the admission document. This will normally involve the preparation of a comprehensive set of verification notes which will seek to confirm the accuracy of each statement of fact, and that there are reasonable grounds for each statement of opinion, contained in the admission document, where possible by reference to independent documentary evidence. Where a statement cannot be verified, the board may decide to alter or qualify that statement in the final admission document. The verification notes and supporting documents may also later provide the directors with the basis for a defence against possible future claims that a statement which is later found to be incorrect was, at the time, made on reasonable grounds and in good faith.

7.8 Due diligence

7.8.1 General

Financial, accounting, commercial and legal due diligence will be conducted by the company's reporting accountants, nominated adviser, and broker and solicitors.

7.8.2 Financial due diligence

The due diligence conducted by the reporting accountants will normally form the basis of long form and short form accountants' reports and reports on working capital and cash flow forecasts and the company's financial reporting systems and procedures, all of which will usually be addressed to the company, its nominated adviser and broker.

The long form report will take the form of a comprehensive financial and commercial analysis of the group and its business. It will focus on a number of areas, including internal management and structure, financial and risk control mechanisms, the market in which the group operates and the group's competitors. It will also highlight material risk factors relating to the group and its business which can then be brought to the attention of potential investors in the admission document.

The short form report will usually contain the group's last three years' statutory audited accounts (or cover such shorter period that the company has been in operation) together with the auditors' reports thereon and notes relating thereto. This will be included in the admission document.

7.8.3 Commercial due diligence

The nominated adviser and broker will conduct their own commercial assessments in relation to the company and its business in order to gauge whether or not the company is appropriate for admission to AIM (the AIM Rules give no guidance as to what is meant by this) and what value investors are likely to attach to the company's securities.

The nominated adviser will also send each director a personal questionnaire which focuses on the matters referred to at 7.5.5(e) above.

In certain circumstances, the nominated adviser and broker may require the company to obtain an independent expert or competent person's report on its business or market or technology. This is particularly likely to apply to companies operating in specialist fields such as biotechnology, oil and gas or mining. They may wish such a report to be disclosed to investors in the admission document.

7.8.4 Legal due diligence

The purpose of the legal due diligence exercise will be to discover whether any steps need to be taken to prepare the group or its structure in connection with admission and to elicit relevant information for the purpose of drafting the additional information section of the admission document. Moreover, any key risks or liabilities unearthed in the legal due diligence report (e.g. invalid patents or major litigation) could question the valuation or indeed the whole basis for the proposed flotation.

The company's solicitors will normally send a comprehensive legal due diligence questionnaire to the company's directors and may then be asked to compile a report addressed to the company and its nominated adviser and broker based upon the company's responses.

Depending on the nature of the group's business, various specific reports may also be required, such as reports on title relating to the group's properties, a patent report from the group's patent agent or an independent patent agent, and counsel's opinion on material litigation affecting the group.

7.9 Financial and accounting procedures

7.9.1 Working capital

The board will be responsible for compiling working capital and cash flow forecasts, usually for a longer period (such as 18 or 24 months) than the 12 months working capital statement required to be made in the admission document.

7.9.2 Financial reporting procedures

A review by the reporting accountants of the group's financial reporting systems and procedures will be of particular relevance where the company is raising new money. In any event, however, the AIM Rules require the nominated adviser to ensure that the company has appropriate financial reporting procedures in place and confirmation of such should be stated on the application form.

7.9.3 Forecasts and projections

Where the admission document is to contain a profit forecast, estimate or projection, the assumptions on which this is based will need to be reviewed by the reporting accountants and disclosed in the admission document. There is no formal requirement under the AIM Rules for the report of the accountants on such matters to be disclosed (as there is under the Prospectus Rules). However, the nominated adviser and broker will be required to confirm in the admission document that it has satisfied itself that the forecast, estimate or projection has been made after due and careful enquiry by the directors and will normally, as a minimum, require a report to be compiled and addressed to them. Companies are usually advised not to include profit forecasts in the admission document on the grounds that investors may bring claims, or the company's share price may suffer, where these are not achieved. However, this can present a dilemma for a very young company with no financial track record but potentially impressive growth prospects.

7.9.4 Indebtedness

Unless the admission document also constitutes a prospectus, there is no express requirement under the AIM Rules to include a statement in the admission document relating to the group's indebtedness. The nominated adviser and broker will, however, often require a review to be undertaken of the group's loan capital, term loans and other borrowings, commitments and obligations (e.g. under hire purchase contracts), and for the reporting accountants to report on this in the long-form report and/or by way of a separate report. Obviously, indebtedness will be one of the factors that contribute to the valuation.

7.9.5 No material adverse change

The company and its directors will often be required to provide the nominated adviser and broker with written comfort that they are not aware that there has been any material adverse change in the group's financial position or prospects since the date of its last audited accounts, save as disclosed in the admission document, and the admission document itself must contain details of any significant change in the issuer's financial or trading position or an appropriate negative statement. This opinion will normally be based upon monthly management accounts produced in respect of this period as well as on the general awareness of the directors.

7.9.6 Taxation

The admission document should contain information relating to tax on income from the securities withheld at source along with an indication as to whether the company assumes responsibility for such withholding and, although not expressly required by the AIM Rules, the admission document will usually include a section on taxation generally. This will, amongst other things, summarise the UK tax position on holding and selling shares, including liability to chargeable gains and stamp duty and in respect of dividends. It may also include a section relating to taxation of overseas shareholders which a taxation specialist will need to draft or review.

7.10 Legal restructuring

7.10.1 General

A number of different issues may arise out of the legal due diligence exercise which requires attention before admission. The following are some of the most common.

7.10.2 Re-registration as a public company

Companies incorporated in England and Wales will often need to be re-registered as public limited companies under the Companies Act 1985. Where the company's net assets are less than its called-up share capital and reserves, however, re-registration will not be permitted and it will instead be necessary to incorporate a new public holding company and effect a group reorganisation, usually by way of a share-for-share exchange, with the new company acquiring the existing trading company.

7.10.3 De-merger

It may be desirable for part of the group's business to be de-merged or hived off prior to admission. This may be the case where, for example, the group owns a business which represents a non-core activity, or which would not be suited to an AIM quoted company, or which would not be of interest to investors. It will be important, however, to ensure that any arrangements put in place for future relations between such businesses avoid potential conflicts of interests and are entered into on an arms'-length basis.

7.10.4 Termination rights and consents

The company may have entered into banking facility arrangements and other material contracts, under which consent requirements or termination rights arise on a flotation or an issue of new shares. This may require consents or waivers to be obtained, or even a refinancing to be effected, prior to admission.

7.10.5 Shareholders' agreements

The company's shareholders may have entered into a shareholders' agreement with the company. Any such agreement will need to be terminated prior to admission unless termination will occur automatically in accordance with the terms of any such agreement.

7.11 Shareholder resolutions

It will often be necessary for the company to pass shareholder resolutions prior to the admission document being issued. Such resolutions may be made conditional upon admission taking place by a certain date.

Shareholders may need to increase the company's authorised share capital and authorise the directors to issue new shares to investors free from pre-emption rights.

A capital reorganisation may sometimes be required in order to ensure that the opening price of the company's shares on admission is at a level which will assist liquidity in the shares. This may involve a consolidation, share split or a bonus issue of shares.

It will also often be necessary to alter the company's articles of association or for the company to adopt a new set of articles which are suitable for a public company quoted on AIM, and which allow for the holding of shares in dematerialised form and for shares to be traded electronically via the CREST system. In particular, any provision hindering free transfer of shares under the articles would have to be changed.

It may be possible for some companies to pass written resolutions signed by all shareholders or to hold an extraordinary general meeting on short notice (usually requiring the written consent of the holders of 95 per cent in nominal value of the company's ordinary shares). Otherwise, the timetable will need to allow for a meeting to be held on the requisite notice (being 14 clear days in respect of ordinary resolutions and 21 clear days in respect of special resolutions).

7.12   Employee share schemes

Companies will often want to set up executive and/or employee share option schemes prior to admission. Consideration will need to be given at an early stage as to which form of scheme is most appropriate, having regard to tax advantages and administrative considerations. If HM Revenue and Customs' approval is required for an approved scheme, then allowance may need to be made for this in the timetable. The extent to which the Revenue is willing to approve an exercise price which is less than the share price on admission may also depend upon the length of the period between the date on which the options are granted and the date of admission. The nominated adviser and broker should be consulted as to the numbers of options to be granted, both on and following admission, and as to the exercise price. Investors will want to be able to identify the maximum level of dilution arising from share options and the circumstances (e.g. are there performance criteria?).

7.13   The board and corporate governance

Although the Combined Code on Corporate Governance does not strictly apply to AIM quoted companies, the company's nominated adviser and broker will generally want the company to have regard to the Code as a means of reflecting best practice. The admission document must contain a statement either confirming that the company complies with the Code or an explanation as to why it does not, and it is usual to see a broad qualification in the admission document that the company complies with the Code in so far as is considered practical, having regard to its size and resources.

Consideration will need to be given as to the balance of the board in terms of numbers of executive and non-executive directors and as to the role of the latter in relation to various board committees, including audit, remuneration and nomination committees. The board will need to consider whether it has adopted appropriate systems to control and manage risk internally and with its customers and suppliers. The company should seek guidance from its nominated adviser and broker in each case. Where new non-executive directors are to be appointed, it will be important to identify them and include them in the admission process at an early stage, so that they are able to become familiar with the group and its business, since they will be jointly responsible for the admission document.

7.14 Placing agreement

If the company is intending to raise money on admission, then one of the documents required will be a placing or underwriting agreement. This will normally be entered into by the company's directors, as well as the company, with the nominated adviser and broker. It will usually be prepared by the solicitors acting for the nominated adviser and broker.

The principal purpose of this agreement is to provide the broker with the authority and comforts it requires to place shares in the company with its placees. The broker will then agree to use its reasonable endeavours to procure such placees and, in the case of an underwritten fund-raising, itself to subscribe for any shares not so placed.

Underwriting is more common where shares are also being offered to the company's existing shareholders by way of a rights issue or open offer, as the company may then want the comfort that the fund-raising is guaranteed once the admission document or prospectus has been published, whatever the level of take-up by shareholders under such an offer. However, given the high cost of, and risks involved in, underwriting (and sub-underwriting), a more common alternative is to make the offer to shareholders conditional upon a successful placing with institutional and other placees procured by the broker, or structure the offer as a placing, subject to claw-back to satisfy acceptances under the offer.

The agreement will include a series of undertakings in favour of the nominated adviser and broker relating to the conduct of the group's business going forward which are designed to protect the broker and its placees in the after-market. However, some or all of these may instead be incorporated into a separate nominated adviser and broker agreement, which will also be entered into prior to admission (*see* Chapter 3, 3.7 and Chapter 5, 5.10).

The company and its directors will normally be required to give representations and warranties in favour of the broker which relate to the accuracy and completeness of the admission document and the quality of the information contained in that document.

There will also be a broad indemnity in favour of the nominated adviser and broker in respect of any losses which they may suffer (e.g. where placees bring a claim against them). Normal carve-outs will include where the nominated adviser and broker have been negligent or in breach of the conduct of business rules of the FSA.

A key negotiating issue will often be the level of any cap on warranty liability, and what other limitations should apply to the directors' liability under the agreement. As a matter of current market practice, executive directors' liability will often be capped by reference to a multiple of, say, two to four times their annual salary or fee from the company. Where higher levels of liability are agreed, directors may wish to arrange to put in place warranty and indemnity insurance (usually at the cost of the company).

The responsibilities of the nominated adviser and broker under the placing agreement will often remain conditional upon a number of factors, including there having been no material breach of the warranties prior to admission and the company not being required under the AIM Rules to publish a supplemental admission document. The broker will also normally have the right to terminate the agreement in certain circumstances, such as in the case of a *force majeure* event occurring prior to admission. These are hardly ever invoked.

The broker's fees and commissions for the placing (and any underwriting commitment) will also be dealt with in the agreement. There will often be a fixed corporate finance fee plus a variable commission based upon the amount raised in the fund-raising (often excluding amounts raised from investors introduced by the board). These will often be supplemented by an option or warrant granted or issued to the broker to subscribe for shares at the placing price following admission.

Where existing shareholders are selling shares as part of a placing, they will usually also be parties to the agreement, so as to authorise the broker to sell their shares. They will generally also be required to give limited warranties, principally relating to title to their shares and their ability to sell. Stamp duty and commissions will usually be deducted by the broker from the sale proceeds.

The lock-in provisions set out in Rule 7 of the AIM Rules are often supplemented or increased in their scope by additional lock-in requirements of the nominated adviser and broker (often going beyond one year and/or extending to persons not required to be locked in under the AIM Rules) to ensure an orderly market for the securities post admission. Such lock-in arrangements may be set out in separate lock-in agreements entered into with the company and its nominated adviser and broker, or may be incorporated into the placing agreement.

7.15   Directors' documents

7.15.1   General

The company's directors will be required to sign a number of documents reflecting their responsibility for the admission document and for managing the company's affairs following admission. The nominated adviser will need to satisfy itself that the directors have been properly advised of their responsibilities and that they have conducted a thorough review of the admission document and all underlying documents.

7.15.2   Responsibility memorandum and statements

The company's solicitors will advise the directors generally as to their responsibilities and continuing obligations as directors of public companies quoted on AIM. This advice will usually be given by reference to a Memorandum setting out such responsibilities and obligations, including relevant areas of civil and criminal liability. The nominated adviser will need to confirm to the Exchange that the directors have received such advice and guidance and will, therefore, usually require some form of written comfort from the company's solicitors. They will usually be required to confirm to the nominated adviser and broker that they have given the directors appropriate legal advice on the AIM Rules and in relation to their responsibilities as directors and that, having done so, they are not aware that the admission document excludes any information which it is required to contain under the AIM Rules. The nominated adviser and broker will also require each director to sign a responsibility letter addressed to them and the company acknowledging that he has read and understood the memorandum and that he takes responsibility for the information contained in the admission document and for the other documents connected with admission.

7.15.3   Dealing rules

In addition to the restrictions imposed under insider dealing and market abuse legislation (for which *see* Chapter 11, 11.9 and Chapter 6, 6.7 of this Guide), directors and employees who hold shares in the company are required under the AIM Rules to adhere to strict dealing restrictions (similar, in part, to those under the Model Code in the Listing Rules), which provide, amongst other things, that they may not deal in shares in the company during a "close" period of two months prior to publication of the company's interim and final results. Further details of these restrictions are set out in Chapter 9.

7.15.4   Service agreements

As part of the due diligence exercise, the nominated adviser will review the existing service agreements and levels of remuneration and benefits of the directors, and the notice periods which apply on termination. Changes may need to be made, for example to ensure that the agreements contain enforceable restrictive covenants preventing the directors from competing with or soliciting employees from the company. The nominated adviser may also want to review the letters of appointment of non-executive directors.

7.15.5   Board meetings

The board of directors of the company will not only have to approve the admission document, but also all of the other key documents relating to the application for admission. Detailed board minutes will need to be prepared for this purpose to ensure that each document is considered carefully and that the directors are fully aware of their individual and collective responsibilities. Board meetings will also need to be held to approve any pathfinder or placing proofs of the admission document and any circular sent to shareholders. The board will often appoint a committee at the pathfinder stage to finalise all documentation, approve the allotment of any new shares on admission and complete the admission process.

7.15.6 Powers of attorney

The directors will usually be required to grant powers of attorney authorising their co-directors to sign on their behalf any document required for admission. The powers of attorney will usually list the main documents which will need to be signed by the directors and give a general power relating to ancillary documents. Authority will also be given to allow non-substantive amendments to be made to those documents referred to and already reviewed by the directors. The giving of powers of attorney means that admission need not be delayed due to the absence of any director.

Powers of attorney may also be sought from existing shareholders proposing to sell their shares as part of the fund-raising on admission. These will facilitate the execution of placing agreements and share transfer forms as required to effect the sale of their shares.

7.16 Financial public relations

A public relations ("PR") agency will sometimes be appointed by the company, initially to help ensure that presentations to potential investors run smoothly, as well as releasing announcements to the Exchange and the media, and generally dealing with the press. Following admission, the PR agency will make announcements on behalf of the company and distribute these as appropriate to the Exchange, media and analysts. The PR agency will also help the company form relationships with the media, analysts and the City in general.

7.17 Application

7.17.1 Ten-day announcement

An issuer seeking admission of new shares must notify the Exchange of certain matters at least 10 business days prior to the expected date of admission. These matters include, *inter alia*:

(a) the name, address/registered office and country of incorporation of the issuer;

(b) a brief description of its business (or in the case of an investing company, details of its investment strategy);

(c) the number and nature of the securities (including details of any treasury shares) and whether there will also be a fund-raising with admission;

(d) the full names and functions of all directors (including any shadow and proposed directors);

(e) insofar as is known, the name of any person who is interested directly or indirectly in 3 per cent or more of the company's securities, together with the percentage of such interest;

(f) the name and address of the nominated adviser and broker.

If any of the details above alter, then the issuer must advise the Exchange immediately.

7.17.2 Three-day announcement

An issuer must then submit to the Exchange not less than three business days prior to the expected date of admission:

(a) An application (together with an electronic version of the admission document). The application contains various declarations from the company relating to working capital, any profit forecast made in the admission document, the company's financial procedures and other such matters. It will be signed by a duly authorised officer of the company. A sample application form can be found in the appendices to this Guide.

(b) A nominated adviser declaration. The nominated adviser will sign a declaration (to be submitted with the application form and admission document) confirming its appointment and also that the directors have received guidance as to the nature of their responsibilities and obligations, that to the best of their knowledge and belief all relevant requirements of the AIM Rules have been complied with and that they are satisfied that in their opinion the company and its securities are "appropriate" to be admitted to AIM. The nominated adviser is likely to seek supporting comfort from the company's directors, solicitors and reporting accountants. A sample declaration can be found in the appendices to this Guide.

(c)   Admission fees and ongoing charges will also be due from the company at the time the three-day announcement is made.

7.17.3   Admission

Admission of the company's securities to trading on AIM will become effective on the publication of a dealing notice by the Exchange.

7.18   Costs and timing

The costs involved in applying for admission will depend upon a number of different factors, such as whether any new money is being raised on admission (and how much), the specific complexities which may arise during the process and the fees agreed by the company with its advisers.

An estimate of expenses will be compiled by the nominated adviser to cover all fees and commissions of advisers, printers and the Exchange. The total will need to be approved by the board prior to the issue of the admission document (and will form the basis of the "net of expenses" figure in that document in relation to any fund-raising). Regard must be had to VAT, some of which will be irrecoverable on a fund-raising.

7.19   Conclusion

The whole of the admission process will generally take around two to four months. Although if a prospectus is required then additional time to obtain the FSA's approval of the document should be factored into the timetable. Much will depend upon the extent to which material issues arise out of the accounting and legal due diligence investigations into the company and its subsidiaries and their business. The admission process will generally involve a great deal of management time, in particular from the directors, and provision should be made for this at the outset so as to ensure that the process runs smoothly and without unnecessarily disrupting the company's business.

Chapter 8

Continuing Obligations and Transactions

Richard Collins

Director
Deloitte & Touche LLP

8.1   Introduction

In contrast to most of the other Chapters, which concentrate on pre-flotation issues, this Chapter concentrates exclusively on post-flotation matters. Once the applicant's shares have been admitted to AIM, there are numerous continuing obligations with which the issuer must comply. These include disclosure of financial and price-sensitive information, rules governing transactions undertaken and further share issues.

This Chapter sets out the continuing obligations of an AIM company with regard to transactions and on a day-to-day basis.

8.2   Announcements

Information that is required to be disclosed by the AIM Rules must be notified to a Regulatory Information Service ("RIS") provider for release to the market. An AIM company must retain a RIS provider to ensure that information can be notified as and when required. Information should be released through the RIS without delay and no later than it is published elsewhere. A list of organisations authorised by the Financial Services Authority to provide regulatory disclosure services for listed companies and who have agreed to provide comparable services to AIM companies is shown in the AIM section of the London Stock Exchange ("the Exchange") website, www.londonstockexchange.com.

115

An AIM company must take reasonable care to ensure that any information it notifies to a RIS is not misleading, false or deceptive and does not omit anything likely to affect the import of such information.

It is presumed that information notified through a RIS is required by the AIM Rules or other legal or regulatory requirements. Any information that is notified to a RIS may be deemed to be price-sensitive. "Drip-feeding" of non-price-sensitive information into the marketplace via RIS announcements is actively discouraged by the Exchange.

Information, which is notified to a RIS, must be in English and in writing. Methods which may be used to transmit the information to the RIS include fax and electronic link. Advice on formatting HTML regulatory announcements can be obtained on the Exchange website.

When notifying information to a RIS, AIM companies should follow the Regulatory News Service Guidelines published by the Exchange.

Any document provided by an AIM company to the holders of its AIM securities must be made available to the public at the same time for at least one month, free of charge, at an address notified to the RIS. Three copies of the document must be sent to the Exchange.

8.3   General disclosure obligations

8.3.1   Price-sensitive information

An AIM company must notify a RIS without delay of any new developments concerning a change in its financial condition, sphere of activity, business performance or expectation of performance, which are not public knowledge and, if made public, would be likely to lead to a substantial movement in the price of its AIM securities.

An AIM company need not notify a RIS about impending developments or matters in the course of negotiation. It may give this information in confidence prior to any announcement to certain parties including its advisers, representatives of its employees or trade unions acting on their behalf and statutory or regulatory bodies or authorities.

116

However, in all cases the company must be satisfied that such confidants are aware that they must not trade in its AIM securities before the relevant information is announced.

If the company has reason to believe that a breach of confidence has occurred or is likely to occur, it must notify a RIS with at least a warning announcement to the effect that it expects shortly to release information which may lead to a substantial movement in the price of its AIM securities.

Where such information has been made public, the company must notify that information to a RIS without delay, notwithstanding the fact that a RIS should be provided with all announcements before they are published elsewhere.

Information that is required to be notified to a RIS must not be given to anyone else (except as set out above) before it has been so notified. Where potentially price-sensitive information is to be announced at a meeting of holders of the company's AIM securities, arrangements must be made for that information to be notified to a RIS no later than the announcement is made to the meeting. This is to ensure that equal information is available to all market participants and that all parties are made aware of this new information, even if they have not managed to attend the relevant meeting.

The Exchange monitors the share prices of all fully listed and AIM companies. It is common for the monitoring team to contact the nominated adviser if an AIM company's share price moves by more than about 10 per cent over a short period and the movement appears unusual in the context of general market or sector movements. In such cases, the Exchange will ask the company and its advisers to consider whether any announcement is necessary under the AIM Rules. The Panel for Takeovers and Mergers ("the Panel") also monitors share price movements and may also ask the AIM company and its advisers to explain the likely reason for a share price movement or unusual trading volumes in the AIM company's shares and request that an appropriate announcement be made through a RIS. The Panel issues similar criteria for the Exchange to monitor share price movements.

8.3.2 Material change

A material change between an AIM company's actual trading performance (or financial condition) and any profit forecast, estimate or projection, which has been included in an admission document or otherwise made public on the company's behalf, should be notified to a RIS. One of the responsibilities of the nominated adviser is to review regularly the actual trading performance and financial condition against any such profit forecast, estimate or projection in order to help the AIM company to determine whether such an announcement is necessary.

In practice, it can be difficult to assess the likelihood of a material change since shortfalls in the short term may be rectified in the medium term, so the directors' assessment of future results may be as important as historical management information. As a general rule, a deviation of more than 10 per cent from previously published indications could be regarded as a material change for these purposes.

Furthermore, a deviation of more than 10 per cent from market expectations of results could be regarded as a material change which should be disclosed as price-sensitive information. For AIM companies which have no broking research, market expectations can be difficult to determine. Factors to consider in these cases include the impression conveyed in general press comment regarding the future trading results of the company, as well as commentary included in interim and annual reports and trading statements issued by the company. An AIM company should consult with its nominated adviser if it is in any doubt.

8.3.3 Significant share interests

An AIM company must notify a RIS without delay of any relevant changes to any significant shareholders, disclosing the information specified in Schedule 5 to the AIM Rules.

For UK registered AIM companies, Sections 198–208 of the Companies Act 1985 ("the Act") provides the mechanism to assist in complying with the changes to the interests of significant shareholders. The Act requires that where a person knows that he has acquired or ceased to have a material interest of 3 per cent or more of the issued share capital of the AIM company, or already has 3 per cent or more of the AIM company's share capital and he increases or reduces his interest across one full percentage point, then he must notify the AIM company within two business days. The AIM Rules apply the 3 per cent threshold to the share capital of the AIM company excluding treasury shares.

If an AIM company becomes aware of a change in a significant interest which should have been disclosed to it under Sections 198–208 of the Act, details must be notified to a RIS as soon as possible. An AIM company should endeavour to ensure that an appropriate announcement is released by the end of the business day following the day of receipt of the information by the AIM company. Such information might, for example, come to the company's attention as a result of a request pursuant to Section 212 of the Act.

Section 212 of the Act allows an AIM company to send a notice to a person or another legal entity to confirm whether or not they have had an interest in the AIM company's share capital at any time within the past three years and to disclose details of their holding, whether they are part of a concert party or to whom their interest was sold.

In addition, an AIM company and transactions in an AIM company's securities will be subject to the Rules Governing Substantial Acquisitions of Shares and the City Code on Takeovers and Mergers, which may accelerate the speed with which the AIM company is notified of any change in its shareholders.

8.3.4 Directors' dealings

Details of any changes to the interests that the directors of an AIM company and their families have in the AIM securities must be notified to a RIS without delay, disclosing the information specified in Schedule 5 to the AIM Rules. Where such a change occurs during a close period (*see* 8.8.4 below), further details are required and these are also set out in Schedule 5 to the AIM Rules. In practice this disclosure must be made by the end of the business day following notification of the change.

The duty of disclosure extends to any dealing (including the grant, acceptance, acquisition, disposal, exercise or discharge) by a director and his family in any option or related financial product relating to the AIM company's securities, or any interest in such option or related financial product.

For UK registered AIM companies, Sections 324–328 of the Act provides a mechanism to assist in complying with the requirement to notify a RIS of changes to directors' holdings. These Sections relate to a director's duty to disclose to the AIM company his shareholdings and those of his spouse and children under 18 in the AIM company, together with, among other things, the grant or exercise of options in the AIM company.

An AIM company which is not subject to the Act is nevertheless subject to the same disclosure requirements as referred to above.

8.3.5 Board changes

An AIM company must notify a RIS of the resignation or dismissal of any director, or the appointment of any new director. In the case of an appointment, the AIM company is required to disclose the information about the new director as set out in Schedule 2(g) to the AIM Rules. This information includes:

(a) current and past (within five years) directorships and partnerships held;
(b) details of any events such as receiverships or compulsory liquidations of any company or partnership where the director was a director or partner at the time or in the 12 months preceding such events; and
(c) details of any public criticisms, censures, unspent convictions and disqualifications from being a director.

8.3.6 Change of nominated adviser or broker

An AIM company must notify a RIS of the resignation, dismissal or appointment of its nominated adviser or broker. If an issuer ceases to have a nominated adviser the Exchange will suspend trading in its securities. If a replacement nominated adviser is not appointed within one month of suspension, trading will be cancelled. It is advisable, therefore, to establish an appropriate period of notice on the engagement of a nominated adviser, for example at least one month, in order to allow sufficient time to find a replacement and thus avoid the potential suspension (or cancellation) of shares.

8.3.7 Change in the number of securities in issue

An AIM company must notify a RIS of the reason for the issue or cancellation of any AIM securities. Any changes in the number of shares in issue requires liaison with AIM Regulation, so that they can arrange the appropriate dealing notice to be released. For new issues of shares, a copy of the AIM company's board minutes allocating such securities or confirmation from its nominated adviser will suffice as evidence that the securities have been unconditionally allotted.

The AIM Rules were amended in December 2003 to cover treasury shares and require an AIM company to notify a RIS of the details of any movement into or out of treasury shares, and the resultant change to the issued share capital of the AIM company less shares held in treasury.

8.3.8 Decision on dividend payment

An AIM company must notify a RIS of any decision to make any payment in respect of its AIM securities, specifying the net amount payable per security, the payment date and the record date. This information may be given in the preliminary statement of annual results or the half-yearly report if appropriate.

8.3.9 Other general disclosure obligations

Notification to a RIS is also required if an AIM company changes its legal name, accounting reference date or its registered office address.

The Exchange may require the company to provide it with such information in such form and within such time limit as it considers appropriate and to publish such information.

The Exchange may disclose any information in its possession:

(a) to cooperate with any person responsible for supervision or regulation of financial services or for law enforcement;
(b) to enable it to discharge its legal or regulatory functions, including instituting, carrying on or defending proceedings; and
(c) for any other purpose where it has the consent of the person from whom the information was obtained and, if different, the person to whom it relates.

8.4   Financial reporting

8.4.1   Publication of annual accounts

An AIM company must publish annual audited accounts prepared in accordance with UK or US Generally Accepted Accounting Practice or International Accounting Standards. These accounts must be sent to the holders of its AIM securities without delay (i.e. once they are finalised and reported on) and in any event no later than six months after the end of the financial period to which they relate.

The Exchange will suspend AIM companies that are late publishing their annual accounts (and late publishing their half-yearly statements – *see* 8.4.2 below). A RIS must be notified of the publication of annual audited accounts and, as with any document sent to shareholders, the annual accounts must be available to the public at the same time for at least one month free of charge at an address notified to a RIS. An electronic copy of the annual accounts must be sent to the Exchange.

Although it is common practice for AIM companies to publish a preliminary statement of annual results, there is no requirement to do so.

It should be noted that the Exchange intends to mandate International Accounting Standards for all AIM companies for financial years commencing on or after 1 January 2007.

8.4.2   Publication of half-yearly report

An AIM company must prepare a half-yearly report within three months of the end of the relevant period and all reports must be notified to a RIS. The report need not be sent directly to shareholders, although AIM companies may choose to do so.

The information contained in a half-yearly report must include at least a balance sheet, an income statement and a cash flow statement and must contain comparative figures for the corresponding period in the preceding financial year. Additionally the half-yearly report must be presented and prepared in a form consistent with that which will be adopted in the AIM company's annual accounts having regard to the accounting standards applicable to such annual accounts. Where the half-yearly report has been audited it must contain a statement to this effect.

The half-yearly report would be expected to contain an explanatory statement covering the figures and an indication of the group's prospects for the current financial year. It is advisable to ensure that the indication of the group's prospects cannot be construed as a profit forecast because that might give rise to an obligation to make further disclosure at a later date.

A profit forecast would include any form of words which expressly or by implication give a floor or ceiling for the likely level of profits or losses for the current financial year, or which contain data from which a calculation of an approximate figure for future profits or losses may be made, even if no particular figure is mentioned and the word profit is not used.

When making profit forecasts, consideration should also be given to the requirements of Section 397 Financial Services and Markets Act 2000 ("Misleading statements and practices"). Under that Section any person who:

(a) makes a statement, promise or forecast which he knows to be misleading, false or deceptive; or
(b) dishonestly conceals any material facts; or
(c) recklessly makes (dishonest or otherwise) a statement, promise or forecast which is misleading, false or deceptive,

is guilty of an offence if he makes the statement, promise or forecast, or conceals the facts for the purpose of inducing, or is reckless as to whether it may induce, another person to enter or offer to enter into, or refrain from entering or offering to enter into, an investment agreement, or to exercise or refrain from exercising any rights conferred by an investment. A person found guilty under Section 397 is liable on summary conviction to a fine and imprisonment for up to six months, or on conviction on indictment to a fine and imprisonment for up to seven years.

If an AIM company changes its accounting reference date such that the accounting period is extended, the company must prepare further reports for each subsequent six-month period expiring prior to the new accounting reference date.

For example, if the year end is changed from 31 December to 31 March such that there is a 15-month accounting period, the company must prepare audited accounts for the year ended 31 December 20X5, then interim reports for the six-month periods ended 30 June 20X6 and 31 December 20X6, followed by audited accounts for the 15 months ended 31 March 20X7.

8.5   Transactions

Certain transactions carried out by an AIM company or its subsidiaries are "classifiable" and may require disclosure and in some cases shareholder approval. A classifiable transaction is any transaction that is *not* either:

(a)   of a revenue nature in the ordinary course of business; or
(b)   carried out in order to raise finance which does not involve a change in the fixed assets of the AIM company or its subsidiaries.

Examples of classifiable transactions might include acquisitions and disposals of shares, businesses and assets, including agreed private deals and public takeovers.

If a transaction is classifiable, certain "class tests" must be applied to determine whether or not disclosure and/or shareholder approval is required. The implications for a substantial transaction (including a disposal resulting in a fundamental change of business), a related party transaction and a reverse takeover are set out at 8.5.2, 8.5.3, 8.5.4 and 8.5.5 respectively below. The varying requirements for these types of transaction mean that an AIM company and its advisers are well advised to consider the class tests at an early stage in the planning of a proposed transaction.

8.5.1 Class tests

The class tests comprise the following ratios, expressed as a percentage, as set out in Schedule 3 to the AIM Rules (where detailed explanations of the calculations can be found):

(a) *gross assets*: gross assets the subject of the transaction – divided by the gross assets of the AIM company;
(b) *profits*: profits attributable to the assets subject to the transaction – divided by profits of the AIM company;
(c) *turnover*: turnover attributable to the assets the subject of the transaction – divided by turnover of the AIM company;
(d) *consideration*: consideration – divided by aggregate market value of all the ordinary shares of the AIM company (excluding treasury shares); and
(e) *gross capital:* gross capital of the company or business being acquired – divided by the gross capital of the AIM company.

In circumstances where the above tests produce anomalous results or where the tests are inappropriate to the sphere of activity of the AIM company, the Exchange may (except in the case of a transaction with a related party) disregard the calculation and substitute other relevant indicators of size, including industry-specific tests. Only the Exchange can decide to disregard one or more of the class tests or substitute another test and the AIM company or its nominated adviser should contact the Exchange at the earliest opportunity if such a dispensation is to be sought.

8.5.2 Substantial transaction

If any of the class tests is 10 per cent or more, the transaction is a "substantial transaction" and the AIM company must notify a RIS without delay as soon as the terms of the transaction are agreed. The information to be disclosed is set out in Schedule 4 to the AIM Rules which sets out detailed particulars on the transaction. In contrast to companies listed on the main market where shareholder approval is required for listed companies wishing to perform a transaction where any of the class tests exceed 25 per cent, AIM companies need only obtain shareholder approval at 100 per cent.

There is no general obligation for an AIM company to inform its shareholders directly of a substantial transaction. However, it may need to do so if shareholders are asked to vote on a related matter, for example on the issue of further shares by the company either to be used as consideration for the particular transaction or to raise sufficient cash to pay for the transaction. It may also wish to do so for investor and public relations purposes.

8.5.3 Disposals resulting in a fundamental change of business

Any disposal by an AIM company which, when aggregated with any other disposal or disposals over the previous 12 months, exceeds 75 per cent in any of the class tests, is deemed to be a disposal resulting in a fundamental change of business. As such the disposal must be conditional on the consent of its shareholders being given in general meeting, notified without delay, disclosing the information specified by Schedule 4 to the AIM Rules and insofar as it is with a related party the additional information required by AIM Rule 13. The required information should be published in a circular. It should also convene the general meeting and be sent to the shareholders.

Where the effect of the proposed disposal is to divest the AIM company of all or substantially all of its trading business activities, the AIM company will, upon disposal, be treated as an investing company and the notification and circular containing the information specified by Schedule 4 to the AIM Rules convening the general meeting must also state its investing strategy going forward.

The AIM company will then have to make an acquisition or acquisitions which constitute a reverse takeover under Rule 14 of the AIM Rules within 12 months of having received the consent of its shareholders.

8.5.4 Related party transaction

Where any transaction whatsoever with a related party exceeds 5 per cent in any of the class tests, an AIM company must notify a RIS without delay disclosing the information set out in Schedule 4 to the AIM Rules, the name of the related party concerned and the extent of its interest in the transaction, and a statement that its independent directors consider, having consulted with its nominated adviser, that the terms of the transaction are fair and reasonable insofar as the holders of its AIM securities are concerned. A related party is defined in the AIM Rules and includes, *inter alia*, the current directors of the AIM company, former directors of the AIM company who have resigned within the previous 12-month period, and shareholders with more than 10 per cent holdings in the AIM company.

Once again, this contrasts with the obligations imposed on a fully listed company which would require a circular to shareholders and shareholder approval for a related-party transaction.

Details of any transaction with a related party (including the identity of the related party, the consideration and all other relevant circumstances) where any class test exceeds 0.25 per cent must be included in the AIM company's next published accounts, whether or not notified to a RIS as described above. Thus if all tests are less than 5 per cent but at least one is greater than 0.25 per cent, this is the only disclosure which needs to be made.

8.5.5 Reverse takeovers

A reverse takeover is an acquisition or acquisitions in a 12-month period which for an AIM company would:

(a) exceed 100 per cent in any of the class tests;
(b) result in a fundamental change in its business, board or voting control; or
(c) in the case of an investing company, depart substantially from the investing strategy stated in its admission document.

A reverse takeover will require shareholder consent and disclosure to a RIS, without delay, of the information set out in Schedule 4 to the

AIM Rules and insofar as it is with a related party, the additional information required for related party transactions.

Unless the subject of the transaction is fully listed or on AIM, upon receiving shareholder approval, trading in the AIM securities of an AIM company will be suspended. If the enlarged entity seeks admission, it must make an application in the same manner as any other applicant applying for admission of its securities for the first time. In addition to the 10-day announcement required by Rule 2 of the AIM Rules, the new entity will need to submit a further fee, an electronic version of its admission document, a nominated adviser declaration and a company application form at least three business days prior to admission. However, the new entity may make an application in advance of the general meeting to approve the reverse takeover such that the securities are admitted on agreement of the acquisition.

Where an AIM company is unable to publish its admission document at the same time as it agrees the terms of a reverse takeover, it will be suspended by the Exchange until it has published such a document (unless the target is a listed company or another AIM company). If the enlarged group does not seek a new admission, trading in the securities of the AIM company will be cancelled.

8.5.6   Aggregation of transactions

Transactions completed during the 12 months prior to the date of the latest transaction must be aggregated with the latest transaction for the purpose of classifying that transaction, where:

(a)   they are entered into by an AIM company with the same person or persons or their families;

(b)   they involve the acquisition or disposal of securities or an interest in one particular business; or

(c)   together they lead to the principal involvement in any business activity or activities which did not previously form a part of an AIM company's principal activities.

8.6 Further share issues

A further admission document will be required for an AIM company only when it is:

(a) required to issue a prospectus under the Prospectus Rules for a further issue of AIM securities; or

(b) seeking admission for a new class of securities; or

(c) undertaking a reverse takeover.

The Exchange may authorise the omission of information from a further admission document in the same circumstances as apply for first-time applicants under Rule 4 of the AIM Rules (unless it also constitutes a prospectus under the Prospectus Rules). In addition, an AIM company may omit the (historical) financial information required by Section 20 of Annex 1 (Annex 1 of Regulation 809/2004 of the European Commission, referred to as the PD Regulation in the FSA Handbook as reprinted in the Prospectus Rules) from any further admission document (a prospectus) provided that the AIM company has been complying with the AIM Rules. In such circumstances the nominated adviser to the AIM company must confirm to the Exchange in writing that equivalent information is available publicly by reason of the AIM company's compliance with the AIM Rules.

Where the further admission document is also a prospectus, application for omission of information should be made to the United Kingdom Listing Authority ("UKLA"). The Exchange itself may not authorise exemptions from any legal requirement under the Prospectus Rules.

At least three business days before the expected date of admission of further AIM securities, the AIM company must submit an application form and where required, an electronic version of any further admission document. An AIM company must also inform the Exchange in advance of any notification of the timetable for any proposed action affecting the rights of the holders of its AIM securities.

Where an AIM company intends to issue AIM securities on a regular basis, the Exchange may permit admission of those securities under a block admission arrangement. Under a block arrangement an AIM company must notify the information required in Schedule 8 to the AIM Rules every six months. However, a block admission cannot be used where the securities to be issued under the block admission exceed more than 20 per cent of the existing class of AIM securities.

If the further issue is in relation to an open offer, there must be at least 15 business days from the date of posting the application form until the close of the offer.

8.7 The City Code on Takeovers and Mergers

If an AIM company is itself the subject of a takeover approach (or the directors are considering seeking a buyer for the company), it should be noted that the City Code on Takeovers and Mergers is likely to apply to the transaction. This, in particular, will be the case for companies which are considered to be resident in the UK, the Channel Islands or the Isle of Man.

8.8 Other eligibility requirements and restrictions

8.8.1 Continuing eligibility

Once admitted to AIM, an AIM company must continue to satisfy the initial eligibility criteria and have in place sufficient procedures, resources and controls to enable compliance with the AIM Rules. In particular, as described below, it must at all times retain a nominated adviser and a broker.

8.8.2 Nominated adviser

An AIM company must continue at all times to retain a nominated adviser. It may only retain the services of one nominated adviser at any one time. If an AIM company ceases to have a nominated adviser, the Exchange will suspend trading in its securities. As mentioned at 8.3.6 above, it is advisable, therefore, to establish a period of notice of at least one month on the engagement of a nomi-nated adviser in order to allow time to avoid the potential suspen-sion of shares.

8.8.3 Broker

An AIM company must retain a broker at all times and must ensure that appropriate settlement arrangements are in place, in particular (unless otherwise agreed with the Exchange), AIM securities must be eligible for electronic settlement.

8.8.4 Directors' share dealing

In addition to the restrictions of the Criminal Justice Act 1993 to prevent insider dealing when a person is in possession of unpublished price-sensitive information, an AIM company must ensure that its directors and applicable employees (any employees who are aware of price-sensitive information) do not deal in any of its AIM securities during a close period. A close period is the period of two months immediately preceding the preliminary announcement of the company's annual results or half-yearly report, or when the company is in possession of unpublished price-sensitive information or any information that is required by the AIM Rules to be notified to a RIS. In addition, the AIM company should not engage in share buy-back activities or early redemption of its securities or sale of any AIM securities held as treasury shares during a close period.

This rule will not apply, however, where such individuals have entered into a binding contract prior to the close period where it was not reasonably foreseeable at the time when such commitment was made that a close period was likely, and provided that the commitment was notified to a RIS at the time it was made.

The Exchange may permit a director or applicable employee to sell his AIM securities during a close period to alleviate severe personal hardship such as the need for a medical operation or to satisfy a court order where no other funds are readily available.

8.8.5 Transferability of shares

An AIM company must ensure that its AIM securities are freely transferable except where any jurisdiction, statute or regulation places restriction on transferability or the AIM company is seeking to ensure that it does not become subject to a statute or regulation if it has a particular number of shareholders domiciled in a particular country.

8.8.6 Securities to be admitted

Only securities which have been unconditionally allotted can be admitted as AIM securities. An AIM company must ensure that application is made to admit all securities within a class of AIM securities.

8.8.7 Precautionary suspension

The Exchange may suspend the trading of AIM securities where:

(a) trading in those securities is not being conducted in an orderly manner;
(b) it considers that an AIM company has failed to comply with the AIM Rules;
(c) the protection of investors so requires; or
(d) the integrity and reputation of the market has been or may be impaired by dealings in those securities.

8.8.8 Cancellation of Admission

The Exchange will cancel the admission of AIM securities where these have been suspended from trading for six months.

Where an AIM company voluntarily seeks a cancellation, it will be conditional upon 20 business days' notice and the consent of not less than 75 per cent of votes cast by its shareholders given in a general meeting, unless the Exchange otherwise agrees. One circumstance in which the Exchange will agree a cancellation is in the case of a takeover offer where an offeror has received valid acceptances in excess of 75 per cent of each class of AIM securities.

8.8.9 Fees (effective 1 April 2005)

An AIM company must pay the fees at the rates published by the Exchange. There are two types of fee payable by an AIM company to the Exchange. The first fee is an admission fee of £4,180 (excluding

VAT) payable by all companies no later than three business days prior to admission to trading. No admission fee is payable by AIM companies for further issues.

The second fee is an annual fee also amounting to £4,180 (excluding VAT) payable by all AIM companies. They are billed in the first week of April for the 12 months commencing 1 April and the fee must be paid within 30 days of invoice date. A pro-rata annual fee is payable by new applicants no later than three business days prior to admission to trading. The fee is calculated by dividing the number of calendar days from and including the admission date to trading up to and including 31 March, divided by 365, and subsequently multiplied by the annual fee. No pro-rata annual fee is payable by the enlarged entity admitted to AIM following a reverse takeover or by a company who has transferred to AIM from the Main Market.

Firms acting as nominated advisers pay an initial fee of £10,250 (excluding VAT) to be approved by the Exchange to act. An annual fee is also payable. This is based on the number of companies represented on the last business day of February, and it ranges from £10,000 to £20,000 (excluding VAT).

8.8.10 Directors' responsibility for compliance

An AIM company must ensure that each of its directors:

(a) accepts full responsibility, collectively and individually, for its compliance with the AIM Rules;
(b) discloses without delay all information which it needs in order to comply with the disclosure requirements under Rule 17 of the AIM Rules, described at 8.3 above (insofar as that information is known to the director or could with reasonable diligence be ascertained by the director); and
(c) seeks advice from its nominated adviser regarding its compliance with the AIM Rules whenever appropriate and takes that advice into account.

In practice these undertakings from the directors are usually dealt with either in the nominated adviser agreement (to which the AIM company and its directors are a party) and/or in comfort letters from the directors to the AIM company (and nominated adviser) given prior to admission.

8.9   Sanctions and appeals

If the Exchange considers that an AIM company has contravened the AIM Rules, it may fine it or censure it or publish the fact that it has been fined or censured, and/or cancel the admission of its AIM securities.

Where the exchange proposes to take any of the steps described in Rules 42 and 43 of the AIM Rules, the Exchange will follow the procedures set out in the Disciplinary Procedures and Appeals Handbook.

Any decision of the Exchange in relation to the AIM Rules may be appealed to an appeals committee in accordance with the procedures set out in the Disciplinary Procedures and Appeals Handbook.

8.10   Conclusion

Aside from possible preferential taxation treatment for shareholders, the less onerous nature of the continuing obligations on AIM is a key factor in influencing the decision of directors to seek admission of their company to AIM as opposed to a main market listing.

The reduced obligations in respect of acquisitions and disposals for AIM companies mean that a company which is likely to engage in substantial merger and acquisition activity is likely to accrue particular benefit from choosing admission to AIM. However, directors of AIM companies should also be conscious of actions required by law and by the company's memorandum and articles of association in such situations.

Compliance with the market abuse provisions of the Financial Services and Markets Act 2000 is also particularly important for directors of an AIM company. It may be advisable to ensure that an executive director and/or the company secretary is tasked with ensuring compliance with the continuing obligations of the AIM company and is always available as a primary contact for the company's nominated adviser.

Chapter 9

Directors' Dealings and Corporate Governance

Anthony Gordon
Partner

Melanie Wadsworth
Associate
Faegre & Benson LLP

9.1 Directors' dealings

9.1.1 Introduction

The directors and certain employees of an AIM company are subject to restrictions on dealing in shares of their company under statute, common law and also under the AIM Rules. The principle behind all regulation of dealings by directors in securities of their company is that no director should be able to take unfair advantage of his position as a director to deal in the company's securities.

Under the AIM Rules, the primary restriction on dealing in the AIM company's securities is set out in a single succinct sentence in Rule 21:

> "An AIM company must ensure that its directors and applicable employees do not deal in any of its AIM securities during a close period."

The rule itself is supplemented by the definitions that apply to the AIM Rules, which are found in the glossary to the Rules. These greatly expand the scope of the restriction beyond what appears at face value to be a straightforward restriction.

The primary responsibility for ensuring compliance with the restriction on dealing that applies to the directors and employees of an AIM company lies with the AIM company itself. Under Rule 31 of the AIM Rules, an AIM company is required to ensure compliance by its directors with the AIM Rules, including the dealing restriction.

9.1.2 To what securities does Rule 21 apply?

The restriction on dealing in securities of an AIM company applies only to securities that have been admitted to AIM. To the extent that a director or applicable employee holds securities issued by their AIM company, whether shares, loan stock, warrants or other securities, that have not been admitted to AIM, the restriction on dealing under the AIM Rules does not apply.

9.1.3 To whom does Rule 21 apply?

The restriction on dealing in Rule 21 applies first to the directors of an AIM company and to any other person who acts as a director, whether or not officially appointed as a director of the company. Although the AIM rules do not use the term "shadow director", they are clearly intended to apply also to persons who, under the Companies Act 1985, would be shadow directors of a company.

The restriction on dealing applies also to "applicable employees", that is, any employee of the AIM company, or a subsidiary or parent undertaking of the AIM company, who is likely to be in possession of unpublished price-sensitive information in relation to the AIM company as a result of their employment. The dealing restriction applies to applicable employees regardless of the size of their holding of, or the nature of their interest in, the AIM securities of the AIM company. Actual possession of unpublished price-sensitive information by the employee is not the test by which an employee is classified by the AIM Rules as an applicable employee and therefore subject to the dealing restriction. The nature of the employee's position and duties will determine whether or not he or she is likely to be in possession of unpublished price-sensitive information and therefore subject to the dealing restriction under the AIM Rules. It is possible, depending upon circumstances, that certain employees will be applicable employees from time to time and, as circumstances change, might cease to be applicable employees.

9.1.4   What are "deals"?

The scope of the restriction that applies to directors and applicable employees on dealings in securities under Rule 21 is expanded considerably by the definition of "deal" in the glossary to the AIM Rules. A "deal" includes both:

> "any change whatsoever to the holding of AIM securities of an AIM company in which the holder is a director or part of a director's family . . . [or] an applicable employee"

and

> "the acquisition, disposal or discharge (whether in whole or part) of a related financial product referenced to AIM securities of an AIM company in which the holder is a director or part of a director's family . . . [or] an applicable employee".

A holding includes any legal or beneficial interest. A director's family comprises his or her spouse and any children under the age of 18 and also other entities in which any of them is interested. A company of which a director or his or her spouse and children under the age of 18 have control or in which they together hold more than 20 per cent of the equity or voting rights in general meeting (excluding treasury shares) is part of a director's family. Any trust of which the director or his or her spouse and children under the age of 18 are trustees or beneficiaries is also part of a director's family, except for any employee share scheme or pension scheme where the director or his or her spouse and children under the age of 18 are beneficiaries and not trustees.

A transaction in AIM securities by a company in which a director (or his or her spouse or children under the age of 18) is interested in 20 per cent of the equity is a deal for the purposes of the AIM Rules. However, for the purposes of the Companies Act 1985, the director might not be interested in the shares in the AIM company and is not therefore required to notify the transaction to the AIM company under Section 324 Companies Act 1985. Under Section 324 of, and Schedule 13 to, the Companies Act 1985 a director of company A is interested in shares of company A if a company (company B) is interested in shares of company A and the director, his or her spouse and children under the age of 18 are entitled to exercise *one-third or more* of the voting power at general meetings of company B.

To comply with the obligation under paragraph 17.2 of Appendix III to the Prospectus Rules to disclose in a prospectus or admission document information as to the directors' ownership of shares in the AIM company, disclosure is usually made of the interests of the directors that must be notified to the company under Section 324 Companies Act 1985 and the interests of persons connected with the directors within the meaning of Section 346 Companies Act 1985. A company in which a director of an AIM company, his or her spouse or children under the age of 18 have an interest in at least 20 per cent of the equity share capital or are entitled to exercise 20 per cent or more of the voting power at any general meeting is "connected" with the director for the purposes of Section 346 Companies Act 1985.

The following transactions are included in the definition of "deal" under the AIM Rules and are therefore subject to the restriction on dealing under Rule 21:

(a) any sale or purchase, or any agreement for the sale or purchase, of AIM securities;
(b) the grant or acceptance of any option relating to AIM securities or any other right or obligation, present or future, conditional or unconditional, to acquire or dispose of AIM securities;
(c) the acquisition, disposal, exercise or discharge of, or any dealing with any option, right or obligation relating to AIM securities;
(d) deals between directors and/or applicable employees;
(e) off-market deals;
(f) transfers for no consideration; and
(g) any shares taken into or out of treasury.

Also included in the definition of "deal" are transactions for the acquisition, disposal or discharge of a related financial product. A related financial product is any financial product whose value, in whole or in part, is determined directly or indirectly by reference to the price of AIM securities or securities which are the subject of an application for admission, including a contract for difference and a fixed odds bet. The widening of the restriction on dealing to include dealings in contracts for difference and similar financial products arose from an admission of a company to AIM where the underwriting of a placing of new shares effected in connection with the admission was effectively sub-underwritten by a director entering into a related financial product.

The following transactions are not deals for the purposes of the AIM Rules and therefore are not subject to the restriction on dealing by directors and applicable employees under Rule 21:

(a) undertakings or elections to take up, and the actual taking up of, entitlements under a rights issue or other pre-emptive offer (including under a scrip dividend alternative);

(b) allowing entitlements to lapse under a rights issue or other pre-emptive offer (including under a scrip dividend alternative);

(c) the sale of sufficient entitlements under a rights issue to allow the take up of the balance of the entitlement;

(d) undertakings to accept, and the acceptance of, a takeover offer.

9.1.5 What is a "close period"?

The restriction on dealing in AIM securities imposed by Rule 21 prohibits dealings by directors and applicable employees of an AIM company whilst the AIM company is in a "close period". A close period is:

(a) the period of two months preceding the publication of annual results (or, if shorter, the period from its financial year end to the time of publication of annual results);

(b) the period of two months immediately preceding the announcement of half-yearly results (or, if shorter, the period from the end of the relevant financial period up to and including the time of the announcement);

(c) if the company reports on a quarterly basis, the period of one month immediately preceding the announcement of its quarterly results (or, if shorter, the period from the end of the relevant financial period up to and including the time of the announcement);

(d) any other period when the AIM company is in possession of unpublished price-sensitive information; and

139

(e)   any time when it has become reasonably probable that the announcement of unpublished price-sensitive information will be required by the AIM Rules.

Determining whether or not an AIM company is in a close period by reference to the announcement of annual, half-yearly or quarterly results will generally not be problematic. Whether or not an AIM company is in possession of unpublished price-sensitive information raises two issues. What is unpublished price-sensitive information and when is an AIM company in possession of such information?

Unpublished price-sensitive information is defined in the glossary to the AIM Rules as information which:

(a)   relates to particular AIM securities or to a particular AIM company rather than to securities or issuers in general;
(b)   is specific or precise;
(c)   has not been made public; and
(d)   if it were made public would be likely to have a significant effect on the price or value of any AIM security.

As a close period includes any time when the AIM company is in possession of unpublished price-sensitive information, at any particular time *all* directors and applicable employees will either be prohibited from dealing or permitted to deal in the company's AIM securities. The AIM Rules do not admit the possibility that only certain directors, or only the directors but not applicable employees, will be prohibited from dealing or permitted to deal at any time.

As applied by the AIM team at the London Stock Exchange, the AIM Rules require an AIM company to demonstrate that the company was not in a close period at the relevant time when any question is raised as to whether or not a dealing by a director or applicable employee was made in compliance with the AIM Rules.

9.1.6   Exemptions from the restriction on dealing

The AIM Rules do provide limited exemptions from the restriction on dealing in a close period. The restriction does not apply where a binding commitment to deal was entered into prior to the AIM company entering a close period and where, at the time the commitment was made, it was not reasonably foreseeable that the company was likely to enter a close period. To rely on the exemption to permit a dealing that would otherwise be prohibited, the commitment must have been announced at the time the commitment was made. Essentially, this exemption will only permit a dealing in a close period which in effect is merely completing a deal that has already been made. Most obviously a conditional contract entered into by a director or applicable employee to buy or sell AIM securities can be completed in a close period. Entering into the contract will be a dealing for the purposes of the AIM Rules which will require announcement. Without the exemption, the completion of the conditional contract during a close period would be a dealing for the purposes of the AIM Rules, as it gives rise to a change in the legal ownership of the securities which are the subject of the transaction.

The AIM Rules also provide for the London Stock Exchange to permit a director or applicable employee of an AIM company to sell AIM securities during a close period to alleviate severe personal hardship. The Guidance Notes that accompany the AIM Rules explain that this exemption is limited to circumstances in which severe personal hardship would otherwise occur to the director or applicable employee or their immediate relatives, such as the urgent need for a medical operation or the need to satisfy a court order where no other funds are reasonably available.

9.1.7 Notification of dealings

An AIM company is required by the AIM Rules to announce without delay any dealing by a director in its AIM securities. The announcement must include:

(a) the identity of the director;
(b) the date on which the AIM company was notified of the dealing;
(c) the date on which the dealing was made;
(d) the price, number and class of the AIM securities which are the subject of the dealing;
(e) the nature of the transaction; and
(f) the nature and extent of the director's interest in the transaction.

141

Where the announcement concerns a related financial product it must include the detailed nature of the exposure under the related financial product.

Compliance by an AIM company with the AIM Rules to announce dealings by directors depends upon the notification of the dealing by the director to the company. As noted above, under the AIM Rules, the AIM company is responsible for ensuring its directors' compliance with the AIM Rules. In relation to dealings in AIM securities, the AIM Rules used to require the adoption of a model code for dealing in AIM securities. This requirement has been dispensed with. However, to ensure compliance with dealing restriction and notification requirements under the AIM Rules, an AIM company must adopt some form of request and decision mechanism for the grant or refusal of permission for directors and applicable employees to deal in AIM securities. In addition, given the extension of the restriction on dealing to a director's family and entities connected with him, an AIM company must have guidance available to be issued to persons connected with a director. This guidance must explain when they can and cannot deal and what information will be required from them, and when, following a dealing in the securities of an AIM company.

9.1.8 Sanctions for breach of dealing restriction

As in any case where it considers that an AIM company has contravened the AIM Rules, in the case of a dealing in breach of the dealing restriction, the London Stock Exchange may:

(a) fine the AIM company;
(b) censure the AIM company;
(c) publish the fact that the AIM company has been fined or censured;
(d) cancel the admission of the AIM company's securities to AIM.

If the London Stock Exchange proposes to take any of these steps, it will follow the procedures set out in the *Disciplinary Procedures and Appeals Handbook*.

9.1.9 Lock-ins for new businesses

In the case of an applicant for admission to AIM whose main business activity has not been independent and earning revenue for at least two years, Rule 7 of the AIM Rules requires the AIM company to ensure that all related parties and applicable employees as at the date of admission to AIM agree not to dispose of any interest in its securities for one year from the date of admission to AIM. The rule applies in the case of an AIM company that effects a reverse takeover and whose main business activity thereafter has not been independent and earning revenue for at least two years.

9.1.10 Who are related parties?

The related parties of an AIM company include the following:

(a) the directors of the AIM company or any subsidiary or parent undertaking, or other subsidiary of its parent undertaking;

(b) substantial shareholders, being any person who holds any legal or beneficial interest directly or indirectly in 10 per cent or more of any class of AIM security of the company (excluding treasury shares) or 10 per cent or more of the voting rights (excluding treasury shares) of an AIM company, excluding any authorised person, or any company with securities quoted on the London Stock Exchange's markets, unless the company is an investing company;

(c) members of a director's family as noted above, and members of the family of any substantial shareholder, which includes a spouse and children under the age of 18 and certain companies and trusts connected with any of them;

(d) any company in whose equity shares any related party thus far mentioned (individually or taken together with his or her family and (in the case of a director of an AIM company) any other director of the AIM company and his or her family) has an interest, or has a conditional or contingent entitlement to become interested, in 30 per cent or more of the votes (excluding treasury shares) able to be cast at general meetings on all, or substantially all, matters or to appoint or remove directors of the company holding a majority of voting rights at board meetings on all, or substantially all, matters;

143

(e)   any company which is a parent or subsidiary undertaking of a company mentioned in paragraph (d) above and any other subsidiary undertaking of any parent undertaking of a company mentioned in paragraph (d) above.

The definition of related party is extended further to include:

(i)   any company whose directors are accustomed to acting in accordance with the instructions or directions of a director of the AIM company or any subsidiary or parent undertaking of the AIM company; and

(ii)   certain companies in which directors of an AIM company, and companies connected with them are able to exercise 30 per cent or more of the votes able to be cast at general meetings on all or substantially all matters.

The net is thus thrown far and wide and, in all but the most straight-forward of situations, detailed analysis is required to determine whether or not a company with which a director of the AIM company is connected is a related party of the AIM company for the purposes of the AIM Rules. For the purposes of Rule 7, an applicable employee of an AIM company is any employee who together with his family has a holding or interest, directly or indirectly, in 0.5 per cent or more of a class of AIM securities (excluding treasury shares). An applicable employee's family for this purpose comprises his or her spouse and any children under the age of 18 and also other entities in which any of them is interested. A company in which an employee or his or her spouse and children under the age of 18 have control of more than 20 per cent of the equity or voting rights in general meeting is part of an employee's family as is any trust of which the employee or his or her spouse and children are trustees or beneficiaries, except for any employee share scheme or pension scheme where the employee or his or her spouse and children under the age of 18 are beneficiaries and not trustees.

In contrast to the general restriction on dealing that applies to the directors and applicable employees of an AIM company, an AIM Rules lock-in applies to all securities of the AIM company, not just those that are admitted to AIM. In addition, Rule 7 does not apply just to securities in the AIM company that are held by related parties at the date of admission to AIM. Rather, Rule 7 is a prohibition on the disposal of any interest in the securities of an AIM company in the period of 12 months following admission. If a related party acquires securities following admission or, for example, were a director or employee to acquire shares on the exercise of an option, a lock-in given in compliance with Rule 7 would prohibit the sale of any of the shares acquired during such lock-in period.

The obligation to ensure compliance with the lock-ins rests with the AIM company. It is customary for lock-ins given in compliance with Rule 7 to be addressed by the related parties to both the company and its nominated adviser.

There are limited exemptions that apply to Rule 7 permitting the disposal by a related party of an interest in the securities of an AIM company in the period of 12 months following its admission to AIM. The exemptions permit a disposal of securities:

(a)   in the event of an intervening court order;
(b)   as a result of the death of the related party;
(c)   by way of the acceptance of a takeover offer for the AIM company which is open to all shareholders.

A substantial shareholder who became so at the time of admission of the company to AIM and at a price more widely available need not be the subject of a lock-in under Rule 7.

9.2   Corporate governance

9.2.1   Introduction

As a concept, corporate governance is poorly defined, notwithstanding that it has succeeded in attracting a great deal of public interest in recent years. In its report published in December 1992, the Cadbury Committee chaired by Adrian Cadbury on the Financial Aspects of Corporate Governance defined corporate governance, narrowly, as "the system by which companies are directed and controlled". Since that report was published, the concept seems to have expanded to include matters as diverse as shareholder democracy, corporate transparency and accountability, and even the way in which a company relates to society at large. According to the QCA Corporate Governance Guidelines (*see* 9.3.1 below), the purpose of good corporate governance is "to ensure that the company is managed in an efficient, effective and entrepreneurial manner for the benefit of all shareholders over the longer term". This is a worthy goal, but there are some who doubt whether an increasingly restrictive corporate governance regime sits comfortably with the concept of entrepreneurial management and the perceived flexibility of the AIM market.

The first point to note when considering the application of general principles of corporate governance to AIM companies is that there is no requirement under the AIM Rules to comply with any of the relevant guidelines. This contrasts with the position of companies listed on the Official List of the UK Listing Authority ("Official List") which are required to state in their annual report and accounts whether or not they have complied, throughout the relevant period, with the provisions of the Combined Code on Corporate Governance appended to the UK Listing Rules ("the Code") and, if not, why not (Rule 9.8.6 of the Listing Rules).

With the ripples of a number of high-profile corporate collapses in the US, including the demise of Enron Corp., still visible some years down the line, corporate governance remains an issue of global concern. Shareholders are demanding greater accountability from the boards of the companies in which they invest and there is renewed focus on the way in which companies are managed and how those in control are rewarded. Shareholder expectations in the area of corporate governance have risen and there is currently no reason to expect that this trend will reverse. Inevitably, such expectations will increase the pressure on AIM companies to address corporate governance issues, regardless of their being under no statutory or regulatory compulsion to do so.

That said, murmurs of dissent are increasingly heard from directors of companies listed on the Official List about "restrictive" and "unrealistic" corporate governance requirements in the UK. The challenge for the London Stock Exchange, therefore, is to protect the credibility of companies listed on its AIM market by addressing shareholder concerns about the standards of corporate governance in smaller companies, while maximising the AIM market's great advantage of offering a lighter regulatory touch. This is quite a balancing act but, with a number of companies in the past year having cited the undue burden of corporate governance requirements as one reason for their transfer from the Official List to AIM, this is a competitive advantage which AIM would do well to preserve.

9.2.2   Corporate governance initiatives in the UK

Following a number of major corporate governance reviews in the 1990s, notably that chaired by Sir Ronald Hampel in 1998, and the publication of the principles of good governance and code of best practice known as the Combined Code, by the end of that decade the UK had a well-established corporate governance model in relation to fully listed companies. Nonetheless, the combination of a difficult trading climate and the very public criticism of the conduct of directors in relation to certain failed US companies created an environment in which the call came for further scrutiny of corporate governance practices in the UK. Accordingly, the last few years have seen the instigation of a number of UK corporate governance initiatives. Paragraphs 9.2.2.1 to 9.2.2.4 below summarise some of the most noteworthy of these.

9.2.2.1   The Higgs Report and the revised Code
The Code, which came into effect for reporting years beginning on or after 1 November 2003, was derived from the findings of a review led by Sir Derek Higgs of the role and effectiveness of non-executive directors. Following a period of speculation that the UK might adopt a prescriptive regime to emulate the US Sarbanes-Oxley law, the Higgs Report was initially well received, with most quarters accepting that a tightening up of the corporate governance regime was required. However, the devil was in the detail and the report ultimately received strong criticism from many in the City who suggested Higgs' proposals were ill-conceived and likely to cause serious damage to the governance of UK-listed companies, particularly smaller ones. Such criticism led the Financial Reporting Council ("FRC") to set up a working party that produced a revised draft of the Code, departing in a number of key areas from the code proposed by Higgs, which was duly adopted in July 2003.

147

Two years on in July 2005, amidst claims that the regulatory burden of the Code, particularly on smaller companies, was too onerous and encouraged a level of bureaucracy which risked stifling entrepreneurship, the FRC issued a "call for evidence" as part of its review of progress in implementing the Code. Around the same time, the chairman of an investment bank whose shares were traded on the Official List announced the board's decision to move the company to AIM and was quoted as saying the Code was a "misconceived piece of quasi-legislation" which did more harm than good. In such a climate it will be interesting to see what views the FRC will receive from listed companies, their directors, investors and other interested parties. The FRC will publish it findings at the end of 2005. If any changes to the Code are recommended there will be a separate consultation in early 2006.

9.2.2.2   *Company law reform*
In March 2005, the Department of Trade and Industry ("DTI") published for consultation a White Paper entitled Company Law Reform ("the White Paper"). The White Paper outlines proposals for extensive modernisation of UK company law and follows on from an independent, three-year company law review commissioned by the DTI in 1998 and the White Paper entitled Modernising Company Law published in July 2002.

The White Paper attempts to address the perceived failures of a company law system based on years of case law and statutory amendment by introducing greater transparency and accessibility. It focuses, in particular, on the needs of smaller companies, with additional or different provisions being brought in for larger companies where necessary.

The proposals with the greatest potential to impact the area of corporate governance include:

(a)   statutory codification of directors' common law duties, with clear guidance to be given to new directors as to what these duties mean;

(b)   enhanced power for proxies so that any proxy will be able to speak, to vote on a show of hands as well as on a poll and to join with others in demanding a poll in general meeting;

(c) a new right for a sufficient body of members of quoted companies to require scrutiny of any poll to be carried out by a registered auditor and disclosed on the company's website; and

(d) new provisions requiring companies to recognise the rights of the holders of beneficial interests in shares and to provide information to such persons in certain cases.

Additionally, the White Paper states that the Government is keen to see institutional investors playing a more effective role in corporate governance. To this end, it proposes that quoted companies should be required to disclose, on their websites and in their annual reports, the results of polls at general meetings and to publish on their websites their annual reporting documents as soon as practicable after they have been approved and the audit report issued. This proposal is made with a view to encouraging greater accountability generally and to give shareholders enhanced opportunities to submit members' resolutions (subject to the existing thresholds) for inclusion in the notice of the imminent annual general meeting, at the company's cost.

9.2.2.3 The Smith Report
In September 2002, the FRC set up an independent group, chaired by Sir Robert Smith, to clarify the role and responsibilities of audit committees and to develop the existing Combined Code guidance. The group's findings were published at the same time as the Higgs Report and included detailed guidance on the composition and responsibilities of the audit committee and specimen terms of reference. These recommendations are included in the Code.

9.2.2.4 The Directors' Remuneration Regulations 2002
Following much criticism of excessive executive remuneration and failure to link pay to company performance, the Directors' Remuneration Report Regulations 2002 (SI 2002/1986) ("the Regulations") came into effect in August 2002 for financial years ending on or after 31 December 2002.

The Regulations require companies whose shares are listed on certain Exchanges (not including AIM) to publish a board-approved report on directors' remuneration as part of their annual reporting cycle and to put the report to a shareholders' resolution at the annual general meeting. The content requirements of the remuneration report are designed to ensure that shareholders will have sufficient information to make an informed decision prior to voting. Broadly, the report must disclose details of:

(a) individual directors' remuneration packages and justification of any compensation packages given in the preceding year;
(b) membership of the remuneration committee;
(c) details of any remuneration consultants used;
(d) a statement of the company's future policy on directors' pay; and
(e) a graph showing company performance for the last five financial years by reference to total shareholder return compared against an appropriate index.

Although payments made to directors do not have to be repaid in the event that the shareholders vote down the remuneration report, the historic defeat of the report of GlaxoSmithKline in May 2003, followed swiftly by a similar fate for Shire Pharmaceuticals Group plc, where there was concern about a pension pay-off for the company's former chief executive, show that the legislation has had an impact.

A report published in November 2004, prepared by Deloitte for the DTI on the impact of the Regulations, found levels of compliance with the Regulations to be high. Notably:

(a) directors' notice periods have been reduced to one year or less and there are disclosure standards of 80 per cent or more in 19 out of the 22 areas covered by the Regulations;
(b) all of the top 350 FTSE companies now put their Remuneration Report to a separate shareholder vote and a number of well-publicised situations have seen remuneration committees changing their policy or practice as a direct result of shareholder voting;
(c) over 90 per cent of shareholders say communications have improved; and
(d) companies are changing their remuneration policies and practices to reflect the link between pay and performance.

However, the Regulations have been criticised for being excessively complex and giving rise to damaging publicity for companies while doing little to address the underlying problems which may have led to shareholder dissent. The Government has stated that the Regulations will be kept under review, but that changes to company law requirements in this area are not needed at this stage.

9.2.3 ABI Guidelines

Some helpful guidance in the area of directors' remuneration is contained in the Principles and Guidelines on Executive Remuneration published by the Association of British Insurers ("ABI").

A useful complement to the Code, the ABI guidelines advise that remuneration policy should aim to establish a clear link between reward and performance. It is preferable for companies to ensure that an appropriate remuneration policy is in place and followed rather than to risk yearly controversy when remuneration outcomes are disclosed in the annual report. The ABI guidelines set out practical suggestions for establishing and implementing such a policy.

These guidelines include the following principles:

(a)　boards should demonstrate that performance-based remuneration arrangements are clearly aligned with business strategy and objectives. It is suggested that simple structures should be relied upon as these enhance the prospects of successful communication with shareholders;

(b)　remuneration committees should maintain a constructive and timely dialogue with their major institutional shareholders on matters relating to remuneration, and contemplated changes to remuneration policy and practice should be discussed with shareholders in advance. Any proposed departure from the stated remuneration policy should be subject to prior approval by shareholders;

(c)　all new share-based incentive schemes should be subject to approval by shareholders by means of a separate and binding resolution, whether or not they are dilutive. Furthermore, where the rules of share-based incentive schemes, or the basis on which the scheme was approved by shareholders, permits some degree of latitude as regards quantum of grant or performance criteria, it is expected that any changes will be detailed in the remuneration report. Any substantive changes in the practical operation of schemes resulting from policy changes or modifications of scheme rules, as previously approved, should be subject to prior shareholder approval;

(d)   there should be transparency on all components of remuneration of present and past directors and, where appropriate, other senior executives. Shareholders' attention should be drawn to any special arrangements and significant changes since the previous remuneration report; and

(e)   remuneration committees must guard against the possibility of unjustified windfall gains when designing and implementing share-based incentives and other associated entitlements. The guidelines state, for example, that schemes should pay out only in respect of the performance period that has elapsed prior to a change of control, and any payment in such circumstances should reflect the underlying financial performance of a company.

9.2.4   National Association of Pension Funds policy

Like the ABI, the National Association of Pension Funds ("NAPF") plays an active role in monitoring corporate governance in the UK, and its Corporate Governance Policy provides detailed voting guidelines on remuneration, including a statement that, where a company does not have a remuneration committee, NAPF will normally recommend a vote against the approval of its remuneration report.

The Government has called on the ABI, NAPF and the Confederation of British Industry to work towards providing a common set of guidelines on directors' contracts (including the remuneration paid under such contracts) by the end of 2005.

9.3   AIM companies and the Code

As previously stated, AIM companies are under no legal obligation to comply with the corporate governance requirements in the code or any other corporate governance guidelines referred to above. Nonetheless, in certain key areas, there is an expectation that AIM companies will adopt, at least in part, the principles of the Code and it is increasingly unusual for an AIM company not to do so.

The Code contains main and supporting principles and provisions. A company listed on the Official List will be required to state in its annual report how it has applied the principles in the Code. It must also confirm that it has complied with the Code's provisions or, where it has not, provide an explanation. Smaller companies on the Official List are exempt from certain of the Code's provisions, although they are encouraged to consider whether it is appropriate to adopt the Code's approach even in relation to exempt matters. Whilst AIM companies are under no compulsion to comply with the Code, their shareholders do, of course, expect such companies to be governed properly and, in the absence of an alternative, will tend to use the Code as their yardstick.

To address this issue, in July 2005 the Quoted Companies Alliance ("QCA") published a set of guidelines for corporate governance of AIM companies ("the QCA Guidelines").

9.3.1 QCA Guidelines

Given that a light regulatory touch is one of AIM's great selling points, publication of the QCA Guidelines gives rise to some concern that, even without the force of law, the guidelines risk codifying a standard for corporate governance which might not be appropriate for every AIM company. In practice, most AIM companies at least fulfil the Code's requirement for a quoted company to appoint an audit committee and a remuneration committee. They will also, generally, seek to comply with the Code's principles in relation to the constitution of the board and the role of non-executive directors.

To an extent, therefore, much of the QCA Guidelines may simply reflect what is already the status quo. That said, the QCA states that compliance with its guidelines should represent a floor for standards of corporate governance, not a cap on them, and encourages AIM companies to aspire to compliance with the Code. Only time will tell what part the QCA Guidelines may play in extending the application of the Code to companies whose shares are traded on AIM, but for now it certainly forms a useful reference point for an AIM company seeking to ensure a high standard of corporate governance.

The main areas of the Code with which the majority of AIM companies currently comply are considered at 9.3.2 to 9.3.4 below. These are all covered by the Code of Best Practice included in the QCA Guidelines.

9.3.2 Independent non-executive directors

The first principle of the Code (Code main principle A.1) is that every company should be headed by an effective board, which is collectively responsible for the success of the company. A further main principle, A.3, states that the board should include a balance of executive and non-executive directors – in particular, independent non-executive directors – such that no individual or small group of individuals can dominate the board's decision making.

The Combined Code offered no guidance on the role of the non-executive director, and the lack of clarity surrounding the role was a central concern of the Higgs review (*see* 9.2.2.1 above). The Code now gives extensive guidance to non-executive directors, both in its supporting principles and in a separate guidance section extracted from the Higgs Report. It states that, as part of their role as members of a unitary board, non-executive directors should constructively challenge and help develop proposals on strategy and support executives in their leadership of the business. Increasingly, the role of the non-executive director is a proactive one: he or she must be well informed about the company, its policies and procedures and the external environment in which it operates with a view to scrutinising and, where necessary, challenging the performance of executive management. It certainly should not be seen as a job which offers the retired executive, seeking a large portfolio of non-executive directorships, an opportunity for a quiet life.

The Code provides that a company outside the FTSE 350 should have at least two non-executive directors determined by the board to be independent (Code provision A.3.2). This requirement is echoed by the QCA Guidelines. Whether a director is or is not independent must be determined by reference to any relationships or circumstances which are likely to affect, or could appear to affect, the director's judgement. The board should state its reasons for deciding that a director is independent, notwithstanding the existence of relationships or circumstances which may appear relevant, including if the director has been an employee of the company within the last five years, has had, directly or indirectly, a material business relationship with the company within the last three years or if he or she has close family ties with any of the company's advisers, directors or senior employees (Code provision A.3.1).

The Code provides that the board should appoint one of the independent non-executive directors to be the senior independent director (Code provision A.3.3). The senior independent director, or SID, should be available to shareholders if they have concerns which they have failed to resolve through the usual channels of chairman, chief executive or finance director or for which such contact is inappropriate. Given the current move towards increased shareholder activism, it is reasonable to expect that shareholders will take advantage of this new line of communication, but it remains unusual for an AIM company to nominate a non-executive director for the SID role.

9.3.3 The audit committee

Main principle C.3 of the Code states that the board should establish formal and transparent arrangements for considering how it should apply the financial reporting and internal control principles of the company and for maintaining an appropriate relationship with the company's auditors. Most AIM companies appoint an audit committee and will look to the Code when drawing up its terms of reference.

9.3.3.1 *The constitution of the audit committee*
Provision C.3.1 of the Code provides that the board should establish an audit committee of at least three or, in the case of a company below the FTSE 350, two members, who should all be independent non-executive directors. It is recommended that appointments should be for up to three years, extendable by no more than two additional three-year periods. Not less than one member of the committee should have recent and relevant financial experience.

9.3.3.2   *The role of the audit committee*

While every director has a duty to act in the interests of the company and, following the principle of the unitary board, remains equally responsible for the company's affairs as a matter of law, the audit committee has a particular role to ensure that the interests of shareholders are properly protected in relation to financial reporting and internal control. Provision C.3.3 of the Code provides that the work of the committee in discharging its responsibilities should be the subject of a separate section in the company's annual report, with a view to giving the audit committee a prominence and authority it might otherwise lack.

The main role and responsibilities of the audit committee should be set out in writing and made available on request and included on the company's website, if it has one. These should be reviewed by the audit committee annually and should include:

(a)   monitoring the integrity of the financial statements of the company and any formal announcements relating to the company's financial performance, including reviewing any significant financial reporting judgements contained in them;

(b)   reviewing the company's internal financial controls (i.e., the systems established to identify, assess, manage and monitor financial risks) and, unless expressly addressed by a separate risk committee composed of independent directors, or by the board itself, reviewing the company's internal control and risk management systems;

(c)   monitoring and reviewing the effectiveness of the company's internal audit function (and where there is no internal audit function, the audit committee should consider annually whether there is a need for such a function and the reasons for its absence should be explained in the relevant section of the annual report);

(d)   making recommendations to the board, for it to put to the shareholders for their approval in general meeting, in relation to the appointment, reappointment and removal of the external auditor and approving the remuneration and terms of engagement of the external auditor. If the external auditor resigns, the audit committee should investigate the issues giving rise to such resignation and consider whether any action is required;

(e)   reviewing and monitoring the external auditor's independence and objectivity and the effectiveness of the audit process, taking into consideration relevant UK professional and regulatory requirements; and

(f)   developing and implementing policy on the engagement of the external auditor to supply non-audit services, taking into account relevant ethical guidance regarding the provision of non-audit services by the external audit firm. If the external auditor provides non-audit services, the annual report should explain to shareholders how auditor independence and objectivity are safeguarded.

Ultimately, the effectiveness of the audit committee will depend upon an open relationship with management and a high level of mutual respect between the committee and the executive. It will also require the audit committee to be properly and promptly informed of all relevant developments and decisions. The audit committee should not hesitate to request additional information and ask difficult questions where it is not satisfied with the explanations of management and the auditors about a particular financial policy procedure. Equally, the executive must ensure that it is quick to canvass, and willing to listen to, the audit committee's views and should take the initiative in supplying all information which the committee may need to discharge its obligations effectively.

9.3.4   The remuneration committee

One of the most controversial and highly publicised areas of corporate governance is the determination of directors' remuneration. Whilst most shareholders accept that levels of remuneration must be sufficient to recruit, retain and motivate directors of the calibre required to run a company successfully, and so increase shareholder value, there has been much criticism of past failures to link rewards to corporate and individual performance.

It is a main principle of the Code (Code main principle B.2) that there should be a formal and transparent procedure for developing policy on executive remuneration and for fixing the remuneration packages of individual directors. No director should be involved in deciding his or her own remuneration. The appointment of a remuneration committee is standard for most AIM companies and, as when appointing an audit committee, such companies will usually base the terms of reference of the remuneration committee on the standards set out in the Code.

9.3.4.1   The constitution of the remuneration committee

The Code provides (in Code provision B.2.1) that the remuneration committee should consist exclusively of independent non-executive directors and should comprise at least three or, in the case of a company below the FTSE 350, two such directors. The remuneration committee should make available on request and on the company's website its terms of reference, explaining its role and the authority delegated to it by the board. These terms should be reviewed and, where necessary, updated annually by the committee.

9.3.4.2   The role of the remuneration committee

The main duties of the remuneration committee should include:

(a)   determining and agreeing with the board the framework or broad policy for the remuneration of the chief executive, the chairman of the company and such other members of the executive as it is designated to consider. As a minimum, the Code provides that the committee should have delegated responsibility for setting remuneration for all executive directors, the chairman and the company secretary;

(b)   determining targets for any performance-related pay schemes operated by the company. It is recommended that the performance-related elements of the remuneration of executive directors should form a significant proportion of the total package and should be designed to align their interests with those of shareholders. The Code contains a schedule of provisions to be followed in designing schemes for performance-related remuneration which should give executive directors a keen incentive to perform at the highest levels;

(c)   ensuring that contractual terms on termination, and any payments made, including pension contributions, are fair to the individual and the company and that a departing director's duty to mitigate his loss is fully recognised. The aim should be to avoid rewarding poor performance, and notice periods should be set at one year or less;

(d) ensuring that provisions regarding disclosure of remuneration, including pensions, as set out in the Directors' Remuneration Report Regulations 2002 and the Code, are fulfilled;

(e) being exclusively responsible for establishing the selection criteria for, selecting, appointing and setting the terms of reference for any remuneration consultants who advise the committee. If such consultants are appointed, a statement should be made available on request and on the company's website as to whether they have any other connection with the company; and

(f) reporting the frequency of, and attendance by members at, remuneration committee meetings in the annual reports.

The remuneration of non-executive directors should be a matter for the chairman and executive members of the board or, where required by the company's articles of association, by the shareholders. It is recommended that non-executive remuneration should reflect the time commitment and responsibilities of the role. Remuneration for non-executive directors should only exceptionally include share options and, if such options are granted, shareholder approval should be sought in advance. Any shares acquired by a non-executive director by exercise of share options should be held until at least one year after the non-executive director leaves the board.

9.4 Conclusion

There is a clear trend amongst companies whose shares are listed on the Official List towards greater accountability to shareholders, particularly in relation to directors' remuneration. It is inevitable that these pressures will make themselves felt in the boardrooms of AIM companies, regardless of whether or not the directors of such companies are under a statutory or regulatory obligation to comply with the increasing volume of guidelines on corporate governance. At the very least, directors of AIM companies will be expected to exhibit an understanding of the relevant issues and, where an AIM company does not comply with the aspects of corporate governance referred to above, it may well find itself having to explain its decision to concerned and expectant investors.

Chapter 10

The Tax Regime

Chilton Taylor
Partner
Head of Capital Markets
Baker Tilly

10.1 Introduction

The tax advantages available in relation to companies whose shares are dealt in on AIM are the same as those which apply to all qualifying unquoted companies. They apply to AIM companies because, for tax purposes, companies on AIM are not regarded as quoted. Recent changes under which AIM became directly regulated by the London Stock Exchange (rather than being subject directly to the European Prospectus Directive) can only strengthen the tax status of AIM, although as AIM has increased in popularity and if even larger companies seek admission to the market then clearly this status may be reviewed by the Treasury.

The tax reliefs available are as follows:

(a) Enterprise Investment Scheme ("EIS");
(b) Venture Capital Trusts ("VCTs");
(c) Corporate Venturing Scheme ("CVS");
(d) Capital Gains Tax ("CGT"):

    (i) business asset taper relief;
    (ii) gift relief;

(e) Inheritance Tax ("IHT"):

    (i) business property relief;

(f) relief for losses.

This Chapter can only provide a brief synopsis of the various reliefs and some of the more common problems and issues that practitioners face. Therefore, it can be no substitute for specialist advice which is always recommended, particularly in respect of the EIS, VCT and CVS regimes because of the complex nature of the legislation which contains widespread anti-avoidance provisions. Advice should only be provided by experienced practitioners familiar with the entirety of the legislation and who regularly advise on it. As the EIS and VCT legislation is specifically more relevant to new equity fundings, this Chapter contains some additional guidance in relation to key issues that should be considered by practitioners in relation to new fundings.

The legislation referred to in this Chapter is that up to the Finance Act 2005.

10.2 Enterprise Investment Scheme and Venture Capital Trusts

The EIS benefits individual investors who can claim generous tax reliefs as an encouragement to invest in qualifying companies. AIM companies which qualify can therefore attract a wider spread of investors, friends and certain family members and (subject to certain conditions) new directors who are able to invest under the EIS.

VCTs are fully listed companies similar to quoted investment trusts whose investors are private individuals who are able to obtain tax reliefs similar to those under the EIS. In this way, investors in VCTs can gain access indirectly to a professionally managed portfolio of unquoted investments – which for this purpose can include shares in qualifying AIM companies. A VCT must invest 70 per cent of its funds in qualifying unquoted companies (which can include those on AIM) broadly within three years of obtaining its quotation, and accordingly VCTs have become an important source of AIM funding particularly in difficult market conditions when other investors are reluctant to invest.

The relevant legislation is contained in the following:

(a)   EIS:

    (i)   Sections 289–312 Income and Corporation Taxes Act 1988;
    (ii)   Schedule 5B Taxation of Chargeable Gains Act 1992;

(b)   VCTs:

    (i)   Section 842AA Income and Corporation Taxes Act 1988;

    (ii)   Schedule 15B Income and Corporation Taxes Act 1988;

    (iii)   Schedule 28B Income and Corporation Taxes Act 1988.

In addition there are various press releases, Revenue interpretations ("RIs") and the HM Revenue & Customs' Venture Capital Schemes Manual ("VCM") which provide further guidance. There are separate regulations in relation to VCTs.

10.2.1   Benefits for investors – EIS

The EIS can benefit individual investors who subscribe for new ordinary shares in AIM companies which qualify as trading companies. Qualifying investments up to £200,000 in aggregate in a tax year (husband and wife may each invest £200,000) entitle an investor to the following tax reliefs.

(a)   Twenty per cent initial income tax relief on investment ("initial relief") but:

    (i)   the investment must remain qualifying and be held for three years to qualify for this relief;

    (ii)   for shares subscribed prior to 6 October in any tax year, a maximum of 50 per cent of each investment and no more than £25,000 in aggregate may be treated as invested in the previous tax year (subject to annual limits);

    (iii)   relief is restricted to the actual income tax liability for the year if less than 20 per cent.

Accordingly investments have an effective initial cost of only 80 per cent of cost.

(b)   Exemption from capital gains tax on disposal but:

    (i)   the investment must be held for three years;

    (ii)   initial relief must not be withdrawn;

    (iii)   the exemption is restricted if initial relief was not given on the full amount or if that amount has been reduced.

Accordingly, subject to the above conditions, any gain after three years is tax free.

(c)   CGT deferral relief:

   (i)   in addition, or as an alternative to, claiming the initial relief, investors may defer assessment to capital gains tax on other gains by reinvesting those gains in subscriptions for new ordinary shares in qualifying companies;

   (ii)   reinvestment of other capital gains must be made up to one year before and three years after the disposal which gave rise to the gain;

   (iii)   the period of deferral is until the investment is disposed of or the investee company ceases to qualify;

   (iv)   there is no limit (up to the amount of the capital gain) that can be deferred in this way;

   (v)   the gain to be reinvested is calculated before deduction of taper relief;

   (vi)   an investor may therefore benefit not only from the 20 per cent initial tax relief and the other reliefs as above (for investments up to £200,000), but also by deferral of assessment to capital gains tax (40 per cent for a higher-rate taxpayer) on the gain which is reinvested;

   (vii)   accordingly it is possible for investors to claim initial tax relief of 60 per cent (for a higher-rate taxpayer) on the first £200,000 (re)invested. However, 40 per cent is a deferral only and is repayable when the investment is disposed of or the investee company ceases to qualify.

Example
This example assumes that the investor is a 40 per cent taxpayer with a capital gain of £100,000 (i.e., a CGT liability of £40,000).

	£
Gross investment in shares	100,000
Less CGT deferral at 40%	(40,000)
Less EIS initial income tax relief at 20%	(20,000)
Net cost of investment	40,000
CGT payable on disposal of shares	40,000*

*subject to taper relief

(d)   Loss relief if the investment fails or is disposed of at a loss:

(i)   this is calculated at an investor's top rate of tax (40 per cent for a higher-rate taxpayer) effectively on the net loss, after taking into account the initial tax relief;

(ii)   losses can be relieved either against capital gains in the year of loss or a subsequent year, or against income in the year of the loss or the previous year.

Whilst loss relief is available for investment in all trading companies, this is enhanced with the EIS and the maximum net loss can thus be restricted to 48 per cent of cost (*see* example below).

Example

	40% taxpayer £	22% taxpayer £
Realised value of shares	Nil	Nil
Original gross cost of investment	(100,000)	(100,000)
EIS income tax relief	20,000	20,000
Loss (80,000)	(80,000)	
EIS loss relief – tax at 40%/22%	32,000	17,600
Net loss	(48,000)	(62,400)

10.2.2   Who can benefit from EIS investment?

Most individual investors, subject to their personal circumstances, should be eligible. Their qualifying status must continue for three years following subscription in new ordinary shares.

However, for initial relief and CGT exemption, an individual:

(a)   need not be UK resident (but must be a UK taxpayer);

(b)   must not be connected with the company as:

(i)   an employee;

(ii)   an existing paid director (but may be a paid director once the issue has been made);

(iii)   a shareholder (with associates[1]) with more than 30 per cent of the share capital, share and loan capital, voting power or

---

[1] Note that associates are partners or linear relations, but not brothers or sisters.

            rights to more than 30 per cent of the assets on a winding up;

  (iv)   otherwise able to control the company;

(c)   may be a new director (but *see* (b)(ii) above);

(d)   can each (individual and spouse) invest up to £200,000 per annum.

For deferral relief, an investor:

(a)   must reinvest a chargeable gain in the period one year before and up to three years after it arises;

(b)   must be a UK resident or ordinarily resident at the time of the original gain, its reinvestment and for three years thereafter;

(c)   can be connected (i.e., control the company or be an employee or director); and

(d)   can reinvest an unlimited amount (up to the amount of the gain(s) deferred).

10.2.3　Benefits for investors – VCTs

Investments in VCTs (whether purchased in the market or subscribed for) of up to £200,000 in a tax year entitle individual investors to the following tax reliefs:

(a)   exemption from tax on dividends;

(b)   exemption from capital gains tax on disposal of shares in the VCT.

In addition, for subscriptions up to £200,000 per annum in new ordinary shares issued by a VCT investors may claim 40 per cent initial income tax relief on the amount invested provided the shares are held for three years.

It is important to note that this rate of relief applies only for the tax years 2004/05 and 2005/06 and will be reviewed. The previous rate was 20 per cent, but investors were also able to claim CGT deferral relief (up to 40 per cent for a higher-rate taxpayer) arising from the disposal of any assets where the gain is reinvested in the shares of the VCT. This benefit was withdrawn when the income tax relief was increased to 40 per cent.

10.2.4   Who can benefit from a VCT investment?

Subject to their personal circumstances, most individual investors should be eligible for VCT relief. There is a maximum limit of £200,000 per annum which both a husband and a wife can invest.

An investor:

(a)   need not be UK resident but must be a UK taxpayer; and
(b)   must hold the investment for three years.

10.2.5   Company qualifying criteria for EIS and VCT investment

Under the EIS and VCT legislation, a qualifying unquoted trading company (which can include those on AIM), subject to its size and other qualifying criteria, can raise up to £16 million of new ordinary share capital.

The legislation is complex. However, the following is a summary of the key criteria that a company must meet.

(a)   Under the EIS the shares issued must be new ordinary shares and must be subscribed for wholly in cash and must be fully paid up at the time of issue.
(b)   There is no limitation to the amount of funds raised under the EIS and from a number of VCTs subject to the gross assets test (*see* (f) below and 10.3.5 below). No single VCT can invest more than £1 million in a 12-month period in an individual company.
(c)   The new ordinary shares issued must carry no preferential rights to dividends or company assets on a winding up and must carry no present or future right to be redeemed.
(d)   A VCT can also invest in loan stock or preference shares where redemption is after five years. However, in the case of AIM issues this is unlikely as most issues are placings or offers of ordinary shares. Thirty per cent of qualifying investments must be in new ordinary shares of investee companies. No holding must be more than 15 per cent of a VCT's investments, and at least 10 per cent by value of a VCT's holding in any one company must be in new ordinary shares.

167

(e) VCT funds and under the EIS all funds raised in the same issue (whether or not they are EIS) must be employed:

    (i)   wholly for the purposes of a qualifying business activity carried on wholly or mainly in the UK;

    (ii)   in the trade as to 80 per cent no later than 12 months from the date of subscription or, if later, commencement of trade (which must commence no later than two years after the issue of shares). The remainder must be used within the following 12 months.

(f) The aggregate gross assets must not exceed £15 million before investment and £16 million immediately after.

(g) Under the EIS throughout the three-year period from the issue of shares or the start of trading if later, and throughout such period as the investment is to be held as a qualifying holding of a VCT:

    (i)   the company must be unquoted – AIM companies are regarded as unquoted for this purpose. A company must be unquoted (which can include a company on AIM) only at the time of the issue of shares under the EIS or to VCTs provided that no arrangements exist at that time for the company to become quoted. For VCTs, where a company's shares become quoted they are treated as being unquoted for VCT purposes for a further five years;

    (ii)   under the EIS (but not when there is a group of companies including a parent and a dormant subsidiary) the company must exist wholly (other than to an insignificant extent) for the purpose of carrying out a qualifying business activity – for which purpose the activities of all companies in a group are considered as one;

    (iii)   if the company is a parent company, the activities of the group as a whole must be substantially qualifying (i.e., this is usually taken to mean up to 20 per cent of activities may be non-qualifying);

    (iv)   the company must either carry on a qualifying trade (i.e., not investment activities) or be the parent company of a trading group. Incidental purposes, which are defined as having no significant effect on activities of the company, can be disregarded;

(v)   it must not be controlled by another company – the definition varies for EIS and VCTs but control is broadly one company's ability to direct the affairs of another through voting rights (under the EIS) or through possession or entitlement to acquire more than 50 per cent of the share capital or voting power, the distributable income of the company or the rights to assets on a winding up (for VCT purposes) – or be a 51 per cent subsidiary (other than a qualifying subsidiary (*see* (vi) below and 10.3.6 below) or under the control of another company and any persons connected with that other company;

(vi)   any subsidiary of the issuing company must be owned as to more than 50 per cent (90 per cent if funds raised under the EIS or VCT are employed in it or for its acquisition) and there must be no arrangements in existence by virtue of which it would cease to be such;

(vii)   there are a number of anti-avoidance measures which include such matters as the purchase of other companies and under the EIS repayment or redemption of shares, and professional advice should be sought. In particular, it is essential that the relevant shares must be issued for commercial reasons and not as part of a scheme or arrangement the main purpose or one of the main purposes of which is the avoidance of tax.

Note: it is possible for the company to apply for provisional approval to HM Revenue & Customs prior to issuing shares to establish whether HM Revenue & Customs consider that the shares to be issued will be eligible and the activities of the company are qualifying. This is considered in further detail below.

10.2.6 Qualifying business activities

Most trades (not investment activities) qualify but some activities do not, including the following:

(a)   property development;
(b)   letting of property;
(c)   dealing in land, commodities, futures, shares or securities;
(d)   dealing in goods other than by normal wholesale or retail;

(e) banking, insurance, money lending, debt factoring, hire purchase or other financial activities;
(f) legal or accountancy services;
(g) farming, market gardening, forestry, woodlands or timber;
(h) operating or managing property-backed establishments such as hotels, guest houses, nursing homes, residential care homes or managing property used for any of these activities;
(i) receipt of licence fees or royalties except where the company or qualifying subsidiary has created the greater part by value of the intellectual property exploited.

10.3 Common problems

Some common problems and other issues are set out below.

10.3.1 The purpose or existence test

This only applies under the EIS and when there is a stand-alone company. Groups do not need to pass this test and may automatically have up to 20 per cent of activities which are not qualifying. However, with stand-alone EIS companies it is important that they exist wholly, other than to an insignificant extent, for the purpose of carrying on a qualifying business activity.

10.3.2 Use of funds test

This may create a limitation on the amount of EIS or VCT funds that may be raised. For example, if a placing is for a research and development company for say £8 million which is to be spent over five years of which only £2 million could be spent in the first two years, then this limits the amount of VCT and EIS funds that can be raised to £2 million and the EIS shares must be issued separately – *see* 10.3.3 below.

Funds may be held on deposit account until employed, but the depositing of funds does not of itself constitute employment of those funds. HM Revenue & Customs manuals indicate that funds may be held on current account and treated as employed to the extent that they may reasonably be said to be necessary or advisable for the purposes of meeting current business requirements. However, this is a grey area and details should be disclosed where possible to HM Revenue & Customs in any advance clearance application to safeguard the company's position.

10.3.3   Separate issues of shares

Where funds from a placing or offer are to be used partly for non-qualifying purposes (for example, employed after the two-year period or in a foreign subsidiary), it is necessary to protect the EIS shareholders where all funds *in the same issue* must be employed in the requisite period *and* wholly for a qualifying business activity for there to be separate issues of shares. Where this is necessary the issues *must be a day apart.*

10.3.4   Royalties and licence fees

HM Revenue & Customs have largely relaxed their interpretation of this requirement over recent years so as not to unduly prejudice software development companies in particular (*see* RI 120 of August 2001). Most software licence agreements will in fact qualify on the grounds that effectively they are not, for EIS or VCT purposes, a licence being granted but a product sold, which is often the case when software products are supplied, technically with a licence, but provided on CD-ROM as a product or package. The terms of the licence agreement should be reviewed and provisional approval sought.

Where it is clear that the income does relate to licence fees or royalties, regard must be had as to whether the greater part of the intellectual property has been derived from the group itself, in which case the income is fully qualifying. Where a subsidiary has created such intellectual property, such a subsidiary must have been part of the group at that time.

10.3.5   Gross assets test

The calculation of the relevant gross assets is often misunderstood. It is calculated by aggregating the gross assets of each group company after eliminating goodwill on consolidation, cost of investment and inter-company balances. It therefore:

(a) *excludes* goodwill on consolidation, and accordingly most service-based companies without much in the way of fixed assets will usually pass this test;

(b) *includes* purchased goodwill and any other assets included on the balance sheet of a company.

The test applies immediately before investment under the EIS or by a VCT and immediately afterwards. Accordingly, if there are other sources of investment it is possible to exceed the gross assets limitations by application of a careful ordering of the various funding sources. HM Revenue & Customs will usually agree that this is acceptable if different issues of shares are effected *a day apart*.

10.3.6 Qualifying subsidiaries

These must be more than 50 per cent owned (90 per cent directly owned if EIS or VCT funds are to be employed in them). This rule was changed with effect for new issues of shares on or after 17 March 2004. Previously a subsidiary had to be at least 75 per cent held, and therefore for older EIS or VCT invested companies it is still possible to disqualify existing EIS or VCT shareholders if a subsidiary is acquired or becomes held as to between 51 per cent and 74 per cent. This must be avoided at all costs as the relief is lost.

10.3.7 Holdings of less than 50 per cent

A holding of less than 50 per cent is, in the first instance, regarded as an investment activity unless it can be argued that it is held for part of the trade of the group. A simple example is if a company is required to hold shares in a buying group. Essentially it is necessary to argue that the holding allows the group to increase its revenues or reduce costs. Specific provisional clearance should be obtained. Care must be exercised when the other shareholders are connected with the EIS or VCT-invested company as this could create control by the company and persons connected with it.

10.3.8 Fifty per cent holdings/joint ventures

Joint ventures are regarded firstly as a potential investment and the points in 10.3.7 above must be addressed. However, there is an additional complication as a result of the case of *Steele* v *EVC International NV* CA [1996] 69 TC 88. Under Section 293(8)(a) and (b) and paragraphs 9(1)(a) and (b) Schedule 28B, ICTA 1988, unless it is a qualifying subsidiary (i.e., more than 50 per cent held) a company cannot be controlled by the EIS or VCT invested company or controlled by it together with another company connected with it and there must be no arrangements for such connection. Accordingly deadlock provisions may constitute such arrangements and it is essential that these are carefully reviewed to ensure that their outcome is not a foregone conclusion in relation to a general meeting. Again this should be specifically provisionally pre-cleared with HM Revenue & Customs to agree that the company is not so controlled whilst not a qualifying subsidiary.

10.3.9   Control

A company must not be controlled by another company or another company and a person connected with it. Again, care must be exercised in connection with corporate trustees of shareholders in this respect and it is often necessary to change from corporate trustees to individuals.

10.3.10   Residence and overseas activities

Residence of a company is itself of no relevance but the funds raised under the EIS must be employed in a business which is carried on wholly or mainly (more than 50 per cent) in the UK throughout the relevant period. The relevant period under the EIS is three years from issue or, if later, commencement of trade, and under the VCT legislation for the whole period a company is regarded as a qualifying holding. Accordingly, for example, a foreign company could raise funds and apply them to its UK subsidiary provided the subsidiary carries out a qualifying trade mainly in the UK and the foreign group meets the criteria for a trading group as set out above. Under the EIS all funds raised under the same issue would have to be employed for a qualifying purpose.

10.3.11   Separate bank accounts

To identify the employment of particular funds raised in a placing or offer it is not essential to hold them in separate bank accounts. The directors should simply state how the funds will be used. HM Revenue & Customs does not seek to examine the use strictly under Clayton's rule (*Devaynes* v *Noble* (*Clayton's* Case) [1816] Mer 572). Nevertheless, if the facts show that the funds have been employed differently and in a non-qualifying manner then this could cause disqualification and accordingly it is advisable to hold the funds in separate bank accounts. It is usually sensible to employ the VCT and EIS funds first to avoid the possibility that the funds may not be employed in the relevant period.

10.3.12 Acquisitions and hive-ups

10.3.12.1 Shares issued before 17 March 2004
Where VCT or EIS funds are to be used for the purpose of the acquisition of shares of another company this will be regarded as an investment activity unless, under Revenue Interpretation 124, it is followed by a hive-up of the trade to the acquiring company as soon as possible.

10.3.12.2 Shares issued on or after 17 March 2004
HM Revenue & Customs relaxed their requirement to hive up the business where target company shares were acquired for shares issued on or after 17 March 2004 and thus certain accounting and valuation issues and the need to assign contracts are avoided.

VCM 12070 should be referred to for further information. It should also be noted that VCT and EIS funds may only be employed in subsidiaries that are at least 90 per cent held directly by the issuing company and therefore it may be necessary to "flatten" the group structure prior to or as soon as possible after the EIS/VCT share issue.

10.3.13 Costs of share issue

Funds used to meet the expenses of issuing the shares are regarded as an expense for the group's trade.

10.3.14 Becoming quoted

A "qualifying company" must be unquoted throughout the relevant period. Under the EIS the relevant period is usually three years from issue of the new shares or, if later, commencement of trade. Under the VCT legislation the period is for as long as the shares are held by the VCT as a qualifying holding. If a company becomes quoted during this period all initial relief is lost and must be repaid, and deferral relief ends.

The shares of the company may subsequently be listed on a recognised Stock Exchange, provided that arrangements are not in existence at the time the shares are issued. If the company ceases to be an unquoted company at a time when its shares are comprised in the qualifying holdings of the VCT, this condition is treated as continuing to be met, in relation to shares or securities acquired before that time, for the following five years.

10.3.15 Sale of company's shares

If an EIS company is acquired or reverses into an AIM company, an EIS investor will lose his income tax relief and CGT exemption under the EIS unless this occurs after the relevant period which is three years from issue or later commencement of trade. For issues prior to 5 April 2000 the relevant period was five years.

For VCT invested companies the VCT regulations provide that, dependent upon certain circumstances, the VCT investment can remain qualifying for a period of between two and five years (*see* VCM 66000).

10.3.16 Issue of shares

There are many references in the EIS and VCT legislation to issue of shares. It should be remembered that issue is when the issue is complete, that is, writing up in the share register and not on allotment. Shares are mostly allotted conditional on admission to AIM. Where it is necessary to have separate issues to protect EIS or VCT investors, conditionality of funds raised from all sources must be considered. It should also be considered if it is necessary for there to be two admissions to trading on AIM, one following a day after the first.

10.3.17 Timetable and planning

It can be seen from the above that a number of issues need to be considered which could limit the amount of EIS or VCT funds to be raised, require restructuring of groups and create timing considerations as additional tax clearances under Section 135 of the Taxation of Chargeable Gains Act 1992 and Section 707 of the Income and Corporation Taxes Act 1988 may be required and which can take 30 days or more to receive. The order of events at completion and for separate allotment and issue of shares also needs careful consideration to preserve EIS reliefs.

10.3.18 Placing letters and application forms

It is worth considering whether the placing letter and or application form should identify the EIS shareholders so that these may be identified for later completion of form EIS 1 (*see* 10.5 below). Complex cases could require separate issues of shares, so identifying the proceeds from each source of funding is particularly important.

10.4 Location of trade

There is a Revenue Press Release dated 30 November 1998 which contains the following guidance. This is very widely drawn so that HM Revenue & Customs is effectively able to argue those factors which are the most appropriate in the specific circumstances. However, as this is a most important consideration the key paragraphs of the press release are reproduced below.

> "(a) The way in which the requirements that the trade should be carried on wholly or mainly in the United Kingdom are applied in any particular case will depend on the precise facts and circumstances. A company may carry on some of the activities of the trade outside the United Kingdom and yet satisfy the requirement, provided that the major part of the trade, that is over one half of the aggregate of the activities of the trade, is carried on within the United Kingdom.
> (b) In looking to see whether the requirement is satisfied, HM Revenue & Customs will take into account the totality of the

activities of the trade. Regard will be had, for example, to where the capital assets of the trade are held, where any purchasing, processing, manufacturing and selling is done, and where the employees customarily carry out their duties. No one factor is in itself likely to be decisive in any particular case. In particular, HM Revenue & Customs will not regard a company's activities as not being carried on in the United Kingdom simply because the goods or services which it manufactures or provides are exported or supplied to overseas customers, or its raw materials are purchased from abroad, or its raw materials or products are stored abroad."

10.5   Obtaining clearance

10.5.1   EIS and VCTs

10.5.1.1   *Provisional approval*
For investors to gain some assurance that an investment in shares in a company should qualify, it is possible to obtain provisional approval from HM Revenue & Customs prior to the allotment of shares, that the shares to be issued will be eligible for the EIS, will be a qualifying holding for VCTs and that the trade will be qualifying. Confirmation that provisional approval has been obtained can be included in the prospectus or relevant document provided to potential investors.

Provisional approval, which can only be obtained by the company, is based solely on the information provided to HM Revenue & Customs and applies only to the conditions that need to be satisfied by the company. It is important for the provisional approval to be valid, to make full disclosure and draw attention to all relevant matters.

The information that is expected to be provided to HM Revenue & Customs' Small Company Enterprise Centre ("SCEC") at Cardiff with the application for provisional approval includes:

(a)   a copy of the latest available accounts of the company and each of its subsidiaries;

(b) an up-to-date copy of the memorandum and articles of association of the company and each of its subsidiaries and details of
any proposed changes;

(c) a copy of the draft of any document to be issued to potential
investors (e.g., admission document);

(d) details of any subscription or similar agreement to be entered
into by the shareholders;

(e) details of all trading or other activities carried on, or to be carried
on, by the company and its subsidiaries; and

(f) the approximate amount to be raised and details of how this will
be used.

10.5.1.2   Timing of provisional approval

SCEC Cardiff allocate the provisional approval application to one of
four SCECs (Dundee, Middlesbrough, Maidstone and Cardiff itself).
For an existing company with a tax reference, the allotted SCEC may
call for the tax files from the local inspector. All this may take time
and it is worth checking that the relevant information has been
received. The application is usually acknowledged as received after
seven to 10 days with an indication that a reply should be given
within 15 days. The timing for the actual response varies depending
upon how busy the relevant SCEC is at the time. It is therefore
prudent to allow up to 30 days for the provisional approval to be
received, although often it is given in around two weeks.

10.5.1.3   Formal EIS approval and issue of EIS certificates

This process applies to both the company and the individual investor
and cannot be applied for until after the later of the date the eligible
shares are issued or four months after the company (or its trading
subsidiary) commences trading.

Form EIS 1 has to be completed by the company and submitted to
SCEC. This form provides SCEC with details about the
company/group, the share issue and other relevant information. If
the SCEC is satisfied that the relevant requirements of the legislation
have been met, formal approval is given by the issue of Form EIS 2
together with blank Form EIS 3. These need to be completed by the
company and sent to the qualifying investors to enable them to make
the relevant claims to their local Tax Inspector. It is important to agree
who is to complete Form EIS 1 and make a diary note as to when it

will be completed and submitted. Obviously submission of the form referring to the provisional approval already obtained should facilitate the approval.

10.5.1.4 *VCT formal approval*

There is no formal approval procedure for investments made by VCTs. However, VCTs do have to provide HM Revenue & Customs with annual returns detailing qualifying investments and are subject to ongoing reviews and declarations.

VCTs issue individual investors with certificates which confirm that eligible shares have been issued to the investor for genuine commercial reasons and are not loan linked. Qualifying investors can then make the relevant claims to relief.

10.5.1.5 *Ongoing HM Revenue & Customs review*

EIS/VCT qualifying companies and VCTs are subject to ongoing review by HM Revenue & Customs (in the case of EIS, for the relevant period).

10.6 Capital gains tax ("CGT")

10.6.1 CGT business asset taper relief

Taper relief was introduced in 1998 and applies to individual investors and trustees. It does not apply to corporate investors. Such individuals and trustees need not be UK resident but the relief relates to UK-chargeable gains in relation to the period the investment is held, and the scales of relief depend upon whether the investment is a "business" or "non-business" asset.

Shares in qualifying AIM companies are classed as "business" assets, which attract significantly higher rates of taper relief – these can reduce the effective rate of tax to 10 per cent for a higher-rate taxpayer after a holding period of two years.

Taper relief reduces the gains made on sales of shares or securities according to the length of the period of ownership. Unlike other reliefs (EIS for example), it does not matter if they are subscribed for in new issues or purchased in the market.

Table 10.1 *Taper relief for disposals on or after 6 April 2002*

No. of whole years in qualifying holding period	Percentage of gain chargeable	
	Business asset	Non-business asset
1	50	100
2	25	100
3	25	95
4	25	90
5	25	85
6	25	80
7	25	75
8	25	70
9	25	65
10	25	60

Notes
(a) Only periods of ownership after 6 April 1998 are included.
(b) The period of ownership is between the exact dates of acquisition and disposal.
(c) Only the last 10 years of ownership are taken into account.
(d) For non-business assets acquired before 17 March 1998 the taxpayer is entitled to a "bonus" year's relief.
(e) Capital losses are effectively restricted because they are set off against gains before taper relief is applied.
(f) An individual taxpayer must be within the charge to UK CGT whether or not resident or ordinarily resident in the UK.

For disposals on or after 6 April 2002, the rates of taper relief are as follows.

10.6.1.1 Criteria

There is no limit to the amount that can be invested by private investors, nor on the size of the company, but to qualify it must, while an investment is held:

(a) be unquoted – for this purpose AIM companies are regarded as unquoted;
(b) be a trading company or the holding company of a trading group (which includes its 51 per cent or more subsidiaries and investments in certain joint ventures);

(c) ensure that any non-trading activities are not substantial (broadly taken to mean 20 per cent).

It is generally of no relevance whether a company is resident in the UK or elsewhere, but investments in certain non-UK companies or collective investment schemes are subject to different rules.

There are a number of anti-avoidance provisions both as regards the activities of the company and the risk exposure of the investor which may be relevant, and professional advice should be taken.

Example
Shares in a qualifying AIM company are disposed of after two years for a gain of £2 million, thereby attracting taper relief of 75 per cent. Ignoring an individual's annual exemption, the CGT computation is as follows.

	£
Gain	2,000,000
Taper relief at 75%	(1,500,000)
Chargeable gain	500,000
Tax at 40%	200,000
Effective tax rate (200,000/2,000,000)	10%

10.6.1.2   Business assets
Business assets include:

(a) shares or securities in qualifying unquoted trading companies. For this purpose shares on AIM are considered to be unquoted and can therefore qualify for business taper relief;
(b) a trading company or the holding company of a trading group. Insubstantial non-trading activities may be undertaken. Broadly these should be no more than 20 per cent (a trading group comprises the company and its 51 per cent or more subsidiaries, plus certain joint venture investments);
(c) investments of at least 5 per cent or all holdings by employees and directors in shares or securities in a quoted trading company;
(d) shares held by directors and employees in any quoted or unquoted non-trading company also qualify as business assets

from 6 April 2000 if the individual holds not more than 10 per cent (including shares held by connected persons).

10.6.1.3 Non-business assets
Non-business assets include shares or securities in quoted companies (unless held by an employee) and non-qualifying unquoted companies.

10.6.1.4 Mixed assets
Mixed assets are those which were business assets for only part of the qualifying holding period. This may arise due to a change in legislation (as was the case at 6 April 2000 when all holdings in unquoted trading companies became eligible for business taper relief), or a change in the status of the company (e.g., ceasing to be a trading company, or becoming quoted by, for example, moving to the Official List), or the circumstances of the individual. For such assets, taper relief is calculated by first apportioning the gain between business and non-business periods. Each part of the gain attracts taper relief at the appropriate rate for the whole of the qualifying holding period. The non-business part is, if applicable, eligible for the bonus year.

10.6.1.5 Relationship with deferral reliefs
Where deferral relief is claimed on reinvestment under the EIS or into a VCT, taper relief on the deferred gain is frozen and that gain is not tapered further over the period of ownership of the EIS/VCT investment.

10.6.1.6 Serial investors
Where the asset giving rise to the gain was itself a qualifying EIS investment and was made on or after 6 April 1998 and the gain on disposal of that asset is reinvested into a second EIS investment, then the period of the taper relief is extended for the entire periods of ownership of the original and new shares (up to the maximum allowed) but ignoring any periods between the disposal of the original shares and the acquisition of the new shares where no asset is owned. This potential maximisation of taper relief encourages serial reinvestment into qualifying companies.

10.6.1.7 Example of a mixed asset
An asset is disposed of giving rise to a gain of £3 million. If the asset has been owned for three years since April 1999, during which time it

was a qualifying business asset for one year and a non-business asset for two years, the taper relief is computed as follows.

	Business asset £	Non-business asset £	Total £
Gain apportioned 1:2	1,000,000	2,000,000	3,000,000
Business taper (three years)	(750,000) (75%)		(750,000)
Non business taper (three years)		(100,000) (5%)	(100,000)
Chargeable gain	250,000	1,900,000	2,150,000

10.6.2 CGT gift relief

There is no general CGT relief for gifts (although transfers between husband and wife are on a no-gain no-loss basis). However, if shares or securities in an AIM trading company are transferred, other than at arm's length, the deemed capital gain arising can be held over; that is, the CGT liability is postponed until a subsequent arm's-length disposal by the transferee, who effectively inherits the transferor's base cost.

The relief must be claimed by both the transferor and transferee within five years and 10 months of the end of the relevant tax year.

10.6.2.1 *Criteria – individuals*
This relief is particularly useful for the transfer or gift of shares within families. The criteria for individuals are as follows:

(a)   the transferee must be resident or ordinarily resident in the UK in the tax year of the transfer and remain so for six years;
(b)   there are no specific requirements for the transferor;
(c)   there is no minimum or maximum holding required; and
(d)   it does not apply to a gift of shares to a company.

Note: The effect of a gift is that the period of ownership for taper relief purposes starts again (except for transfer between husband and wife) and there is no taper relief for the previous period of ownership.

Where the donee emigrates within the six-year period following the gift and fails to settle any tax arising on the gifted asset as a result of their emigration, the held-over gain may in certain circumstances be recoverable from the transferor.

10.6.2.2   Criteria – companies

For shares to be eligible for gift relief companies must be:

(a)   unquoted trading companies (including those on AIM) and holding companies of trading groups;

(b)   trading companies where the person making the gift holds at least 5 per cent of the voting rights.

Residence is not relevant.

10.6.3   Inheritance tax ("IHT")

10.6.3.1   Business property relief

Investments in qualifying AIM trading companies can attract 100 per cent relief from IHT provided that the investment is held for at least two years before a chargeable transfer for IHT purposes.

10.6.3.2   Who can benefit from IHT relief?

Estates and beneficiaries of UK-domiciled individuals who are likely to be assessed for IHT on a chargeable transfer, which include the following:

(a)   death of the shareholder;

(b)   death of the donor, if the shares were gifted within seven years of death; or

(c)   chargeable lifetime transfer (e.g., into a discretionary trust).

Individuals who are not regarded as domiciled in the UK enjoy certain benefits in respect of investments which are not regarded as situated in the UK for tax purposes. The rules are complex and different for CGT and IHT.

10.6.3.3   Which companies qualify?

IHT is more concerned with the individual's domicile and accordingly a company need not be UK resident. Most trades qualify, but a company's business must not be wholly or mainly that of:

(a)   dealing in securities, stocks and shares;

(b)   dealing in land or buildings; or

(c)   making or holding investments (unless that of a market maker or discount house).

Restrictions apply where the company owns excepted assets not used for the purposes of the trade.

10.7   Corporate Venturing Scheme

The Corporate Venturing Scheme ("CVS") is a tax incentive scheme which has been introduced to encourage companies ("investing companies") to invest in small higher-risk trading companies ("issuing companies") to form wider corporate venturing relationships.

The scheme has been described as the equivalent of the EIS for companies because of the similarities in the issuing companies that qualify and reliefs available to investing companies. The CVS entitles investing companies to the following tax reliefs.

(a)   Twenty per cent corporation tax relief on investment but:

   (i)   the investment must be in new ordinary shares in qualifying companies;

   (ii)   the investment must be held for at least three years;

   (iii) there is no limit on the amount that can be invested subject to:

   – the gross assets of the issuing company not exceeding £15 million before investment and £16 million immediately after, or

   – 30 per cent control by the investing company;

   (iv)   relief is limited to the tax liability of the investing company in the tax year of investment if this is less than 20 per cent of the investment.

(b)   Deferral of tax on CVS gains but:

   (i)   a gain arising on the disposal of shares invested under the CVS may be deferred if it or part of it is reinvested into another investment under the CVS;

(ii)   there is no limit to the amount that can be reinvested subject to the gross assets and control tests as above;

(iii)   reinvestment must be made in a different company to that in respect of which the gain arose;

(iv)   reinvestment must be made in the period from one year before to three years after the date when the original gain arose.

(c)   Relief against income for capital losses but:

(i)   the loss on disposal is calculated net of the initial corporation tax relief of 20 per cent;

(ii)   the loss is set against taxable income of the year in which the loss arises and, if unrelieved and a claim is made, against income of the previous 12 months;

(iii)   a claim to carry back the loss must be made within two years of the end of the period in which the loss arises.

10.7.1 Which companies can benefit?

There are various conditions that need to be met by the investing company. It must:

(a)   either exist wholly for the purpose of carrying on non-financial trade(s) or be the holding company of a group carrying on such activities;

(b)   (together with any connected persons) not control the issuing company or hold, directly or indirectly, or be entitled to acquire, more than 30 per cent of the:

(i)   ordinary share capital, or

(ii)   the voting rights, or

(iii)   the combined share capital and loan capital of the issuing company.

The Finance Act 2002 introduced new legislation which exempts corporate gains on the disposal of substantial shareholdings (10 per cent or more of the share capital) in trading companies provided certain conditions apply. While these rules potentially apply to all trading groups (i.e., not only qualifying AIM or other unquoted companies) they may be of specific relevance to companies investing under the CVS such that deferral relief for tax on gains may become less significant in the future.

10.7.2   Company qualifying criteria

The legislation is complex, but the key criteria that a company must meet are similar to those under the EIS and VCT, with an additional qualifying period of three years. A company must not be in partnership with another company or a party to a joint venture with another.

Note that it is possible for the issuing company to apply to HM Revenue & Customs for advance clearance.

10.7.3   The investing company

Similar considerations to those for the EIS apply. The investing company must be subject to corporation tax to benefit from the CVS reliefs.

10.7.4   Provisional approval

Potential issuing companies can apply to HM Revenue & Customs for an advance clearance notice prior to a share issue. The application should include the information noted above (at 10.2–10.5) for EIS/VCTs as well as other information to confirm the qualifying criteria summarised in that section of this Chapter are satisfied. The advance clearance notice will confirm whether, based on the information provided, HM Revenue & Customs is satisfied that the issuing company is qualifying, the necessary requirements are to be met for both the shares and the money raised and also that there will be no prearranged exit or tax avoidance.

Although similar to the provisional approval application in respect of the EIS and VCTs, this advance clearance notice is dealt with under specific legislation rather than on a non-statutory basis. HM Revenue & Customs has a time limit of 30 days in which to process the application and either issue the advance clearance notice or request additional information if it considers this necessary.

10.8   Loss relief

Should an investment in an unquoted trading company (which for this purpose includes an AIM company) fail or be disposed of at a loss, tax relief for the loss may be available. The relevant legislation is contained in Sections 574–576 ICTA 1988.

The amount of loss is enhanced under the EIS as described at 10.2 above.

10.8.1   Qualifying companies

To qualify, a company must:

(a)   be an unquoted trading company (including AIM) at the date of disposal;

(b)   have qualified for a continuous period of six years ending on disposal or entire period of ownership if less;

(c)   carry on a qualifying activity (essentially as under the EIS) wholly or mainly in the UK.

10.8.2   Qualifying investors

To qualify, investors must be:

(a)   individuals or trustees who are resident or ordinarily resident in the UK; and

(b)   the loss must arise as a result of a sale at arm's length, a liquidation or where the investor is able to claim that the investment has become of negligible value.

10.8.2.1   *Relief*

The loss may be relieved against capital gains in the year of disposal or a subsequent year. For losses under the EIS for new shares subscribed, the loss may instead be relieved against income of that year or the previous year. If there is any loss available after claiming relief against income, such loss is available for relief against capital gains either in the current or subsequent years.

A similar relief applies to investment companies, which are able to claim loss relief under similar circumstances to those described above for individuals.

Chapter 11

The Broker and the Trading Rules

John Wakefield
Director and Head of Corporate Finance
Rowan Dartington & Co Limited

11.1 Introduction

The AIM Company ("AIM Co.") has been successfully admitted to trading on AIM. An investor – whether a private individual or institutional fund manager – intending to buy or sell shares in AIM Co. is likely to be concerned with three main issues: price, payment and delivery. How do investors find out about AIM Co., in particular how shares are bought and sold, and the practicalities of dealing on AIM?

This Chapter examines the trading and regulatory environment in which shares in AIM Co. are traded and which regulate the trading activities of the market practitioners – the nominated adviser, the broker and the market maker.

11.2 The trading system

Information on AIM quoted shares is disseminated by the Stock Exchange Automated Quotations ("SEAQ") or the Stock Exchange Alternative Trading System Plus ("SEATS") trading systems which are operated by the London Stock Exchange plc ("the Exchange") and published via a public display system such as those operated by third-party service providers, including Reuters and ICV Datastream. SEAQ is used by Exchange member firms to publish the prices of listed securities in real time. A SEAQ security is a domestic equity market security for which a minimum of two market makers display two-way prices and for which there is a "normal market size" (i.e. the minimum quantity of securities in which the market makers are obliged to quote a firm two-way price).

SEATS Plus is an extension of the SEAQ system and is used to provide similar information on SEATS securities. A SEATS security is defined by the Rules of the London Stock Exchange ("the Exchange Rules") as "a security which is traded on SEATS Plus". SEATS Plus is used for publishing prices and information on securities in which there is only one or no market maker prepared to quote two-way prices. In practice, this means thinly traded, fully listed as well as AIM securities.

The principal difference between SEAQ and SEATS Plus is that SEAQ is a quote-driven trading service whereas SEATS Plus is a hybrid trading service, incorporating features of the SEAQ system and of the Stock Exchange Electronic Trading Service ("SETS"), which is an order-driven trading service used in connection with securities for which there is a multiplicity of market makers ensuring shares are available to be traded at the keenest prices.

SETS is a trading mechanism used for trading highly liquid shares comprised in the FTSE 100 and FTSE 250 indices and it enables member firms to execute bargains electronically by "accepting" the published orders to buy or sell securities in the size and at the price for which details are given on screen.

On SEATS Plus a member firm which is a market maker may quote a price at which it is willing to deal (a "firm exposure order"); and a non-market maker member firm may publish an order at which it will buy or sell stock. This is capable of becoming a bargain binding the parties simply by being accepted by another member firm (a "hit order"). Either way, the published price will be treated as firm and binding on the member firm. The hit order mechanism under the SEATS Plus system is sometimes referred to as the "Bulletin Board".

In practice, most trading in AIM stocks is undertaken through market makers in accordance with the quote-driven system in SEAQ except where there is only one market maker.

11.3   Information requirements

A public display system will usually give the following information on an AIM security to enable investors to make appropriate judgements on whether to buy or sell:

(a)   the date the information was last updated;
(b)   the Stock Exchange Daily Official List ("SEDOL") or International Securities Identification Number ("ISIN") code;
(c)   the industry sector;
(d)   the number of shares in issue;
(e)   the approximate free market capital ("FMC") as a percentage of shares in issue. FMC excludes shares owned by directors, connected persons (*see* Companies Act 1985 ("the Act"), Section 326), and shareholders owning 5 per cent or more;
(f)   the expected dates of announcement of preliminary and interim results;
(g)   the company's final or interim turnover, whichever is later;
(h)   the net interim and (if available) final net dividend figure;
(i)   the volume of shares traded in the last 12 months; and
(j)   the volume of shares traded to date during the current month.

This information is usually input by the company's corporate broker.

A typical SEAQ page on an AIM traded security, as published by ICV Datastream, is as follows.

The example shows that CODASciSys has four market makers – Teather and Greenwood ("TEAM") Robert W Baird ("BARD"), KBC Peel Hunt ("KBC") and Winterflood Securities ("WINS"). All are making a market in 1,000 shares (the normal market size). The "bid" price at which the market maker will buy is 390p (BARD and KBC) or 395p (TEAM and WINS) and the "offer" price at which the market maker will sell is 410p (BARD and KBC) and 415p (TEAM and WINS), giving a "spread" of 20p, which is equivalent to 5 per cent of the respective mid-market price and from which the market makers will derive their "turn" or profit on the trade. The best price at which a market maker will buy and the same or another market maker will sell, is called the "touch" and is indicated by a yellow strip in the centre of the screen. In this example, the touch is 395–410p.

Figure 11.1 SEAQ page for an AIM traded security

CODASCISYS PLC ORD 25P

Symbol	CSY.L	ISIN	GB0001520757	Local	CSY
Currency	GBX	Sector	SOFTWARE		
News		Country	UK London SE	Settlement	C
Segment	AIMI MQP	Mkt Sect	AIMT NMS 500	PL	3,000

Open	402.5	Close on	15 Aug 05		402.5	Close Bid/Ask		395–410
Trade		Volume		Cum. Vol		Current Price		NetChg
						402.5		+0
			Trade Hi			Curr Hi	402.5	+0
			Trade Lo			Curr Lo	402.5	+0
			YVol	24,350				

ROWAN DARTINGTON & CO LD				NBR		57328
2		TEAM WINS	395–410	BARD KBC		2

BARD	390	410	1x1	07:58	TEAM	395	415	1x1	07:53
KBC	390	410	1x1	08:00	WINS	395	415	1x1	07:30

As CODASciSys has four market makers, the Bulletin Board trading facility available in SEATS Plus is not in use.

The following example shows the SEATS Plus facility in use in relation to CityBlock Plc, published by ICV Datastream.

As CityBlock only has one market maker (WINS), the Bulletin Board mechanism is available to enable member firms to publish "hit orders" at which they will deal and which are capable of being accepted electronically by member firms. In the example, no orders are currently being displayed.

Figure 11.2   SEATS Plus system

CITYBLOCK PLC ORD 0.5P

Symbol	CLK.L	ISIN	GB0033272237 Local CLK	
Currency	GBX	Sector	REAL ESTATE DEV.	
News		Country	UK London SE	Settlement
Segment	AIM2 MQP	Mkt Sect	AIMS NMS 5,000	PL 30,000

Open 55	Close on 15 Aug 05	55		Close Bid / Ask	45–65
16 Aug 2005					
Trade 10:14	Volume		Cum. Vol	Current Price	NetChg
45	750		750	55	+0
		Trade Hi	45	Curr Hi 55	+0
		Trade Lo	45	Curr Lo 55	+0
		Yvol			

1		WINS	45–65 WINS	1

WINS 45 65 5x5 07:31	

Buy	Sell

In practice, the designation "AIM2" (as opposed to "AIM1") indicates that a company has only one market maker and its shares are traded on SEATS Plus, where the quote-driven price set by the market maker is supplemented by the Bulletin Board hit order facility.

The Exchange is developing a new trading platform which combines the characteristics of the Bulletin Board and market making. SETSmm enables shares to be traded over the SETS electronic trading system, already in use for FTSE 100 and FTSE 250 (fully listed) companies, and to be dealt in by market makers under the well-established quote-driven system. The Exchange is rolling out SETSmm to the FTSE Small Cap index and it is likely to be only a matter of time before it is further extended to the largest, more liquid AIM companies.

11.4   The market practitioners

One of the main benefits and distinguishing features of AIM is the relative simplicity of the procedures governing eligibility and admission to the market, in contrast to the more onerous requirements of the Official List. This is also generally true of the environment in which AIM quoted securities are traded following admission. By and large, it is up to the market practitioners to ensure a satisfactory trading environment in which the securities can be traded freely within the regulatory framework established by the Exchange.

Although the nominated adviser is responsible to the Exchange for confirming that AIM Co. is appropriate to be admitted to AIM and ensuring compliance by AIM Co. and its directors with the AIM Rules, the nominated adviser is not required to be a member firm of the Exchange. The trading rules are contained in the Exchange Rules (not the AIM Rules) which apply to member firms and compliance with them is the principal responsibility of the broker who is such a member firm. In addition, the (buying or selling) broker (who need not be the corporate broker) is responsible for trade reporting and settlement, generally within the CREST system (*see* 11.8 below).

The role of the nominated adviser is the subject of Chapter 3.

11.4.1   The role of the broker

It is a requirement of the AIM Rules that a company whose shares are quoted on AIM must retain a broker at all times (Rule 35). Although there are no specific duties imposed on the broker under the AIM Rules, the mandatory language of Rule 35 effectively makes the appointment of a broker a requirement of achieving admission, and the retention of a broker is a continuing requirement in order to maintain the dealing facility.

The Guidance Notes contained in Part Two of the AIM Rules explain that, by agreeing to act as broker to AIM Co., the firm (an Exchange member firm) is required to use its best endeavours to match bargains in AIM securities in which there is no registered market maker during the mandatory quote period (08:00–16:30 during business days). This means finding a willing buyer to "match" a willing seller (or vice versa), which is an order-driven process using the Bulletin Board facility, rather than responding to opportunities generated by the competing quotes published by market makers.

It should be noted that, where AIM securities are traded on such a matched bargain basis, the price may not be a true reflection of market value in the absence of firm continuous two-way prices.

Only two types of order for AIM securities can be input by member firms on SEATS Plus:

(a) "firm exposure order" – where the member firm is prepared to deal at firm bid/offer prices;
(b) "hit order price" – which may be accessed automatically by member firms.

In addition, the Exchange may declare prices to be "indicative only" in certain specified circumstances and to maintain an orderly market. A firm order will also be treated as indicative for a limited period of 30 minutes following an announcement by the company on the Regulatory News Service ("RNS") operated by the Exchange.

In practical terms, the broker supplies liquidity by identifying and matching buyers and sellers without taking a principal position, unlike the market maker.

11.4.2 The role of the market maker

A market maker is a member firm of the Exchange which wholesales lines of stock and takes a principal position by owning securities for resale. This enables shares to be freely traded and, as a result, the price fluctuates or "floats" according to the market makers' perception of supply and demand.

Unlike the broker, who is remunerated by charging clients (buying or selling) a commission based on the value of the transaction, the market maker earns its revenue by exploiting the difference between the price at which it is prepared to buy (the "bid" price) and the price at which it is prepared to sell (the "offer" price) the shares. The difference between the two prices is called the "market maker's turn".

It should be noted that only a member firm that is registered as a market maker in a security can quote prices on SEAQ or SEATS Plus.

A registered market maker in an AIM security is required to display firm, continuous, two-way prices in not less than the minimum quote size of 500 shares. If at least one market maker is displaying firm, continuous, two-way prices in a security, all market makers' prices in that security must also be firm, continuous, two-way prices.

Where a market maker quotes a price on the telephone that is higher than the one on display, it is obliged to deal at that price and size. Where a market maker quotes a price over the telephone to another market maker in a security for which it is registered, but is displaying an indicative price (i.e. outside the mandatory quote period or where the Exchange has declared the price of the security indicative in the interests of maintaining an orderly market), that quotation will be treated as firm and the market maker is obliged to deal at the quoted price.

There are three control mechanisms which the market maker can use to regulate its risk in holding AIM Co. securities and to encourage trading:

(a) to mark the price up or down in response to demand;
(b) to widen the bid/offer spread; and
(c) to increase or reduce the size at which it is prepared to buy or sell (but not below the minimum quote size of 500 shares).

As the market maker's income derives from its level of trading activity, its role in correctly judging market demand is crucial both as regards its own profitability and generally in providing liquidity, thereby determining the current market value of AIM Co.

The choice and selection of a market maker is generally dealt with by the broker. The broker will take care to ensure that the market maker is kept informed of developments in the AIM Company's trading activities and also that the market maker has an opportunity to participate in issues of new shares and significant transactions in existing shares conducted "on exchange".

At the time of writing there were over 80 member firms registered as market makers who may make markets in AIM securities. Analysis of the latest available Exchange statistics shows that 97 per cent of AIM companies have at least two market makers, and approximately 35 per cent have four or more market makers. As at July 2005, 1,268 companies were quoted on AIM with market capitalisations ranging from under £1 million to over £1 billion, with the majority of companies falling within the £10–25 million band. It would be a reasonable inference to conclude that there is a correlation between the size of the company and the number of market makers registered to deal in its stock.

Detailed rules govern how firm and indicative orders may be executed in a particular security, depending on whether the order is "all or nothing" or a "limit order", and when the order was first given in relation to competing orders in the same security. For example, before completing a transaction, a market maker must check to see whether there are any firm exposure orders at the same price or at a more competitive price. If there are, it must satisfy the displayed order unless it is an "all or nothing" order and the proposed transaction is for a lesser number of shares with the result that the price available for completing the balance of the order would be prejudiced.

11.5   Liquidity

The price of quoted securities is driven by supply and demand which, actual or perceived, is influenced by many factors, but none more so than the trading performance of the company in relation to market expectations.

A great deal has been written about liquidity, or the lack of it, in AIM securities, the implication generally being that trading in an AIM company is *per se* less liquid than for a fully listed security.

A great many influences affect liquidity, ranging from macroeconomic factors such as interest and exchange rates (which are outside the company's control) to sector and stock-specific factors. Certainly the size of company is an important factor, if only for the reason that larger companies tend to be more dependent on outside capital and therefore have a wider "free market capital" ("FMC") – the number of shares in the marketplace which are available for trading in response to market demand – so increasing opportunities for active trading to take place.

Liquidity – the ease with which AIM shares can be freely bought and sold – is determined by the availability of shares at prices and in sizes which will attract investors wishing to deal. In practice, liquidity is supplied by the market makers' preparedness to quote continuous bid/offer prices, and their willingness to do so will reflect their perception of demand for a share relative to supply in the marketplace. While investors wish to trade shares in order to earn an investment return, the availability of shares is a function of FMC. Great care must be taken by the broker to ensure that the supply of, and demand for, a share does not become out of kilter and result in distortion of prices in relation to the underlying financial characteristics, such as price/earnings and dividend yield, by which a share is ultimately valued.

The ideal scenario is a trading environment where company performance is in accordance with, or better than, market expectations, and the FMC is such that shares are readily available for trading in response to judicious pricing by competing market makers.

This creates a virtuous cycle in which there is sufficient trading activity for several market makers to provide competing quotes at the keenest prices; it is the environment in which FTSE 100 companies trade.

Generally speaking, it is usually the case that the smaller the company, the lower the FMC and the greater the reluctance of the market makers to make "keen" prices, which is reflected in a wide bid/offer spread. However, this is not seen as a function of AIM, but of the size of the company in terms of market capitalisation. As a company expands, so generally does its need to access outside capital, which in turn results in the issue of further shares, so increasing the FMC and trading opportunities.

11.6   The after-market

Liquidity is, of course, also influenced by the activity and effectiveness of the broker in publicising information amongst its client base and creating and managing a demand environment.

Brokers take on companies where they are convinced of the prospects for above-average growth, either because of the quality of the management or the products/services on offer, or market sentiment towards the sector. If brokers are unable to assess such factors, it is unlikely that they will wish to be associated with the stock or actively encourage their clients to make an investment.

So far as new issues are concerned, brokers look to price companies at a level which is designed to give investors a modest premium of around 10 per cent in initial dealings as an inducement for the risk of holding a "new" share. Ideally, the opening price should go to and remain at this level until there is an announcement justifying a price adjustment, usually the first set of figures after flotation. To maintain an active and orderly after-market, brokers will be in frequent contact with companies. Estimates for the current year and future performance are updated in the light of trading conditions. Certainly, brokers would look to publish research notes following the interim results or preliminary announcement of full-year results, as well as general and more comprehensive updates on companies following significant transactions or further capital-raising exercises (unless the company is in a quiet period as, for example, when it is in an "offer period" (as defined by the City Code) when publication of any forecasts could risk divulging price-sensitive information or which would lead to further unhelpful rumour and speculation. It has become the practice for the house broker not to publish research material at these times).

The relationship between the broker and the company will usually be defined by an agreement which would be expected to cover such routine matters as publication of research notes, organising institutional presentations and shareholder analysis, as well as one-off, specific projects.

11.7   Relations with investors

The broker is responsible for maintaining an active dialogue between AIM Co. and its investors who might otherwise only hear from the company on a twice-yearly basis (on publication of its interim results and preliminary announcement), as well as at the annual general meeting. The broker will also arrange institutional presentations at which the executive directors, usually the chief executive/managing director and finance director would have one-to-one meetings with the institutional shareholders.

This process is crucial if AIM Co. has ambitions to raise further equity capital, such as an acquisition to be financed by an entitlement issue (rights issue or open offer) or a vendor consideration placing. In such circumstances, the broker will normally seek the agreement of the institutional shareholder that it be made an insider prior to the commencement of discussions designed to establish the level of support for a particular transaction. In addition, the broker will seek to involve the market maker in "agency crosses" (riskless transactions in the existing shares between member firms) to allow the market maker to fulfil any limit order or to level a long or short position.

11.8   Reporting and settlement

Most transactions conducted on the Exchange are settled in CREST. CREST is the system used for settling Stock Exchange bargains in uncertificated (or dematerialised) form. It is operated by CRESTCo Limited (under the authority and supervision of the Bank of England) and has been operational since 15 July 1996.

CREST effectively matches all buying and selling transactions (by crediting and debiting stock and consideration electronically) to or from the buyer's or seller's account, which is operated by the 20 CREST member accounts.

The Exchange Rules require CREST trades to be reported by 21:00 on the day of the trade if the transaction was carried out during the trade reporting period (07:15–17:15 on days when the Exchange is open for business) or by 20:00 on the following day if it was conducted outside the trade reporting period.

Where a trade report is required, the trade must be submitted to the Exchange within three minutes of the execution of the transaction, except where it is effected outside the trade reporting period, in which case it must be reported to the Exchange between 07:15 and 08:00 during the next trade reporting period. The Exchange Rules prescribe the detailed information to be included in a trade report. All AIM transactions must be trade reported except "riskless principal transactions" (matched bargains, sometimes referred to as "agency crosses") or where the transaction is "put through" the Exchange, at the same price and size.

All risk trades are published three business days after the day of trading; riskless transactions are published as soon as the Exchange receives details.

Settlement, unless otherwise agreed, is three days after the transaction date (the date on which the transaction is effected). The minimum period for settlement on CREST is delivery on the same day, the maximum period is delivery within one year.

An alternative method of settlement is "residual settlement" (for very illiquid stocks). This involves the physical delivery of stock to the marketplace generally within three days of the transaction.

11.9   Market regulation

11.9.1   Insider dealing

11.9.1.1   Criminal liability
An individual must ensure that he does not deal in an AIM security (or any publicly quoted security) on the basis of "inside information".

This prohibition is, therefore, not confined to AIM and is part of the general criminal law contained in Part V of the Criminal Justice Act 1993 ("CJA 1993").

A detailed analysis of the nature and extent of the prohibition is outside the scope of this Guide. In summary, the legislation creates an offence of "insider dealing" and prohibits the use of inside information, which may be defined generally as confidential price-sensitive information for the purposes of dealing in the securities of a quoted company and thereby deriving an advantage. The legislation, which only applies to individuals, extends beyond any individuals in possession of inside information who themselves deal in the securities in question. It also applies to encouraging or procuring another person to deal, whether or not that person knows he is dealing on the basis of inside information.

The difficulty is to identify confidential price-sensitive information because much depends on the particular circumstances of each case.

Section 56, CJA 1993 defines "inside information" as information which:

(a) relates to a particular security or issuer, and not to securities or issuers generally;
(b) is specific or precise;
(c) has not been made public; and
(d) if it were made public would be likely to have a significant effect on the price.

According to Section 57, CJA 1993, a person has information as an insider if and only if:

(a) it is, and he knows it is, inside information; and
(b) he has the information and knows that he has it from an inside source, that is:

  (i)   from a director, employee or shareholder; or
  (ii)   from a person who has access to such information by virtue of his employment, office or profession; or
  (iii) directly or indirectly from any such person referred to in (i) and (ii).

The general principle is that any information which is not already in the public domain and can reasonably be construed as having a bearing on the value of quoted securities, and thereby requiring an announcement to be made, constitutes confidential price-sensitive information. In borderline cases, caution must be exercised and before dealings take place an announcement must be made to prevent a false market from arising.

Under Section 53, CJA 1993, it is a defence if the individual:

(a) does not expect the dealing to result in a profit because the information is price sensitive; or
(b) believes on reasonable grounds that the information has been disclosed sufficiently widely, so that no one taking part in the transaction could be prejudiced by not having the information; or
(c) still would have dealt even if he did not have the information.

11.9.1.2 *Special defences*
Paragraph 1 of Schedule 1 to the CJA 1993 provides a defence if an individual acted in good faith in the course of his business as, or his employment in the business of, a market maker.

For these purposes, a market maker is defined as a person who "holds himself out at all normal times in compliance with the rules of a regulated market or an approved organisation as willing to acquire or dispose of securities". An "approved organisation" is defined as "an international securities self-regulating organisation approved by the Treasury under any order made under Section 22 of the Financial Services and Markets Act 2000". It therefore appears that a market maker registered as such under the Exchange Rules is clearly covered by this definition and so is within the scope of the defence.

11.9.1.3 *Civil liability*
In addition, it is possible to institute civil proceedings for insider trading (effectively for breach of statutory duty) with a view to obtaining restitution or compensation, as appropriate, from the defendant.

There have been remarkably few successful prosecutions and even fewer successful civil actions. Successful action under either criminal or civil law would not necessarily render the offending transaction void, voidable or otherwise unenforceable.

11.9.1.4   Further developments

The Financial Services and Markets Act 2000 ("FSMA 2000") creates a new offence of "market abuse". The intention appears to be to catch behaviour which is damaging to markets but which does not constitute any of the existing offences. This is in part in response to technological developments such as the wider use of the internet and increased levels of execution-only trading by relatively unsophisticated individuals, which have seen instances of unscrupulous behaviour by some stock tipsters buying securities for their own account shortly before publishing "buy" recommendations.

The legislation applies to all persons (individuals and corporations) and has an extra-territorial dimension in that it applies to prevent market abuse on a "prescribed market" (including the Exchange), regardless of where the abuse takes place.

In addition, Section 397, FSMA 2000 creates an offence of making or engaging in misleading statements and practices in relation to the market in or price or value of listed or quoted shares.

The Market Abuse Directive ("MAD"), which came into force with effect from 1 July 2005, imposes additional requirements on fully listed companies to maintain lists of persons (including employees and advisers) who are privy to confidential price-sensitive information. The FSA's Guidance Manual confirms that MAD does not apply to AIM listed companies.

11.9.1.5   Exchange requirements

For directors and "applicable employees", Rule 21 imposes additional constraints on dealing. Directors and certain employees are considered to be generally in possession of more information regarding a company's affairs than is publicly available. An "applicable employee" is defined in Schedule 9 to the AIM Rules as someone who, together with his family, has an interest directly or indirectly in 0.5 per cent of a class of AIM securities, or is likely to be in possession of price-sensitive information in relation to the AIM Company because of his employment with the company or a member of the group. Such individuals are prohibited from dealing within two months prior to the publication of interim results or the preliminary announcement for the full year (or after the relevant period end has elapsed, until publication of the results, if earlier).

AIM Co. must ensure that its directors and applicable employees do not deal in its securities during a "close period". A close period is defined in the AIM Rules as any one of the following:

(a)   the two-month period preceding the publication of the company's annual results or, if shorter, the period from its financial year end to the time of publication;

(b)   the two-month period immediately preceding the notification of the company's half-year results (or, if shorter, the period from the relevant financial period end up to and including the time of notification),

where the company reports on a half yearly basis;

(c)   where the company reports on a quarterly basis, the period of one month immediately preceding the notification of its quarterly results or, if shorter, the period from the relevant financial period end to the time of notification;

(d)   any other period when the company is in possession of unpublished price-sensitive information; and

(e)   any time when it has become reasonably probable that such unpublished price-sensitive information will be required by the AIM Rules to be notified to the Company Announcements Office.

These particular obligations mirror the principal restrictions contained in the Model Code of Directors' Dealings in the Listing Rules of the UKLA. It is good practice to require dealings by a director or applicable employee to obtain the chairman's approval.

It is important to emphasise that these restrictions are in addition to the criminal law which applies in all cases.

In certain instances, discussions will need to take place between a company looking to raise further capital (e.g. to finance an acquisition or improve its balance sheet) and its major shareholders. In these circumstances, the position is regulated by general company law. Where an underwriting or capital raising is in prospect by way, for example, of a selective marketing or placing, discussions will need to be held with a company's major shareholders for the purposes of determining the level of support for the proposals and as part of the pricing mechanism. In practice, most firms of brokers seek to make their major institutional clients insiders, thereby depriving those shareholders of the opportunity of dealing until a full public announcement is made. When the outcome is known and the acquisition, for example, can proceed, an announcement will be required under Rule 10.

11.9.2 Dealing announcements

Announcement of certain transactions is required in accordance with general company law, as supplemented by the AIM Rules and the Substantial Acquisition of Shares Rules ("SARs") monitored by the Take-over Panel in accordance with the City Code on Takeovers and Mergers.

11.9.2.1 *Dealings by directors*
Any dealing by a director or person in whose shares the director is deemed to be interested (typically a spouse or minor children) and any "interest in shares" must be disclosed to the company within five business days and then, in accordance with Rule 17, by the company "without delay". The requirements of the Companies Act 1985 are deemed not to be satisfied if certain information is not contained in the announcement, including the price and date of dealing.

11.9.2.2 *Substantial interests*
A person (or persons acting in concert) who acquires an interest in shares amounting to 3 per cent or more of a company is required under the Companies Act 1985 to inform the company within two business days of the transaction. Thereafter, any subsequent dealing which takes the shareholder through one whole percentage point, upwards or downwards, or as a result of which the shareholder ceases to have a substantial interest (i.e. less than 3 per cent), must be reported to the company, which must then make an appropriate announcement by the next business day.

Under Section 209(8) of the Companies Act 1985 an interest in shares held by a market maker for the purposes of his business (only in so far as it is not used for the purpose of intervening in the management of the company) is disregarded. For these purposes a market maker is a person authorised under the law of a Member State to deal in securities and to deal on a relevant Stock Exchange, and who holds himself out at all normal times as willing to acquire and dispose of securities at prices specified by him and in so doing is subject to the rules of that Exchange.

Market makers are therefore exempt from the requirement to notify companies of their substantial interests, but they must nevertheless inform the Exchange. The Exchange publishes announcements via the RNS at its discretion.

11.9.2.3   *Substantial Acquisition Rules ("SARs")*
Where a person (or persons acting in concert) has acquired 15 per cent or more of the voting shares in a public company, he (they) must disclose to the Exchange, by 12 noon on the next business day following the transaction, any subsequent transaction which causes the shareholding to rise or fall by one whole percentage point. The Exchange then notifies the Takeover Panel which monitors compliance with the SARs.

Market makers are subject to the requirements of the SARs.

11.9.3   Integrated Monitoring and Surveillance System ("IMAS")

The Exchange operates an integrated surveillance system to monitor trading on the London markets. IMAS is a sophisticated computer system which highlights irregularities such as large fluctuations in share prices or volumes of trades.

The system works in real time during market hours. It monitors trades and quotes continuously and pinpoints deviations from the norm.

Generally speaking, an unexplained price movement of 10 per cent or more on one day will lead to an informal enquiry of the company's broker by the Exchange surveillance team.

11.10   Information about AIM companies

Where does an actual or prospective investor in AIM Co. look for information about the company?

There are six main sources of information:

(a)   SEAQ and SEATS Plus, which can be accessed by a member firm, usually a broker acting on behalf of the investor.

(b)   With effect from 2005, the Exchange introduced new indices of the leading AIM companies by market capitalisation. Details of the companies which constitute the top 50 and top 100 AIM companies, as well as the FTSE AIM All-Share, can be found on the Exchange's website (www.londonstockexchange.com).

(c)   Brokers' research notes – information prepared by corporate brokers for their private and institutional clients, include a résumé of the company and the nature of its business, an estimate of projected trading performance for the next two to three years, and a commentary on the latest published figures.

(d)   Financial press – the FT publishes the latest share prices of AIM quoted companies on a daily basis. It should be noted that the price/earnings ratios ("PERs") quoted by the FT are historic as opposed to the PERs in brokers' notes. Other publications, such as *Investors Chronicle* and *AIM and Ofex News*, follow the more actively traded and fashionable AIM stocks.

(e)   Published annual and interim report and accounts. The FT provides a free distribution service for many AIM companies.

(f)   In addition to the websites of particular companies, the website of the London Stock Exchange provides information on all AIM quoted securities: www.londonstockexchange.com.

11.11   Conclusion

The role of the broker is key to promoting the investment profile of the AIM Company to the market, as represented by existing investors and market makers and also to prospective investors.

The broker's functions broadly cover the following:

(a)   maintaining a two-way dialogue between the company and the market, including regular updates on actual and expected performance of the company and its peer group;
(b)   equity distribution to finance acquisitions or rights issues;
(c)   advising the company on the presentation of corporate information to the market and generally acting as a sounding board on the appropriateness and proposed financing of acquisitions.

The broker is therefore a key member of the company's team and supplements the work of the company's other advisers in ensuring that actual and prospective investors, including the market makers, are kept regularly informed of all material developments and the broker's views on expectations and trends.

In addition, the AIM Rules require the broker, in cases where there is only one registered market maker, to supplement the role of the market maker in using its best endeavours to match buyers and sellers of the company's shares.

Chapter 12

Overseas Companies and the Fast-track Route

Nick Williams
Partner

Andrew Whalley
Senior Solicitor
Hammonds

12.1   Introduction

As the economies of the world have become increasingly globalised, so too have its capital markets. Competition between markets for overseas members continues to be strong.

12.2   Why might an overseas company choose AIM?

12.2.1   AIM's objectives

AIM describes itself as "the international market for growing companies" and is keen to attract as many overseas (i.e. non-UK) companies to AIM as possible. It has succeeded in attracting a good number of overseas companies per year in recent years, and noticeably more since 2004 (*see* 12.3 below). In May 2003, admission to trading on AIM was made potentially easier for certain companies quoted on a number of overseas exchanges. These are exchanges which have been designated by AIM as fulfilling certain criteria described at 12.5.1 below and identified as "AIM Designated Markets". Companies which have been quoted on an AIM Designated Market for at least 18 months may take advantage of the "fast-track route", which is an expedited procedure previously only available to companies transferring to AIM from the Official List.

213

12.2.2 Less regulation

One of AIM's key attractions is the fact that it is less regulated and therefore more flexible than, for instance, the UK Listing Authority ("UKLA") Official List ("the Official List"). For example, AIM has less requirements for shareholder approval than the Official List in relation to transactions (*see* Chapter 8), no requirement for a three-year track record, no minimum market capitalisation requirement and no requirement for a minimum amount of shares to be publicly held.

12.2.3 Availability of capital

When many stock markets were in the grip of a severe bear market, AIM had continuing success in raising new funds. In 2001, 2002 and 2003, there were 177, 160 and 162 new admissions to AIM respectively. In 2004 there were 355 admissions to AIM, raising £2,775.9 million in aggregate, and 1,330 further issues by companies already admitted to AIM, raising £1,879.9 million in aggregate. The directors of an overseas company will want to be comfortable that it will be able to raise funds on AIM and that analysts reporting on the London markets will provide it with sufficient coverage.

12.2.4 Failure of competing markets

In September 2002, the Deutsche Börse announced it would close its high-growth technology offshoot, Neuer Markt. Nasdaq Europe closed down in November 2003. This meant there were fewer markets competing with AIM for smaller and medium-sized European companies seeking to raise money on a capital market. Since it opened in May 2005, Alternext, the Euronext market designed for small and midsized companies, had listed just 16 companies by the middle of November 2005, and its success has yet to be proven.

12.3 How successful has AIM been in attracting overseas companies?

As at 31 August 2005, of the 1,292 companies admitted to AIM, 175 of them (13.54 per cent) were overseas companies. For these purposes,

AIM counts any company incorporated outside the UK as an overseas company.

There was a steady number of admissions of overseas companies in 2001, 2002 and 2003 (15, 13 and 16 overseas companies respectively). However, in 2004 there were 61 overseas companies admitted to AIM. This higher figure needs to be read in the context of a greater overall number of admissions to AIM in 2004 (355 in 2004 versus 162 in 2003, 160 in 2002 and 177 in 2001), but even so, it is remarkable. The rate of admissions in the first eight months of 2005 was even higher: 356 admissions, of which 67 were attributable to overseas companies. The overseas nations with companies admitted to AIM were (as at 31 August 2005): Australia (34 companies), Canada (33 companies), Ireland (24 companies), US (20 companies), Bermuda (15 companies), Israel (12 companies), British Virgin Islands (11 companies), Cayman Islands (10 companies), Belize (four companies), Cyprus, Germany, Luxembourg and the Falkland Islands (two companies each) and Italy, Denmark, Norway and New Zealand (one company each).

A breakdown of the 175 overseas companies admitted to AIM as at 31 August 2005 by sector reveals that the sectors with the most overseas companies were mineral extractors and mines (37 companies), oil and gas – exploration and production (25 companies), "other" financial (17 companies), gold mining (15 companies), software (eight companies) and investment companies (five companies). No other sector contains more than four overseas companies. This reveals that mining-related companies represented approximately 29 per cent of all overseas AIM companies and oil and gas exploration and production companies represented approximately 14.3 per cent of all overseas AIM companies.

It should be borne in mind that these figures do not take account of overseas companies which have, for whatever reason, decided to establish a new UK plc holding company prior to admission to AIM.

12.4 Legal and regulatory considerations for overseas companies

12.4.1 Eligibility requirements under the AIM Rules

Overseas companies are subject to the eligibility requirements described in Chapter 2 in the same way as UK incorporated companies. In this regard, an overseas company will consider in particular the following requirements.

The shares in an AIM company must be freely transferable (Rule 32). There are two exceptions. The first is where "in any jurisdiction, statute or regulation places restrictions upon transferability". The second is where "the AIM company is seeking to limit the number of shareholders domiciled in a particular country to ensure that it does not become subject to statute or regulation".

There have been instances of UK holding companies being set up where the method of transferring shares in an overseas company is not compatible with AIM.

Rule 36 states that an AIM company must ensure that appropriate settlement arrangements are in place. In particular, all AIM securities (including where the relevant AIM company is incorporated outside the UK) must be eligible for electronic settlement save where London Stock Exchange plc ("the Exchange") otherwise agrees. Although CREST is the usual form of electronic settlement used by AIM companies, Rule 36 does not expressly limit "electronic settlement" to CREST or even to an electronic settlement system administered in the UK. The Guidance Notes to the Rules state that the Exchange will only grant a derogation from the requirement to be eligible for electronic settlement in the most exceptional circumstances, which could include the situation where the local law of an AIM company prohibits such settlement.

Advisers should therefore liaise as appropriate with AIM, CREST and/or the company's registrars at an early stage in the admission process about the above issues. Chapter 13 considers particular aspects of electronic settlement for overseas companies.

12.4.2 The Prospectus Rules

If an overseas applicant company is not taking advantage of the fast-track route (*see* 12.5 below), it will have to produce an admission document including the information required by Schedule 2 to the AIM Rules. Schedule 2 requires, amongst other things, that certain of the content requirements set out in Annexes I and III of the Prospectus Rules are included in the admission document and, if the admission document is issued in respect of an offer to the public for the purposes of the Prospectus Rules, the content requirements of the Prospectus Rules will apply in full (*see* Chapters 6 and 7 for more details). These requirements of the AIM Rules (and, where applicable, the Prospectus Rules) are applicable to overseas companies, for instance the principal rules on the financial information which must appear in the admission document, which are set out in Section 20 of Annex I to the Prospectus Rules. These provide, amongst other things, that the last three years' accounts should be included in the admission document (or such shorter period as the issuer has been in operation). Also, note that the whole of the admission document (including the accounts) must be in English (Rule 30).

12.4.3 Using a UK plc as a new holding company

An alternative to an overseas company seeking admission is to effect a reorganisation prior to admission so that a UK plc becomes the parent company, owning 100 per cent of the shares in the overseas company.

The decision to do this may be driven by tax considerations or because a UK plc is seen by institutional investors as a preferable form of entity in which to invest, or because the method of transferring shares in the overseas company is not compatible with Rule 32 (*see* 12.4.1 above).

Apart from the legal issues involved in such a reorganisation, there may be UK or overseas securities regulations and tax and stamp duty implications to consider.

12.4.4   Continuing obligations

An overseas AIM company is subject to the continuing obligations under the AIM Rules described in Chapter 8. It will need to address the following requirements in particular:

(a)   Rule 10 (Principles of disclosure): where an AIM company is required to make an announcement through a regulatory information service, the information must be announced no later than it is published elsewhere. This means that, for instance, if an AIM company is also quoted on another exchange, the announcements must be coordinated;

(b)   Rule 19 (Annual accounts): AIM companies must publish annual audited accounts prepared in accordance with UK GAAP, US GAAP or International Accounting Standards; and

(c)   Rule 30 (Language): all admission documents, any documents sent to holders of AIM securities and any information required by the AIM Rules must be in English. Where the original document or information is not in English, an English translation must be provided.

12.5   The fast-track route for certain companies quoted on AIM Designated Markets

12.5.1   Key features of the fast-track route

On 28 May 2003, the AIM Rules were amended to provide for an expedited admission procedure (the fast-track route) to be available to certain companies quoted on certain overseas exchanges, as well as companies transferring to AIM from the Official List.

Rule 3 provides that a company which has had its securities traded upon an AIM Designated Market (*see* below) for at least 18 months prior to applying to have those securities admitted to AIM, and which seeks to take advantage of that status in applying for admission (a "quoted applicant"), is not required to produce an admission document when it applies for admission (unless otherwise required in accordance with the Prospectus Rules).

The Exchange has established certain criteria for markets that the Exchange may designate as suitable for the fast-track route. These criteria are set out in the AIM fact sheet entitled *AIM Designated Markets* available at www.londonstockexchange.com. The Exchange may designate a market as an AIM Designated Market if the market:

(a) has a domestic equity market capitalisation, excluding investment trusts, of not less than €200 billion;

(b) has not less than 100 companies with securities traded upon it;

(c) has the securities of at least 15 companies that are non-domestic traded upon it;

(d) has an owner/operator which is a member of the World Federation of Exchanges;

(e) is properly operated according to the law in any relevant jurisdiction;

(f) has been proposed by either the Exchange or two nominated advisers where at least one such adviser has acted in a principal corporate finance advisory role for an initial public offering on that market;

(g) has admission rules which require companies with securities traded upon it to disclose equivalent information to that required by the Public Offers of Securities Regulations 1995. Note that the text of this paragraph has not changed, even though the POS Regulations have now been repealed; and

(h) has ongoing disclosure requirements no less exacting than those required by the AIM Rules.

The Exchange may waive a specific requirement under criteria (g) or (h) where it is satisfied that this can be met by other means.

Notwithstanding the above, the Exchange will only designate a market where it is satisfied that sufficient disclosure and transparency exists in such market for the proper information and protection of investors.

The Exchange publishes a list of AIM Designated Markets, which may be downloaded from its website at www.londonstock exchange.com. As at 31 August 2005 these were the main markets of:

219

(a)   Euronext;
(b)   Deutsche Börse;
(c)   Stockholmsbörsen;
(d)   Swiss Exchange;
(e)   Nasdaq;
(f)   Australian Stock Exchange;
(g)   Johannesburg Stock Exchange;
(h)   New York Stock Exchange;
(i)   Toronto Stock Exchange; and
(j)   UKLA Official List.

It will be noted that the Official List is an AIM Designated Market. The fast-track route makes an expedited procedure previously available only to companies transferring to AIM from the Official List available to companies on qualifying overseas exchanges, which either wish to transfer to AIM or to obtain an additional quotation on AIM. The Exchange may at any time remove a market from its list of AIM Designated Markets where that market no longer satisfies the relevant criteria.

12.5.2   Disclosure requirements

If a company is seeking to rely on the fast-track route, the requirements for it to make a pre-admission announcement (in accordance with Rule 2 of the AIM Rules – *see* Chapter 7 for further details) are modified in two ways. First, the information specified in Schedule 1 to the AIM Rules must be provided to the Exchange at least 20 (as opposed to 10) business days (any day upon which the Exchange is open for business) before the expected date of admission. In addition, a quoted applicant must provide at the same time the information specified in the supplement to Schedule 1 to the AIM Rules.

The supplement to Schedule 1 to the AIM Rules requires a quoted applicant to provide the Exchange with the following additional information:

(a)   the name of the AIM Designated Market upon which its securities have been traded;
(b)   the date from which its securities have been so traded;

(c)   confirmation that, following due and careful enquiry, it has adhered to any legal and regulatory requirements involved in having its securities traded upon such market;

(d)   an address or website address where any documents or announcements which it has made public over the last two years (in consequence of having its securities so traded) are available. The Guidance Notes provide that such documents or announcements must be made available for at least 14 days following admission;

(e)   details of its intended strategy following admission including, in the case of an investing company (any company which, in the opinion of the Exchange, has a primary business of investing its funds in the securities of other companies or the acquisition of a particular business), details of its investment strategy;

(f)   a description of any significant change in the financial or trading position of the applicant which has occurred since the end of the last financial period for which audited statements have been published. The Guidance Notes provide that this should include any significant change to indebtedness;

(g)   a statement that its directors have no reason to believe that the working capital available to it or its group will be insufficient for at least 12 months from the date of its admission;

(h)   details of any lock-in arrangements pursuant to Rule 7;

(i)   a brief description of the arrangements for settling transactions in its securities;

(j)   a website address detailing the rights attaching to its securities;

(k)   information equivalent to that required for an admission document which is not currently public. The Guidance Notes explain that information made public is that which is made available at an address in the UK or at a website address accessible to users in the UK;

(l)   a website address of a page containing its latest published annual report and accounts which must have a financial year end not more than nine months prior to admission. The accounts must be prepared according to UK or US GAAP or International Accounting Standards, although the Guidance Notes concede that a reconciliation to UK or US GAAP or International Accounting Standards may be presented where its accounts are not prepared under those standards. Where more than nine months have elapsed since the financial year end to which the latest published annual report and accounts relate, a website address of a page containing a set of fully audited interim results covering the period from financial year end to which the latest published annual report and accounts relate and ending no less than six months from that date; and

(m) the number of each class of securities held as treasury shares.

Other consequences of using the fast-track route are:

(a) under Rule 2, the Exchange may delay the expected date of admission for a quoted applicant by 20 business days (as opposed to 10 business days for other applicant companies) if in the Exchange's opinion the information contained in the pre-admission announcement has significantly changed prior to admission;

(b) under Rule 5, a quoted applicant is required to submit to the Exchange at least three business days before the expected date of admission an electronic version of its latest report and accounts (instead of an electronic version of an admission document, which is the requirement where the fast track is not being used). All applicants are required in addition to submit a completed application form and a nominated adviser's declaration and to pay the admission fee; and

(c) under Rule 39 and Schedule 7 to the AIM Rules, a nominated adviser to a quoted applicant is required to confirm that to the best of its knowledge and belief, having made due and careful enquiry, the requirements of Schedule 1 to the AIM Rules and its supplement (contents of the pre-admission announcement) have been complied with. This contrasts with the requirement for confirmation of compliance with all relevant AIM Rules for other applicant companies, which a nominated adviser must give under Schedule 6 to the AIM Rules.

For the avoidance of doubt, Rule 7 (lock-ins for new businesses) and Rule 9 (other conditions) specifically state that they apply to quoted applicants.

12.5.3 The role of the nominated adviser in the fast-track route

Although there is no requirement under the fast-track route for a quoted applicant to produce an admission document, the nominated adviser still has an obligation (which flows from Rule 39) to confirm that a quoted applicant is suitable for AIM. It will therefore have to determine the extent of the legal and financial due diligence which is to be carried out with respect to a particular quoted applicant. The Exchange will not give any guidance as to the level of due diligence it expects a nominated adviser to carry out in relation to a quoted applicant and considers it a matter for the nominated adviser in each case. Whether or not a nominated adviser would take any comfort from the fact that a quoted applicant is already quoted on an AIM Designated Market, and would therefore undertake a lesser amount of due diligence, will no doubt depend on the circumstances of each case, including the relevant nominated adviser's own policy, the standing of the quoted applicant's professional advisers and the particular market on which the quoted applicant is already quoted.

Similarly, the nominated adviser will need to consider the extent of the work to be undertaken in relation to reporting on the quoted applicant's sufficiency of working capital. The working capital statement which is given by the directors of a quoted applicant (as required by paragraph (g) of the supplement to Schedule 1 to the AIM Rules) is that the "directors have no reason to believe that the working capital available to it or its group will be insufficient for at least 12 months from the date of its admission". This is less robust than the statement required in an admission document, to the effect that in the opinion of the directors, "having made due and careful enquiry, the working capital available to the [applicant company] and its group will be sufficient for its present requirements, that is for at least twelve months from the date of admission of its securities".

12.5.4 The Prospectus Rules and the fast-track route

Companies intending to use the fast-track route and simultaneously raise funds in the UK will have to consider whether the fund-raising amounts to an "offer to the public" in the UK for the purposes of the Prospectus Rules. If it does, the fast-track route will be of marginal assistance, since the admission document will have to comply with the content requirements of the Prospectus Rules. The Guidance Notes to Rule 3 provide that where there is a requirement for a prospectus, because the quoted applicant is making an offer to the public in the UK or under the legal or regulatory requirements of another jurisdiction, the prospectus should be made available to the public under Schedule 1 to the AIM Rules as if it were an admission document.

However, certain types of offers of shares in the UK are not treated as offers to the public. Common examples in the context of an AIM fund-raising are offers to fewer than 100 persons and offers to persons who are "qualified investors" (for more on these exemptions *see* Chapter 6). In these cases, a prospectus complying with the content requirements of the Prospectus Rules is not required to be published, although any offer falling within the exemptions is still likely to involve the production of an information memorandum.

12.5.5   The impact of the fast-track route

Although the exemption from producing an admission document provided by Rule 3 is of potential assistance to a quoted applicant, if any fund-raising is undertaken in the UK at the time of the admission, a prospectus will still be required if a public offer of shares is made. In these circumstances, the prospectus will have to comply with the content requirements of the Prospectus Rules, and so eligibility for the fast-track route will not result in any significant advantage.

If one of the exemptions described at 12.5.4 above can be relied on, it is still likely that a fairly substantial information memorandum will be produced in relation to an offering of shares. In these circumstances, the removal of the need to comply with the content requirements for AIM admission documents set out in Schedule 2 to the AIM Rules will no doubt often lead to a degree of saved time and cost. However, the fast-track route will provide the most significant advantage over a standard AIM admission where a quoted applicant seeks admission to AIM by way of an introduction, that is, without undertaking a fund-raising, since no information memorandum will be necessary.

Regardless of the extent to which the fast track may speed up a quoted applicant's admission to AIM, issues such as the quoted applicant's future ability to raise funds on AIM and its expected profile on AIM are likely to be of paramount importance to its decision whether to seek admission.

Chapter 13

Settlement Arrangements – CREST

Jane Tuckley
Partner
Travers Smith

13.1   Introduction

The AIM Rules require that every AIM company must have appropriate settlement arrangements in place. Unless the Exchange otherwise agrees, this means that the securities traded on AIM must be admitted to one of the electronic settlement systems. While CREST is not the only such system, it is the one most commonly used by the AIM market.

The Exchange will grant a derogation from this rule in only the most exceptional of circumstances – thus, some years ago, when an AIM facility first became very popular among overseas companies, a mechanism had to be found for overseas securities (not normally eligible for admission to CREST) to become transferable by means of the CREST system.

13.2   What is CREST?

CREST is an electronic system for the holding and transfer of securities in electronic form. Its arrangements also facilitate:

(a)   the making of payment simultaneous with transfer; and
(b)   the effecting of various corporate action-related operations in relation to securities held within its system (proxies can be appointed by means of CREST; takeovers accepted; rights taken up and so on).

The CREST system is operated by CRESTCo Limited, a member of the Euroclear group. However, it is a system separate and distinct from the Euroclear system.

Unless an AIM company were to decide that all its shares were to be capable of being held *solely* in CREST (a very unusual step), the CREST system enables holders to decide whether they want to become members of the CREST system and hold their securities within the system, or whether they would prefer to continue to hold them in paper form. Securities held in the system are termed "uncertificated"; securities in paper form are "certificated". The system facilitates the transfer of securities from certificated to uncertificated form and vice versa. These facilities are known as the paper interface.

13.3   The CREST legal framework

13.3.1   General

Until the CREST system became operational in 1996, English company law provided that shares were to be evidenced by means of a share certificate and transferred by means of a stock transfer form. Legal changes were therefore required to enable title to be transferred by means of an electronic system; these came in the form of the Uncertificated Securities Regulations 1995. While the regulations, often referred to as the "USRs", make no mention of CRESTCo, they provide a framework which generally fits the manner in which the CREST system operates. CRESTCo has been approved as an operator for the purposes of the USRs. The USRs have been re-enacted and amended a number of times since the original 1995 version.

The USRs apply to both shares and other securities or interests in securities, for example debenture and loan stocks, bonds, warrants, nil-paid and fully-paid rights and depository interests (depository receipts). The USRs in some senses are little more than a piece of framework legislation. They amended the key legal obstructions to the operation of an electronic settlement system in the UK and address certain regulatory and other issues. It was always intended, however, that any system operating under the USRs would be complemented by a detailed contractual structure. In relation to AIM companies, the key relevant elements of the contractual structure are:

(a)   the Security Application Form (*see* 13.4.2 below);
(b)   the CREST Manual; and
(c)   the CREST Rules.

13.3.2   Non-UK securities

The USRs only govern the holding and transfer in CREST of securities constituted under the laws of England and Wales, Scotland or Northern Ireland. Securities constituted under the laws of the Republic of Ireland, Jersey or the Isle of Man can also be held and transferred in CREST under similar regulations passed in each of those jurisdictions. Guernsey-constituted shares are also eligible for CREST provided particular CREST rules are complied with. These securities are together referred to as "domestic securities".

The securities of no other jurisdiction can be admitted *directly* to the CREST system. These securities ("overseas securities") are settled by the CREST system using an indirect mechanism (*see* 13.6 below).

13.4   Admitting domestic securities to CREST

13.4.1   Are the securities eligible for CREST?

In relation to any transaction involving the issue of securities by an AIM company, early consideration should be given to whether the securities are eligible for CREST. Eligibility is determined by a combination of jurisdictional issues (see above), the USRs, the terms of issue of the securities and the CREST Rules. In particular, in the case of shares:

(a)   the company's articles of association must be consistent with the USRs and the holding and transfer of the shares in uncertificated form or an overriding directors' resolution must have been passed in accordance with regulation 16 of the USRs and remain in effect; and

(b)   the conditions set out in the CREST Rules must be met (most notably Rule 7). The rules contain provisions which, for example, relate to the fungibility of the shares within the class (so, for example, partly paid shares cannot be admitted to CREST because they are required by law to be individually numbered and are therefore not fungible), the free transferability of the shares and their unconditional issuance.

Additional rules apply in respect of Guernsey shares and depositary interests (Rules 8 and 9 respectively) and to other securities which are not shares.

It is not necessary for securities to be listed or subject to any trading facility in order for them to be eligible for CREST. Theoretically, therefore, the shares of any private company might be eligible for CREST, although there is little demand for such a facility in relation to these shares. Where, however, the allotment or issue of a security is *conditional* upon, say, admission to trading on AIM, the security must not be admitted to the CREST system until that condition has been satisfied (*see* 13.4.2 below).

13.4.2   The admission mechanics

Admission is made by means of a Security Application Form. This is available from the CRESTCo website (www.crestco.co.uk), but the company's registrar is also likely to have a ready supply. The company's registrar will assist the company with the completion of the form – CRESTCo has published guidance notes for the completion of the form, which form part of its Application Procedures. The registrar will submit the form to CRESTCo on the company's behalf. However, the form must be signed by the company itself. CRESTCo guidelines require the submission of the form no later than two business days before the security is to be enabled in CREST. When the timetable permits (as might be usual in the case of an initial public offering ("IPO")), the registrar will usually try to submit the form to CRESTCo approximately 10 business days in advance of the date on which the shares are to become enabled within CREST. Arrangements can often be made to expedite the processing of the form by CRESTCo, including when necessary the faxing of the completed form to CRESTCo and its processing on the same day, but such arrangements are at CRESTCo's discretion and allow no leeway for identification and correction of errors. If the form is faxed to CRESTCo, the hard copy must follow promptly.

It is not necessary for all of the criteria for the security to be eligible for CREST to be satisfied at the time the form is submitted. It is possible to indicate on the form that some conditions for admission to the CREST system remain to be satisfied – a special box is included for this purpose. If the form indicates that the conditions are not satisfied, CRESTCo may take some preparatory steps in relation to setting the security up in its system, but will not enable the security in the system until it receives confirmation that all conditions for admission of the security have been satisfied. This confirmation, commonly referred to as an enablement letter, must be given in writing by either the issuer or its agent. It is common that the last condition to be satisfied will be the admission of the securities to trading on AIM, since the allotment and issue of at least some of the securities to be admitted to CREST will normally be expressed to be conditional upon this event.

The preparatory steps taken by CRESTCo to set a security up in its system prior to receipt of an enablement letter will permit steps to be taken to ensure prompt settlement of securities once enablement occurs. These may include the entering into the system of settlement instructions (for example, for the delivery of securities to the placees) or the provisional crediting of CREST accounts by the registrar in preparation for the enablement of the security. If provisional credits are made, the credits will be of no legal effect until the security is enabled in the system.

The Security Application Form requires the company to state the date on which the company would like the security to be enabled in CREST. If no outstanding conditions exist at the time the form is submitted, CRESTCo will adhere to this date (unless it receives notification to the contrary before the security has been enabled). If there are outstanding conditions CRESTCo will only adhere to this date if it has received an enablement letter.

An approximate CREST application timetable in relation to a typical AIM IPO will therefore run as follows:

D minus 14 days: Security Application Form completed and sent to CREST. (Form indicates that some conditions remain outstanding. Form sets the security start date at D.)
D minus three days: Settlement instructions entered into the system and/or provisional crediting of the relevant CREST accounts by the registrar.

D: Securities admitted to trading on AIM.
Enablement letter faxed to CRESTCo.
CRESTCo enables the security and settlement commences.

13.4.3   Admitting further securities to CREST

The permission for securities to be admitted to CREST does not apply to a fixed number of securities, it applies to the whole class and to any further securities of that class which may be issued from time to time provided that they are absolutely identical. Therefore, no further application needs to be made in relation to a new issue where this is the case. However, it is common to see further issues of shares of an existing class made on terms that the new shares will not qualify for a dividend in relation to a period just ended or about to end. In this case, the new shares would not be absolutely identical and a new application would need to be made for the further shares. Arrangements would be made with CREST for the two lines to be merged once the old shares are marked ex dividend.

13.5   The relationship between the AIM company and CREST

The relationship between CRESTCo and the company operates on a number of different levels.

13.5.1   The technical interface

Almost all companies (save for a handful with very large registers) appoint agents (registrars and receiving agents) to send and receive messages through CREST on their behalf. Therefore, there is normally no need for the company itself to have the technical capabilities required for a link to the CREST computer system.

13.5.2   The legal relationship

Notwithstanding that a company does not communicate electronically with the CREST system, each company whose securities are admitted to CREST has a contractual relationship with CRESTCo. This contract is entered into on the terms of the Security Application

Form, which incorporates the CREST rules and manual as from time to time in force. Changes to the rules and manual are not notified directly to issuers – they are sent to their registrars.

CRESTCo's liability to a company is subject to the limitations and exclusions set out in the CREST Manual.

13.5.3 Registers of securities – England and Wales, Scotland and Northern Ireland

The USRs governing UK securities make provision for a system known as electronic transfer of title, or "ETT".[1] In essence this means that certain records maintained within the CREST system are the prima facie evidence (or, in relation to Scottish securities, sufficient evidence) that the persons named are the holders of the number of securities stated in the record. Therefore, in relation to securities held in uncertificated form, the CREST computer records themselves constitute the relevant register of holders. The principal effect of this is that transfer of title occurs in relation to UK securities simultaneously with settlement of a transaction within the CREST system.

Where the securities are shares, the company is still required to keep a composite register of members, containing the details (which it, not CREST, holds) of the holders of shares in certificated form and copy details (obtained from CREST) of the holders of shares in uncertificated form. To the extent that the details of uncertificated holders shown on the company's (composite) register of members and those shown on CREST's register differ, the CREST register prevails.

CREST has made complex rules identifying which of its system records form part of the register of securities (*see* CREST Rule 14).

As each transaction settles in CREST, the relevant issuer (through its registrar) receives details of the transfer which has been effected. This enables the registrar to maintain a running record of the holders (in effect, a duplicate of the register maintained in CREST). It is this

---

[1] ETT was introduced in 2001. Prior to that time, issuers continued to maintain the register of members/holders and the CREST records were distinct from the register, the latter being updated to reflect each transfer recorded in CREST a short time later.

record which the issuer uses for day-to-day purposes, for example in processing corporate actions. The USRs provide that, as long as a company has regularly reconciled its record with the register in CREST, a company will not be liable if it relies on its record for processing purposes and that record subsequently proves to be incorrect.

13.5.4 Registers of securities – Ireland, Jersey, Guernsey and the Isle of Man

An equivalent of the ETT regime has not yet been adopted for the other (i.e. non-UK) domestic securities and therefore CREST does not maintain the register of holders of legal title to these securities. Accordingly, in these jurisdictions, legal title does not pass at the point of settlement in CREST: at the point of settlement an equitable interest (or its equivalent in the relevant jurisdiction) is acquired by the transferee. Simultaneously, the relevant registrar is notified electronically (through CREST) of the transaction, and legal title transfers when the registrar updates the register of holders (normally within two hours of CREST settlement).

13.6 Overseas securities – depository interests

13.6.1 General

The CREST legal framework permits only those securities constituted under the laws of one of the domestic jurisdictions to be admitted to the CREST system. The mechanism for permitting CREST settlement of overseas securities therefore involves creating a domestic security which represents the underlying overseas security but is separate and distinct from it. A number of slightly different structures can be used, although all tend to involve the creation of a type of depository interest, similar to the American depository receipts and global depository receipts with which the markets are familiar, under which a depository holds the relevant underlying overseas securities on trust for the holders from time to time and issues to the holders (i.e. the beneficiaries under the trust) depository interests which represent the entitlement to the overseas security. Typically, one unit of a depository interest represents one share of the overseas security held. The depository may either hold the overseas securities in its own name or appoint a nominee to hold them on its behalf. The structure is created by a deed poll or similar instrument.

The depository interests are typically constituted under the laws of one of the UK jurisdictions. They are therefore governed by the USRs (and any relevant CREST requirements) and will behave in the CREST system much as any other UK security, with a register maintained by CREST.

In addition to complying with the rules generally applicable to securities admitted to CREST, depository interests are required to comply with the additional rules contained in Chapter 9 of the CREST Rules.

While there is no prescribed depository interest mechanism, a number of structures are commonly seen. These are described below and a comparative table of their key features is included at 13.6.6.

13.6.2   CREST Depository Interests ("CDIs")

CRESTCo operates an international service which relies on a series of automated links which it has established with its counterparts in other jurisdictions. The service is based on a depository interest mechanism – a CRESTCo subsidiary holds (directly or indirectly) the overseas securities on trust for the relevant CREST members who are issued with CDIs representing their overseas securities.

The CDIs are not themselves admitted to trading on AIM. The overseas securities will be admitted to trading in the normal way and will be allocated an international stock identification number (known as an "ISIN" – the unique identification number by which securities are identified in trading, settlement and other systems). The CDIs are regarded as a mere settlement mechanism – a trade in the underlying overseas security will be settled by means of a transfer of CDIs which represent the securities traded. For this reason, the CDIs are identified within the CREST system by the same ISIN as the underlying overseas security.

The CDIs are generally only capable of existing in uncertificated form. There is therefore no effective paper interface in relation to these securities, but otherwise they behave in CREST in broadly the same way as other domestic securities admitted to the system.

The international service, as an established structure, is convenient and does not involve the overseas issuer in additional cost in the establishment or ongoing operation of its own depository interest structure (the costs are borne by the CREST members holding the CDIs and not the issuers). It does not, however, have universal coverage and not all links operate on a with-payment basis (some of the links facilitate the transfer of the securities but not payment for them, with the result that separate bilateral payment arrangements need to be made between the parties to the transaction). The CREST international service is described in detail in the CREST International Manual (*see* the CREST website at www.crestco.co.uk) and includes facilities for the processing of corporate actions. While some specific additional arrangements can be made with CRESTCo in individual cases, the CREST international service inevitably does not have the flexibility of some of the bespoke arrangements described below.

Companies wishing to establish a CREST settlement facility for their overseas securities should contact CREST at an early stage in order to identify whether the security is already settled by means of the international service (this is quite often the case where the security has an overseas listing). If it is not, the company should check whether it would be eligible for the service and, if so, the service to which it would be admitted. The arrangements for introducing new securities to the service can also, of necessity, vary considerably depending on the local requirements in the relevant overseas jurisdiction. Therefore, this should also be raised with CRESTCo at an early stage.

It is important to identify whether a security has already been admitted to the international service even if a company proposes to establish its own bespoke depository arrangements. The CREST system has no means of distinguishing between two different securities (a CDI and a bespoke depository interest) which bear the same ISIN within its system and, for this reason, will only admit one security per ISIN.

13.6.3 Bespoke Depository Interests ("DIs")

The bespoke depository interest structure emerged initially to permit a form of CREST settlement for those securities which are not eligible for the CREST international service, although some companies whose securities would be eligible have since established a bespoke service.

These DI structures tend to be offered by some of the larger registrar groups. They involve a member of the registrar's group acting as depository and (either itself or through a nominee or custodian on its behalf) holding the underlying overseas securities on behalf of the holders; and, as with the CREST structure, issuing DIs (typically constituted under English law) representing the underlying securities in uncertificated form in CREST to those holders. Since the number of overseas securities held within the DI structure tends not to be static (it is a requirement that there is a ready facility for the crediting and withdrawal of the underlying securities to and from this structure), the registrar may also either itself hold the register of overseas securities or have arrangements with an entity which does.

At the time these DI structures were developed there was some concern that the London Stock Exchange ("LSE"), in its capacity as the UK's national numbering agency, would not permit the DIs to share the same ISIN as the underlying security, or that the Financial Services Authority ("FSA"), as the UK's listing authority, may require the DIs to be listed instead of relying on the listing of the underlying overseas security. Confirmation was obtained from the LSE and the FSA respectively that the same ISIN could be used and that no separate listing would be required provided that the DIs meet the following criteria:

(a)　they are created as legal instruments in their own right;

(b)　they are created under and subject to UK law;

(c)　they are subject to the USRs;

(d)　they use the same ISIN code as the underlying security to which they relate and, accordingly, they are not separately traded or priced from those underlying securities;

(e)　they will be available for use by the underlying security's holder at its sole discretion;

(f)　they are freely convertible into the underlying listed security (subject only to fair and reasonable costs);

(g)　they benefit from all the rights attaching to the underlying security, including voting rights, dividends and participation in corporate actions;

(h)　they are settled electronically through a "relevant system" for the purposes of the USRs (the CREST system is currently the only such system);

(i)   they are created and used in respect of a UK listed security issued by a non-UK incorporated issuer;

(j)   they are structured and established such that the promotion of the DIs is not subject to the restrictions on financial promotions under Section 21 of the Financial Services and Markets Act 2000; and

(k)   that the use of the DIs to effect electronic settlement will not contravene the law of the jurisdiction governing the underlying security.

The same criteria are applied in relation to DIs representing AIM traded securities.

Accordingly, like the CDIs, the DIs have no separate trading facility on AIM and no separate ISIN. They are merely regarded as a settlement mechanic – a trade in the underlying overseas security can be settled by the delivery of DIs through CREST. As if to emphasise this, requirement (f) necessitates an interchange between the uncertificated DIs and the certificated underlying security (the DIs themselves not being permitted to exist in certificated form outside CREST). The normal CREST paper interface messaging and forms are used to achieve the conversion, although additional support is required either from the constitutional documents of the underlying issuer or appropriate board or other resolutions (depending on the requirements of local law). The provisions must achieve the following key objectives:

(a)   That on receipt of a dematerialisation request form (which ordinarily simply requests the conversion of a security from certificated form to uncertificated form in the name of the same holder):

   (i)   the company may treat this as a request to transfer the securities to the depository's nominee to be held for the account of the holder; and

   (ii)   the depository may treat it as a request to issue DIs to the CREST account of the holder.

(b)   That on receipt of a CREST transfer form (which ordinarily simply requests the conversion of a security from certificated form to uncertificated form in the name of a new holder):

236

(i)   The company may treat this as a request to transfer the securities to the depository's nominee to be held for the account of the new holder; and

(ii)   the depository may treat it as a request to issue DIs to the CREST account of the new holder.

(c)   That on receipt of a stock withdrawal message in CREST (which ordinarily simply requests the conversion of a security from uncertificated to certificated form either in the name of the same holder or a new holder, as specified in the message):

(i)   the depository may treat this as a request to collapse the affected DIs; and

(ii)   the company may treat it as a request to transfer the underlying securities from the depository's nominee to the person specified in the message.

The DIs have the advantage that they can be adapted to the individual company's circumstances and requirements (within the limitations of the criteria prescribed by the FSA and LSE – *see* above), although the costs of the service are borne by the company.

To establish a DI structure the following documents and resolution must be put in place:

(a)   a Depository Agreement – entered into by the depository and the overseas company, this is a framework agreement which sets out the terms on which the depository agrees to establish the DIs for the overseas company;

(b)   a Deed Poll – executed solely by the depository, this key document constitutes the DIs and contains the declaration of trust which sets out the terms on which the depository holds the overseas company's securities on trust as DIs for CREST member holders; and

(c)   a board resolution of the overseas company – the Deed Poll contains the necessary provisions to establish the mechanics of the paper interface (as described above) and the overseas company's constitution must permit these arrangements. Accordingly, the overseas company normally passes a board resolution (or, depending on the requirements of local law, other arrangements for the amendment of its constitution) confirming that the paper interface arrangements are valid under its constitution.

13.6.4   Global Depository Interests ("GDIs")

While based on the same basic depository interest concept, GDIs differ from CDIs and DIs in a number of key respects:

(a)   they are admitted to trading on AIM as a security in their own right, with their own ISIN (distinct from any ISIN allocated to the underlying security);

(b)   as such, for the purposes of the Prospectus Regulations and the AIM rules, it is the depository itself which is the issuer of the security to be traded and accordingly some information needs to be included in relation to it (at the time of writing, no GDIs had been admitted to trading on AIM under the new Prospectus Regulations and accordingly it is difficult to gauge the level of information which would be regarded as sufficient in relation to the depository, but under the predecessor regulations limited information was required) and/or appropriate derogations obtained;

(c)   if a certificated option is available, it is the GDI itself which will be available in certificated form – the GDI is not simply a settlement mechanism and can (if its terms provide) have an existence outside CREST.

Very few GDI structures have been put in place in relation to AIM trading facilities – the predominant structures are those relating to DIs and CDIs.

13.6.5   Admitting DIs and GDIs to CREST

Once the DI structure (as described at 13.6.3 above) is in final form, the depository must apply to CREST for admission of the DI. It is the depository, and not the underlying overseas company, which has the legal relationship with CRESTCo in relation to the DIs. Application to CRESTCo involves the submission of the following documents:

(a)   a Legal Opinion[2] – assuming that the Deed Poll is governed by English law, this must be provided by a firm of English solicitors

---

[2] At the time of writing, CRESTCo was reviewing the necessity for the legal opinion in relation to certain jurisdictions. Current requirements should be checked with CRESTCo on a case-by-case basis.

acting for the depository in the standard CREST form which confirms key legal criteria, under English law, in relation to the DI structure and the depository, and, under the relevant foreign law, in relation to the issuer. Accordingly, in order to be able to give the opinion, the solicitors acting for the depository will need to procure a foreign legal opinion.[3] The pro-forma opinion is available from the CREST legal department;

(b)   a Security Application Form – this is the same form as for the admission of domestic securities and the same process as described at 13.4.2 above applies save that, for a DI, the issuer of the security to be admitted to CREST is the depository and not the overseas company and, therefore, the depository arranges for the submission of the form; and

(c)   an Operational Bulletin – this is provided by the depository and published by CRESTCo. It sets out, for informational purposes for CREST members and the market, the date of admission of the DI and the arrangements in relation to the paper interface. The pro-forma bulletin is available from CREST or registrar depositories.

All of the above documents must be received by CREST either five or 10 business days prior to the date of admission of the DI to CREST. The deadline depends on whether trades in the overseas company's securities (of the same ISIN as the proposed DI) are already being settled through the CREST residual settlements mechanism.[4] If not, the deadline will be five business days and, if so, 10 business days (to allow such trades to settle) prior to the admission date. On a new primary listing or issue of a new class of share the deadline will typically only be five days before the admission date. This should be checked with CREST early on in the process.

The admission process for a GDI is similar but, given the infrequency with which such instruments are admitted, the specific timing should be confirmed with CRESTCo.

---

[3] If the issuer maintains a share register in a jurisdiction other than (a) that in which it is incorporated, or (b) the UK, an additional opinion in relation to the jurisdiction in which the register is located will also be required.

[4] The CREST residual settlements mechanism makes use of parts of the CREST paper interface functionality to facilitate traditional certificated settlement on a T+10 timeframe.

13.6.6 Comparison of key aspects of the different depository interest mechanisms

	CREST Depository Interests	Bespoke Depository Interests	Global Depository Interests
Are the costs of the service borne by the company?	No. CREST makes no charge to the company.	Yes. Charges typically include a one-off establishment fee plus ongoing costs.	Yes. Charges typically include a one-off establishment fee plus ongoing costs.
Are the depository interests separately traded on AIM?	No. It is the underlying overseas security and not the CDI which is admitted to trading.	No. It is the underlying overseas security and not the DI which is admitted to trading.	Yes. The trading facility relates to the GDI itself and not the underlying overseas security.
Do the depository interests share the same ISIN as the underlying security?	Yes.	Yes.	No. The GDIs have their own ISIN.
Can the holder participate in corporate actions relating to the underlying security?	Yes.	Yes.	Yes.
Is the holder able to exercise voting rights on the underlying security?	Not a standard service.	Yes.	Yes.
Can the CREST paper interface be used to obtain a certificate?	No.	Yes. The DI will be cancelled and a certificate for the underlying overseas security issued to the holder.	Yes. The GDI can normally exist in certificated or uncertificated form.

13.7 Conclusion

The requirement in the AIM rules that appropriate electronic settlement arrangements should be in place is met simply in relation to UK and other domestic securities. With the increased popularity of AIM as a forum for trading other overseas securities it has been necessary to become more innovative in order to meet the settlement requirements. However, over time a range of products has been developed so that it is normally possible to find a solution suitable for each issue.

Appendices

Appendix 1   AIM Admission Document   245

Appendix 2   Specimen AIM Documents List   305

Appendix 3   AIM Admission Timetable   311

Appendix 4   Specimen AIM Completion Board Minutes   321

Appendix 5   Application to be signed by the Company   341

Appendix 6   Declaration by the Nominated Adviser   347

Appendix 1

AIM Admission Document

THIS DOCUMENT IS IMPORTANT AND REQUIRES YOUR IMMEDI-ATE ATTENTION. If you are in any doubt as to the contents of this document or as to the action you should take, you are recommended to consult a person authorised under the Financial Services and Markets Act 2000 ("FSMA"), who specialises in advising on the acquisition of shares and other securities.

This document is an AIM admission document and has been drawn up in accordance with the AIM Rules. This document does not constitute a prospectus within the meaning of section 85 of FSMA, has not been drawn up in accordance with the Prospectus Rules and has not been approved by or filed with the Financial Services Authority. This document does not constitute an offer of transferable securities to the public within the meaning of FSMA, the Act or otherwise.

The Directors of the Company, whose names appear on page 257 of this document and the Company, accept responsibility, collectively and individually, for the information contained in this document. To the best of the knowledge of the Directors and the Company (having taken all reasonable care to ensure such is the case) the information contained in this document is in accordance with the facts and contains no omission likely to affect the import of such information.

Annex I
1.1, 1.2
Annex III
1.1, 1.2

Application [will be/has been] made for the Ordinary Shares issued and to be issued pursuant to the Placing to be admitted to trading on AIM, a market operated by the London Stock Exchange ("AIM").

AIM is a market designed primarily for emerging or smaller companies to which a higher investment risk tends to be attached than to larger or more established companies. AIM securities are not admitted to the Official List of the United Kingdom Listing Authority. A prospective investor should be aware of the risks of investing in such companies and should make the decision to invest only after careful consideration and, if appropriate, consultation with an independent financial adviser. The London Stock Exchange plc has not itself examined or approved the contents of this document.

AIM Sch 2(e)

The whole of the text of this document should be read. You should be aware than an investment in the Company involves a high degree of risk. Your attention is drawn to the risk factors set out in Part II of this document.

Annex I
5.1.1

CONAME PLC

Annex I
5.1.2
Annex III
4.1
Annex III
4.4

Incorporated and registered in England and Wales with registered number •

Placing of • ordinary shares of £• each at £• per share
and

AIM
Sch 2(e)

**Admission to trading on
AIM
Nominated Adviser and Broker
[NOMAD]**

The Placing Shares will, on Admission, rank *pari passu* in all respects with the Existing Ordinary Shares including the right to receive all dividends or other distributions declared, paid or made after Admission.

Annex III
10.1 [NOMAD] which is authorised and regulated by the Financial Services Authority, is acting exclusively for the Company and no-one else in connection with the Placing and Admission. [NOMAD] will not regard any other person as its customer or be responsible to any other person for providing the protections afforded to customers of [NOMAD] nor for providing advice in relation to the transactions and arrangements detailed in this document. [NOMAD] is not making any representation or warranty, express or implied, as to the contents of this document.

This document does not constitute an offer to buy or to subscribe for, or the solicitation of an offer to buy or subscribe for, Ordinary Shares in any jurisdiction in which such offer or solicitation is unlawful. In particular, the Ordinary Shares offered by this document have not been, and will not be, registered under the United States Securities Act of 1933 as amended (the "Securities Act") or qualified for sale under the laws of any state of the United States or under the applicable laws of any of Canada, Australia or Japan and, subject to certain exceptions, may not be offered or sold in the United States or to, or for the account or benefit of, US persons (as such term is defined in Regulation S under the Securities Act) or to any national, resident or citizen of Canada, Australia or Japan. Neither this document nor any copy of it may be sent to or taken into the United States, Canada, Australia or Japan, nor may it be distributed directly or indirectly to any US person (within the meaning of Regulation S under the Securities Act) or to any persons with addresses in Canada, Australia or Japan, or to any corporation, partnership or other entity created or organised under the laws thereof, or in any country outside England and Wales where such distribution may lead to a breach of any legal or regulatory requirement.

Copies of this document will be available free of charge to the public during normal business hours on any day (Saturdays, Sundays and public holidays excepted) at the offices of [NOMAD] from the date of this document for the period ending one month after Admission.

CONTENTS

	Page
Placing Statistics	252
Expected Timetable of Principal Events	253
Definitions and Glossary	254
Directors, Secretary and Advisers	257
PART I – Information on the [CONAME] Group	259
PART II – Risk Factors	267
PART III – Accountants' Report	269
PART IV	273
Part A – Accountants' Report on the Unaudited Pro Forma Statement of Net Assets of the Group	273
Part B: Unaudited Pro Forma Statement of Net Assets of the Group	274
PART V – Additional Information	275

PLACING STATISTICS

Placing Price   • p

Number of Existing Ordinary Shares in issue prior
to the Placing   •

Number of Placing Shares being issued to Placees*   •

^{Annex III}_{9.1} [Number of Sale Shares being sold to Placees by the   •
Selling Shareholders pursuant to the Placing]

Number of Ordinary Shares in issue following the Placing   •

Percentage of the enlarged issued ordinary share capital   • per cent.
available to Placees in the Placing (excluding the Sale Shares)

Estimated gross proceeds of the Placing   £• million

Estimated net proceeds of the Placing receivable by the   £• million
Company

Market capitalisation following the Placing at the Placing   £• million
Price

* N.B. Annex III paragraph 9.2 requires a mandatory disclosure of the amount and percentage of immediate dilution in the case of a subscription offer to existing Ordinary Shareholders (or other equity holders) in the event that such holders do not subscribe to the offer.

EXPECTED TIMETABLE OF PRINCIPAL EVENTS

Admission and dealings in the Ordinary Shares to commence on AIM • 200[ ] Annex III 4.7

CREST accounts credited • 200[ ]

Despatch of definitive share certificates, where applicable • 200[ ]

DEFINITIONS AND GLOSSARY

The following definitions [and glossary terms] apply throughout this document unless the context requires otherwise:

"Act"	the Companies Act 1985 as amended
"AIM"	AIM, a market operated by the London Stock Exchange
"AIM Rules"	the rules published by the London Stock Exchange entitled "AIM Rules for Companies" governing admission to, and the operation of, AIM as amended from time to time
"Articles"	the articles of association of the Company
"Board" or "Directors"	the board of directors of the Company currently comprising the persons whose names are set out on page 257 of this document
"Combined Code"	the principles of good governance and code of best practice applicable to companies which are listed on the Official List, as amended from time to time
"Company" or "[CONAME]"	[CONAME] plc
"CREST"	the relevant system (as defined in the CREST Regulations) for paperless settlement of share transfers and the holding of shares in uncertificated form which is administered by CRESTCo Limited
"CREST Regulations"	the Uncertificated Securities Regulations 2001 (SI 2001/3755) as amended
"Existing Ordinary Shares"	the • Ordinary Shares in issue as at the date of this document
"FSA"	the Financial Services Authority
"FSMA"	the Financial Services and Markets Act 2000 as amended
"Group" or "[CONAME] Group"	the Company and its subsidiaries
"London Stock Exchange"	London Stock Exchange plc

"New Ordinary Shares"	the • new Ordinary Shares to be issued by the Company and placed with Placees
"NOMAD"	[NOMAD]
"Official List"	the Official List of the UK Listing Authority
"Ordinary Shares"	ordinary shares of £• each in the capital of the Company
"Participant ID"	the identification code or membership number used in CREST to identify a particular CREST member or other CREST participant
"Placees"	subscribers for Placing Shares procured by [NOMAD] on behalf of the Company pursuant to the Placing Agreement
"Placing"	the arrangements for the procurement of subscribers for the New Ordinary Shares [and purchasers for the Sale Shares] procured by [NOMAD] (as agent for the Company [and the Selling Shareholders] pursuant to and on the terms of the Placing Agreement)
"Placing Agreement"	the conditional agreement dated • 200[ ] between (i) [NOMAD], (ii) the Company, (iii) the Directors and (iv) certain shareholders of the Company [including the Selling Shareholders] relating to the Placing, further details of which are set out in paragraph of Part V of this document
"Placing Price"	•p for each Placing Share
"Placing Shares"	the New Ordinary Shares [and the Sale Shares]
"Prospectus Rules"	the Prospectus Rules of the FSA brought into effect on 1 July 2005 pursuant to Commission Regulation (EC) No. 809/2004 and the Prospectus Regulations 2005 (SI 2005/1433)
["Sale Shares"	the • Ordinary Shares to be sold to purchasers by the Selling Shareholders pursuant to the Placing]
["Selling Shareholders"	• and • of [business address] both of whom have been [principal shareholders/directors/other] of the Company]
"Share Option Scheme(s)"	the share option scheme(s) adopted by the Company further details of which are set out in paragraph of Part V of this document

Annex III 7.2

Annex III 7.1

"Shareholder(s)"	(a) person(s) who is/are registered as holder(s) of Ordinary Shares from time to time
"subsidiaries"	any subsidiary as defined in the Act
"UK" or "United Kingdom"	United Kingdom of Great Britain and Northern Ireland
"UK Listing Authority"	the Financial Services Authority acting in its capacity as competent authority for the purposes of Part VI of FSMA
"uncertificated" or "in uncertificated form"	recorded on the register of Ordinary Shares as being held in uncertificated form in CREST, entitlement to which by virtue of the CREST Regulations, may be transferred by means of CREST
"£" or "sterling"	UK pounds sterling

[The rate of exchange used for the purposes of this document is £1: •, being the rate of exchange as at the close of business on • 200[   ], the latest practicable date prior to the date of this document.]

DIRECTORS, SECRETARY AND ADVISERS

Directors	[	]	Annex I 1.1
Company secretary	[	]	
Registered office of the Company	[	]	
Nominated adviser and broker °	[	]	
Solicitors to the Company	[	]	
Auditors* and reporting accountant	[	]	Annex I 1.1 Annex I 2.1
Solicitors to the nominated adviser and broker	[	]	
Financial public relations	[	]	
Registrars	[	]	
[Expert†]	[	]	

° Insert name and registered office/principal trading address of each adviser

* Membership in professional body must be disclosed and if the historical financial information was prepared by more than one statutory auditor then all names and addresses should be included (Annex I, 2.1)

† Include if expert report (e.g. patent agent's report) and refer to Annex III, 10.3 for further disclosure requirements

PART I
INFORMATION ON THE [CONAME] GROUP

Introduction

[   ]

History of the Group

[Include a description of the important events in the development of the Annex I 5.1.5 Company's business.]

Principal Activities

[Include a description of, and key factors relating to, the nature of the Annex I 6.1.1 Company's operations and its principal activities, stating the main categories of products sold and/or services performed for each financial year for the period covered by the historical financial information; and]

[Include an indication of any significant new products and/or services that Annex I 6.1.2 have been introduced and, to the extent the development of new products or services have been publicly disclosed, give the status of development.]

[Investment Business

Where the Company is an investing company, provide details of its invest- AIM Sch 2(i) ing strategy which must include, as a minimum requirement, such matters as:

- the precise business sector(s), geographical area(s) and type of company in which it can invest;

- how long it can exist before making an investment or having to return funds to Shareholders;

- whether it will be an active or passive investor;

- whether it will spread its investments; and

- what expertise its directors have in respect of evaluating its proposed investments and how and by whom any due diligence on those investments will be effected.]

The market

[   ]

Products

[   ]

Customers

[   ]

Suppliers

[   ]

Sales and marketing strategy

[   ]

[Intellectual property rights

^{Annex I} Include information regarding the extent to which the Company is depen-
^{6.4} dent upon patents or licences, industrial, commercial or financial contracts, or new manufacturing processes if relevant.]

[Competition

^{Annex I} If included, state the basis for any statements regarding the Company's
^{6.5} competitive position.]

Financial record

The following audited financial information on the Group has been extracted from the Accountants' Report set out in Part III of this document.

	200[ ] £'000	200[ ] £'000	200[ ] £'000

Current trading and prospects

^{Annex I}
¹²

[Include information on:

(i)   the most significant recent trends in production, sales and inventory, and costs and selling prices since the end of the last financial year to the date of the admission document; and

(ii) any known trends, uncertainties, demands, commitments or events that are reasonably likely to have a material effect on [CONAME's] prospects for at least the current financial year.]

[Profit forecast

AIM
Sch 2(d)

Where the admission document contains a profit forecast, estimate or projection (which includes any form of words which expressly or by implication states a minimum or maximum for the likely level of profits or losses for a period subsequent to that for which audited accounts have been published, or contains data from which a calculation of an approximate figure for future profits or losses may be made, even if no particular figure is mentioned and the words "profit" or "loss" are not used) the document must include:

(i)   a statement by the Directors that such forecast, estimate or projection has been made after due and careful enquiry; AIM Sch 2(d)(i)

(ii) a statement of the principal assumptions for each factor which could have a material effect on the achievement of the forecast, estimate or projection. These assumptions must be readily understandable by investors and be specific and precise; and AIM Sch 2(d)(ii)

(iii) confirmation from [NOMAD] to the Company that it has satisfied itself that the forecast, estimate or projection has been made after due and careful enquiry by the Directors. AIM Sch 2(d)(iii)

Such profit forecast, estimate or projection must be prepared on a basis comparable with the historical financial information.] AIM Sch 2(d)(iv)

Reasons for the Placing and use of proceeds

[Provide the reasons for the Placing and, where appropriate, the estimated net amount of the proceeds broken into each principal intended use and presented by order of priority for such uses. If the Company is aware that the anticipated proceeds will not be sufficient to fund all the proposed uses, state the amount and sources of other funds needed, details must be given with regard to the use of the proceeds, in particular, when they are being used to acquire assets, other than in the ordinary course of business, to finance announced acquisitions or other business, or to discharge, reduce or retire indebtedness.] Annex III 3.4

The Placing and Admission

• New Ordinary Shares are being placed, representing • per cent. of the enlarged issued Ordinary Share capital of the Company following the Placing. This does not include [the Sale Shares being placed by [NOMAD] on behalf of the Selling Shareholders which already form part of the issued Ordinary Share capital or] any Ordinary Shares reserved for the exercise of options to subscribe for Ordinary Shares pursuant to Share Option Schemes, as described below in Part I of this document. At the Placing Price, the Placing of New Ordinary Shares will raise approximately £• million (net of expenses) for the Company.

[NOMAD] has agreed, pursuant to the Placing Agreement and conditional, inter alia, on Admission, to use its reasonable endeavours to place the Placing Shares with institutional and other investors. The Placing is conditional, inter alia, upon:

• the Placing Agreement becoming unconditional and not having been terminated in accordance with its terms prior to Admission; and
• Admission becoming effective not later than • 200[　], or such later date as [NOMAD] and the Company may agree, being not later than • 200[　].

Application has been made to the London Stock Exchange for the Ordinary Shares, issued and to be issued, to be admitted to trading on AIM. Admission is expected to become effective and dealings in the issued Ordinary Shares are expected to commence on • 200[　]. The Placing Shares will be placed free of expenses and any stamp duty and will rank pari passu in all respects with the Existing Ordinary Shares including the right to receive all dividends and other distributions declared, paid or made after the date of issue.

Further details of the Placing Agreement are set out in paragraph of Part V of this document.

Lock-ins and orderly market arrangements

_{AIM Sch 2(f)} In accordance with Rule 7 of the AIM Rules each of the Directors, certain Shareholders and applicable employees have agreed, subject to certain limited exceptions, not to dispose of any of their interests in Ordinary Shares for a period of twelve months from Admission.

_{Annex III 7.3} [Provide details of any lock-in agreements, including the parties involved, the contents and exceptions of the lock-in agreement and an indication of the period of the lock-in.]

[Selling Shareholders

Include the following information if applicable:

Annex III
7.1, 7.2

(i)   the name and business address of the person or entity offering to sell shares, the nature of any position, office of other material relationship that that Selling Shareholder has had in the past three years with the Company or any of its subsidiaries or its predecessors/affiliates:

(ii) the number and class of shares being offered by each of the Selling Shareholders.]

Directors and senior management

[Should include ages and previous names if applicable]

AIM Sch
2(g)(i)

[Staff and Employees

If not included in Part III, include <u>either</u> the number of employees at the end of the period <u>or</u> the average for each financial year for the period covered by the historical financial information up to the date of the admission document (and changes in such numbers, if material) and, if possible and material, a breakdown of persons employed by main category of activity and geographic location. If [CONAME] employs a significant number of temporary employees, include disclosure of the number of temporary employees on average during the most recent financial year.]

Annex I
17

Share Option Scheme(s) [and other incentive schemes]

In order to provide an incentive to employees of the Group, the Company has established the Share Option Scheme(s). Details of the Share Option Scheme(s) and the options that have been granted thereunder are set out in paragraphs 2.3 and 2.4 and of Part V of this document.

Annex I
17.3

Dividend Policy

[Provide a description of the Company's policy on dividend distributions and any restrictions thereon. Unless covered in the Accountants' Report in Part III, where applicable, include a description of the amount of the dividend per share for each financial year for the period covered by the historical financial information adjusted, where the number of shares in the issuer has changed, to make it comparable.]

Annex I
20.7

Corporate Governance

Annex I 16.4 The Company intends, so far as is practicable for a company of its size and nature, to comply with the provisions of the Combined Code which applies to companies which are admitted to the Official List. The Company has appointed three non-executive Directors to bring an independent view to the Board, and to provide a balance to the executive Directors.

Annex I 16.3 [If relevant provide a summary of the terms of reference of the Audit, Remuneration and Nominations Committees including the name of each committee member.]

The Directors are required to comply with Rule 21 of the AIM Rules relating to Directors' and applicable employees' dealings in the Company's securities and to this end the Company has adopted an appropriate share dealing code.

Annex III 4.3 **Settlement and CREST**

CREST is a paperless settlement procedure enabling securities to be evidenced otherwise than by a certificate and transferred otherwise than by a written instrument. The Company has applied for the Ordinary Shares to be admitted to CREST and it is expected that the Ordinary Shares will be so admitted and accordingly enabled for settlement in CREST on the date of Admission. It is expected that Admission of the Ordinary Shares issued and to be issued will become effective and that dealings will commence on • 200[　]. Accordingly, settlement of transactions in Ordinary Shares following Admission may take place within the CREST system if any Shareholder so wishes. CREST is a voluntary system and Shareholders who wish to receive and retain share certificates will be able to do so. Persons acquiring Ordinary Shares as a part of the Placing may elect to receive such shares in uncertificated form if, but only if, that person is a "system-member" (as defined in the CREST Regulations) in relation to CREST.

AIM Sch 2(k) **[General Duty of Disclosure – Not a specific head but a reminder!**

There should be inserted into the admission document (as and where appropriate) any other information which the Company reasonably considers necessary to enable investors to form a full understanding of:

(i) the assets and liabilities, financial position, profits and losses, and prospects of the applicant and its securities for which admission is being sought;

(ii)   the rights attaching to those securities; and

(iii)   any other matter contained in the admission document.]

Further information

Your attention is drawn to the additional information set out in Parts II to V of this document.

PART II
RISK FACTORS

Investment in AIM traded securities

Investment in shares traded on AIM is perceived to involve a higher degree of risk and be less liquid than investment in companies whose shares are listed on the Official List. The AIM Rules are less demanding than those of the Official List. It is emphasised that no application is being made for the admission of the Company's securities to the Official List. An investment in the Ordinary Shares may be difficult to realise. Prospective investors should be aware that the value of an investment in the Company may go down as well as up and that the market price of the Ordinary Shares may not reflect the underlying value of the Company. Investors may therefore realise less than, or lose all of, their investment.

Share price volatility and liquidity

The share price of quoted companies can be highly volatile and shareholdings can be illiquid. The price at which the Ordinary Shares are quoted and the price which investors may realise for their Ordinary Shares will be influenced by a large number of factors, some specific to the Company and its operations and some which may affect quoted companies generally. These factors could include the performance of the Company, large purchases or sales of the Ordinary Shares, currency fluctuations, legislative changes and general economic, political or regulatory conditions.

International Financial Reporting Standards

On 12 October 2004, AIM changed its regulatory status and it is now regulated by London Stock Exchange. Therefore, it is no longer a regulated market under European Union regulations. On 7 October 2004, London Stock Exchange issued guidance which stated that London Stock Exchange intends to mandate International Financial Reporting Standards ("IFRS") for all AIM companies for financial years commencing on or after 1 January 2007. AIM companies are encouraged to prepare for this change well in advance of this date. It is expected that there will be significant continuing developments in IFRS between now and the date of adoption of IFRS by the Company and consequently there is uncertainty about exactly what IFRS will require at that time.

In the meantime, the UK Accounting Standards Board is adopting a phased transition to the conversion of existing UK financial reporting standards

("UK FRS") to IFRS and as a result is in the process of issuing a number of new standards or revisions to existing standards over the next two years. However, it is likely that, by the IFRS implementation date set by London Stock Exchange, UK FRS will not be fully aligned with IFRS. Therefore the transition of UK FRS to IFRS and/or the adoption of IFRS could possibly have a material impact on the Group's reported financial position and results, although it is not possible for the Directors to quantify the impact at this time.

Risk factors

It may be necessary for the Company to raise additional capital to enable the Group to progress through further stages of development.

[The Group's business may be materially affected by the inability to recruit sufficient personnel of the right quality or qualifications, or by the loss of key personnel.]

[There may be a change in government regulation or policies which materially adversely affects the Group's activities.]

[The Company is subject to regulation by • and its registration is subject to annual renewal.]

[There can be no assurance that the Company will be able to •.]

[The • division has been operating for a relatively short period and accordingly there is a relatively short trading history on which to base any judgment of the growth prospects of this division.]

[There can be no assurance that the Company will be able to achieve the level and rate of growth of sales envisaged by the Directors.]

[The Group operates in a market which is subject to rapid technological change. There can be no assurance that the Group will be able to keep pace with technological developments and respond to customer requirements.]

[Competition]

[Loss of key management could have adverse consequences for the Group. While the Group has entered into service agreements with each of its key personnel, the retention of their services cannot be guaranteed.]

PART III
ACCOUNTANTS' REPORT

Annex I
20

Set out below is the text of a report on the Company by •, registered auditors, chartered accountants and reporting accountants.

The Directors
[CONAME] Plc
[   ]

The Directors
[NOMAD] Limited
[   ]

• 200[   ]

Dear Sirs

[CONAME] plc ("Company") [and its subsidiaries (together "the Group")]

[   ]

[Note: must include a statement that in Auditors' opinion, the historical annual financial information in the report gives a true and fair view in accordance with the auditing standards applicable in the relevant EC Member State or an equivalent standard.]

[Note: refer to Annex I, Rule 20 for full details of the disclosures required in connection with the financial information concerning the Company's assets and liabilities, financial position and profits and losses.]

For the purposes of Schedule Two of the AIM Rules we are responsible for this report as part of the Admission Document and declare that we have taken all reasonable care to ensure that the information contained in this report is, to the best of our knowledge, in accordance with the facts and contains no omission likely to affect its import. This declaration is included in the Admission Document in compliance with Schedule Two of the AIM Rules.

Yours faithfully

[   ]

Chartered Accountants
Registered Auditors

^{Annex I}_{20.1} [Note: The last year of audited financial information may not be older than (a) 18 months from the date of issue of document if audited; (b) 15 months from date of issue of the document if unaudited.

If the audited financial information is prepared according to national accounting standards, such information must include at least:

(a)   balance sheet;

(b)   income statement;

(c)   a statement showing either all changes in equity or changes in equity other than those arising from capital transactions with owners and distributions to owners;

(d)   cash flow statement; and

(e)   accounting policies and explanatory notes.

^{Annex I}_{20.6.1} If the Company has published quarterly or half yearly financial information since the date of its last audited financial statements, these must be included in the admission document.

^{Annex I}_{20.6.2} If the admission document is issued more than nine months after the end of the last audited financial year, interim financial information, which may be unaudited, covering at least the first six months of the financial year must be included. These should include a comparison with the same period in the prior financial year.

^{Annex I}_{20.3} If the Company prepares both its own and consolidated annual financial statements, include at least the consolidated annual financial statements in the document.

^{Annex I}_{20.4.3} Any financial data which is not audited should be stated to be such and the source of the data should be given.]

[Note: The lawyer should check that the following information is contained in this Part III or in Parts I or V:

Investments

^{Annex I}_{5.2} (a)   a description (including the amount) of the Company's principal investments for each financial year for the period covered by the historical financial information up to the date of the document;

(b)   a description of the Company's principal investments that are in progress, including the geographic distribution of these investments (home and abroad) and the method of financing (internal and external); and

(c)   information concerning the Company's principal future investments on which its management bodies have already made firm commitments.

Holdings

Information relating to the undertakings in which the Company holds a proportion of the capital likely to have a significant affect on the assessment of its own assets and liabilities, financial position or profits and losses.

Annex I 25

Related Party Transactions

Annex I 19

Details of related party transactions (which for these purposes are those set out in the standards adopted according to the Regulation (EC) No 1606/2002), that the Company has entered into during the period covered by the historical financial information and up to the admission document, must be disclosed in accordance with the respective standard adopted according to Regulation (EC) No 1606/2002 if applicable.

If such standards do not apply to the Company, the following information must be disclosed:

(a)   the nature and extent of any transactions which are – as a single transaction or in their entirety – material to the Company. Where such related party transactions are not concluded at arm's length provide an explanation of why these transactions were not concluded at arm's length. In the case of outstanding loans including guarantees of any kind indicate the amount outstanding; and

(b)   the amount or the percentage to which related party transactions form part of the turnover of the Company.]

PART IV
PART A: ACCOUNTANTS' REPORT ON THE UNAUDITED PRO FORMA STATEMENT OF NET ASSETS OF THE GROUP

Annex I
20.2

Set out below is the text of a report on the Group by •, registered auditors, chartered accountants and reporting accountants.

The Directors
[CONAME] Plc
[   ]

The Directors
[NOMAD] Limited
[   ]

• 200[   ]

Dear Sirs

[CONAME] plc ("Company") [and its subsidiaries (together "the Group")]

[   ]

[Note: must include statement that in Auditors' opinion:

(a)   the pro forma financial information has been properly compiled on the basis stated; and
(b)   that basis is consistent with the accounting policies of the Company.]

For the purposes of Schedule Two of the AIM Rules we are responsible for this report as part of the Admission Document and declare that we have taken all reasonable care to ensure that the information contained in this report is, to the best of our knowledge, in accordance with the facts and contains no omission likely to affect its import. This declaration is included in the Admission Document in compliance with Schedule Two of the AIM Rules.

Yours faithfully

[   ]

Chartered Accountants
Registered Auditors

^{Annex}_{II} PART B: UNAUDITED PRO FORMA STATEMENT OF NET ASSETS OF THE GROUP

The following unaudited pro forma statement of net assets of the Group following the Placing and Admission (the "Transaction") has been prepared for illustrative purposes only to provide information about the impact of the Transaction on the Group and because of its nature may not give a true reflection of the financial position of the Group. It has been prepared on the basis that the Transaction was undertaken as at • 200[ ] and on the basis set out in the notes.

	As at • 200[ ] (note 1)	Adjustment for net Placing proceeds (note 2)	Pro forma net assets of the Group
	£000	£000	£000
Fixed assets			
Current assets			
Creditors: amounts falling due within one year			
Net current (liabilities)/assets			
Net assets			

Notes:

The pro forma statement of net assets has been prepared on the following basis:

1. The net assets of the Group at • 200[ ] have been extracted from the financial information set out in Part III of this document.
2. This adjustment reflects the net proceeds from the Placing, being [£•] net of expenses of approximately [£•].
3. No adjustments have been made to reflect the trading results of Group since • 200[ ].

[Note: Pro forma financial information is only required by Annex I, 20.2 in the case of significant gross change. On occasions, whilst perhaps not required, it is considered helpful to include pro forma financial information. In either case, if included, it should demonstrate how the transaction might have affected the assets and liabilities and earnings of the Group, had the transaction been undertaken at the commencement of the period being reported on or at the date reported.]

[Note: The pro forma information must be presented as set out in Annex II.]

PART V
ADDITIONAL INFORMATION

1. The Company and its subsidiaries

1.1 The Company was incorporated and registered in England and Wales under the Act on • under the name of • Limited with registered number • as a private company with limited liability under the Act. The Company was re-registered as a public company on •. Annex I 5.1.3–4

1.2 The Company is the holding company of the following trading subsidiary companies, all of which are incorporated in England and Wales and are wholly owned: Annex I 7.1–2

Name	Date of Incorporation	Issued share capital (fully paid)
• Limited	•	• ordinary shares of £• each
• Limited	•	• ordinary shares of £• each
• Limited	•	• ordinary shares of £• each
• Limited	•	• ordinary shares of £• each

1.3 The registered office of the Company and each of its subsidiaries is at • and the telephone number of the registered office is •. The ISIN for the Ordinary Shares is •. Annex I 5.1.4 Annex III 4.1

2. Share capital
Annex III 4.2

Annex I 21.1.7
2.1 The Ordinary Shares have been created pursuant to the Act. The Company was incorporated with an authorised share capital of • represented by • ordinary shares of £• each of which • were issued to subscribers • and •. The following alterations in the issued share capital of the Company have taken place since incorporation:

(i) on • 200[ ] each of the issued and unissued ordinary shares of £• each in the capital of the Company was sub-divided into • Ordinary Shares;

(ii) on • 200[ ] the authorised share capital of the Company was increased from £• to £• by the creation of an additional • Ordinary Shares which includes the New Ordinary Shares to be placed with Placees; Annex III 4.6

(iii) on • 200[ ] • Ordinary Shares were allotted and issued to certain investors;

(iv) [describe any other changes];

275

Annex III 4.6

(v)   on • 200[   ], in substitution for any previous authority, the Directors were generally and unconditionally authorised, in accordance with section 80 of the Act to allot all relevant securities (as defined in that section and which includes the New Ordinary Shares to be placed with Placees) up to a maximum aggregate nominal amount of relevant securities of £• provided that this authority will expire (unless previously renewed, varied or revoked by the Company in general meeting) at the conclusion of the next annual general meeting of the Company following the passing of the resolution, or if earlier, the date falling fifteen months after the date on which the resolution was passed, save that the Directors may, before the expiry, make an offer or agreement which would or might require relevant securities to be allotted after such expiry and the Directors may allot relevant securities pursuant to such offer or agreement as if the authority had not expired; and

Annex III 4.6

(vi)   on • 200[   ] the Directors were given power in accordance with section 95 of the Act to allot equity securities (within the meaning of section 94 of the Act and which includes the New Ordinary Shares to be placed with Placees) pursuant to the authority conferred by the resolution details of which are set out in paragraph 2.1 (v) above as if section 89(1) of the Act did not apply to the allotment provided that such power will expire (unless previously renewed, varied or revoked by the Company in general meeting) at the conclusion of the next annual general meeting of the Company following the passing of this resolution, or if earlier, the date falling fifteen months after the date on which this resolution was passed save that the Directors may, before the expiry make an offer or agreement which would or might require equity securities to be allotted after such expiry and the Directors may allot equity securities pursuant to such offer or agreement as if the authority had not expired.

Annex I 21.1.1

2.2   The authorised and issued share capital of the Company (i) as at • 200[   ] and at the date of this document and (ii) following completion of the Placing and Admission is set out below:

Authorised				Issued and fully paid	
	£	Number		£	Number
(i)	•	•	Ordinary Shares	•	•
(ii)	•	•	Ordinary Shares	•	•

The number of Ordinary Shares outstanding at the beginning of the year was • and the number of Ordinary Shares outstanding as at the financial year ending • 200[ ] is •. [If more than 10% of capital has been paid for with assets other than cash within the period covered by the Accountants' Report include details].

2.3   As at the date of this document and in addition to the options ^{Annex I 21.1.6} detailed in paragraph 5.2 below, there are • share options granted under the Share Option Scheme(s) which are outstanding as set out below:

Option Holder	Date of Grant	No. of Ordinary Shares	Exercise Price	Earliest Exercise Date	Latest Exercise Date
•	• 200[ ]	•	£•	• 200[ ]	• 200[ ]

2.4   Save as disclosed in paragraph 2.3 above and paragraph 5.2 below, ^{Annex I 18.4} no capital of the Company is proposed to be issued or is under option or is agreed to be put under option.

2.5   There are • [convertible securities/exchangeable securities/securi- ^{Annex I 21.1.4} ties with warrants] in the Company [describe procedure for conversion/exchange/subscription].

2.6   [If applicable provide details of any shares which do not represent ^{Annex I 21.1.2} capital, including the number and main characteristics of such shares.]

2.7   [If applicable, provide details of the number, book value and face ^{Annex I 21.1.3} value of shares in the Company held by or on behalf of the Company itself or by subsidiaries of the Company.]

2.8   [If applicable, provide information about and terms of any acquisi- ^{Annex I 21.1.5} tion rights or obligations over authorised but unissued capital or any undertaking to increase the capital.]

2.9   [If applicable, include details of any takeover bids by third parties in ^{Annex III 4.10} respect of the Company's shares which have occurred during the last financial year and the current financial year including details of the price/exchange terms and the outcome.]

3.   Constitutional documents and other relevant laws and regulations

Annex I
21.2.1 **3.1   Memorandum of Association**

The principal objects of the Company, which are set out in clause •
of its Memorandum of Association, are to carry on the business of a
general commercial company.

3.2   Articles of Association

The Articles of Association of the Company contain, *inter alia*, provisions to
the following effect:

3.2.1   *Voting rights*

Annex I
21.2.3 Subject to paragraph 3.2.6 below, and to any special rights or restrictions as to voting upon which any shares may for the time being be
held, on a show of hands every member who (being an individual)
is present in person or (being a corporation) is present by its duly
appointed representative shall have one vote and on a poll every
member present in person or by representative or proxy shall have
one vote for every Ordinary Share held by him. A proxy need not be
a member of the Company.

3.2.2   *Variation of rights*

Annex I
21.2.4 Whenever the share capital of the Company is divided into different
classes of shares the special rights attached to any class may be
varied or abrogated either with the consent in writing of the holders
of three-fourths in nominal value of the issued shares of that class or
with the sanction of an extraordinary resolution passed at a separate
general meeting of the holders of the shares of that class and may be
so varied and abrogated whilst the Company is a going concern or
during or in contemplation of a winding up. To every such separate
general meeting (except an adjourned meeting), the quorum shall be
two persons at least holding or representing by proxy one-third in
nominal value of the issued shares of that class. These conditions are
not more significant than required by law.

3.2.3   *Alteration of capital*

Annex I
21.2.8 The Company may by ordinary resolution increase its capital,
consolidate and divide all or any of its share capital into shares of a

larger nominal value, sub-divide all or any of its shares into shares of a smaller nominal value, cancel any shares not taken, or agreed to be taken, by any person and diminish the amount of its capital by the amount of the shares so cancelled.

The Company may, subject to any conditions, authorities and consents required by law, by special resolution reduce or cancel its share capital or any capital redemption reserve or share premium account.

Subject to and in accordance with the provisions of the Act, the Company may purchase its own shares (including any redeemable shares) with and subject to all prior authorities of the Company in general meeting as specified under the Act provided that the Company may not purchase any of its shares if as a result of the purchase of the shares there would no longer be any member holding shares in the Company other than redeemable shares.

These conditions are not more stringent than required by law.

3.2.4   *Transfer of shares*

A member may transfer all or any of his shares (1) in the case of Annex III 4.8 certificated shares by transfer in writing in any usual or common form or in any other form acceptable to the Directors and may be under hand only and (2) in the case of uncertificated shares, in the manner provided for in the rules and procedures of the operator of the relevant system and in accordance with and subject to the CREST Regulations. The instrument of transfer of a certificated share shall be signed by or on behalf of the transferor and, if the share is not fully paid, by or on behalf of the transferee. Subject to paragraph 3.2.6 below, the Articles contain no restrictions on the free transferability of fully paid shares provided that the transfer is in respect of only one class of share and is accompanied by the share certificate and any other evidence of title required by the Directors and that the provisions in the Articles relating to the deposit of instruments for transfer have been complied with.

The Company will not close the register of members in respect of a share, class of share, renounceable right of allotment of a share or other security (title to units of which is permitted to be transferred by computer-based systems and procedures in accordance with the CREST Regulations) without the consent of the operator of the computer-based system and/or procedure. The registration of transfers may be suspended at such times and for such periods as the Directors may determine either generally or in respect of any class of shares. The register of members shall not be closed for more than thirty days a year.

Subject to the requirements of the UK Listing Authority and/or the London Stock Exchange, as appropriate, the Company shall register a transfer of title to any uncertificated share or any renounceable right to allotment of a share held in uncertificated form in accordance with the CREST Regulations but so that the Directors may refuse to register such transfer in any circumstance permitted or required by the CREST Regulations.

The Directors may also decline to register a transfer of shares representing 0.25 per cent. or more in nominal value of the issued shares of their class after there has been a failure to comply with any notice under section 212 of the Act requiring the disclosure of information relating to interests in the shares concerned unless the shareholder has not, and proves that no other person has, failed to supply the information. Such refusal may continue until the failure has been remedied, but the Directors shall not decline to register:

(a)   a transfer pursuant to acceptance of a takeover offer for the Company (within the meaning of section 428 of the Act); or

(b)   a transfer in consequence of a sale made through a recognised investment exchange (as defined in FSMA) or any other stock exchange outside the United Kingdom on which the shares are normally traded; or

(c)   a transfer which is shown to the satisfaction of the Directors to be made in consequence of a sale of the whole of the beneficial interest in the shares to a person who is unconnected with the member and with any other person appearing to be interested in the shares.

3.2.5   *Dividends*

Annex I
20.7

(a)   Subject to the Act or any other statutes in force, the Company may by ordinary resolution in general meeting declare dividends provided that no dividend shall be paid otherwise than out of profits available for the purpose and no dividend shall exceed the amount recommended by the Directors. The Directors may from time to time declare and pay interim dividends on shares of any class of such amounts and on such dates in respect of such periods as appear to the Directors to be justified. All divided payments shall be non-cumulative.

(b)   Subject to the rights of any persons, if any, holding shares with special dividend rights, and subject to paragraph 3.2.6 below, all dividends shall be apportioned and paid pro rata according to the amounts paid or credited as paid on the shares during any portion or portions of the period in respect of which the dividend is paid. No amount paid or credited as paid in advance of calls shall be regarded as paid on shares for this purpose.

(c)   All dividends unclaimed for a period of 12 years from the date on which such dividend was declared or became due for payment shall be forfeited and shall revert to the Company.

(d)   There is no fixed date on which an entitlement to dividend Annex III 4.5 arises.

(e)   There are no dividend restrictions attaching to the Ordinary Annex I 20.7 Shares, provided they are fully paid up. Payments of dividends may be made by any method the directors consider appropriate and on a cash dividend there are no special arrangements for non-resident Shareholders. The Directors may make such arrangements as they consider expedient in connection with a dividend payment in shares to deal with any legal or other difficulties that may arise in any territory in which non-resident shareholders are present.

3.2.6   *Suspension of rights*

If a member or any other person appearing to be interested in shares of the Company fails after the date of service of a notice to comply with the statutory disclosure requirements then:

(a)   if the shares are held in certificated form from the time of such failure until not more than 7 days after the earlier of (a) receipt by the Company of notice that there has been a transfer of the shares by an arm's length sale and (b) due compliance, to the satisfaction of the Company, with the statutory disclosure requirements (if the Directors so resolve) such member shall not be entitled to vote or to exercise any right conferred by membership at meetings of the Company in respect of the shares which are the subject of such notice. Where the holding represents more than 0.25 per cent. of the issued shares of that class, the payment of dividends may be withheld, and such member shall not be entitled to transfer such shares otherwise than by an arm's length sale.

(b)   if the shares are held in uncertificated form, the Directors may serve upon the registered holder of such shares a notice requiring the holder to convert his holding of uncertificated shares into certificated form within such period as is specified in the notice and require the holder to continue to hold such shares in certificated form for so long as such failure continues. If the holder shall fail to convert his holding within the specified time, the Directors are empowered to authorise some person to take all such steps and issue such instructions as may be necessary in the name of the holder of such shares to effect the conversion of such shares to certificated form. Such steps shall be as effective as if they had been taken by the registered holder of the relevant uncertificated shares. Once such conversion to certificated form has been effected, the above rules in relation to shares in certificated form shall apply.

3.2.7   *Return of capital*

Annex III
4.5

Subject to any preferred, deferred or other special rights, or subject to such conditions or restrictions to which any shares in the capital of the Company may be issued, on a winding-up or other return of capital, the holders of Ordinary Shares are entitled to share in any surplus assets pro rata to the amount paid up on their Ordinary Shares. A liquidator may, with the sanction of an extraordinary resolution of the Company and any other sanction required by the Act, divide amongst the members in specie or in kind the whole or any part of the assets of the Company (whether or not the assets shall consist of property of one kind or shall consist of property of different kinds), those assets to be set at such value as he deems fair. A liquidator may also vest the whole or any part of the assets of the Company in trustees on trusts for the benefit of the members as the liquidator shall think fit.

3.2.8   *Pre-emption rights*

Annex III
4.5

There are no rights of pre-emption under the Articles in respect of transfers of issued Ordinary Shares.

Annex I
21.2.6

In certain circumstances, Shareholders may have statutory pre-emption rights under the Act in respect of the allotment of new shares in the Company. These statutory pre-emption rights would require the Company to offer new shares for allotment to existing Shareholders on a *pro rata* basis before allotting them to other persons. In such circumstances, the procedure for the exercise of such statutory pre-emption rights would be set out in the documentation by which such shares would be offered to the Company's shareholders.

3.2.9   *General meetings*

An annual general meeting of the Company shall be held in each year in addition to any other meetings which may be held in that year and at such time and place as may be determined by the Directors, but so not more than fifteen months shall elapse between the holding of any two successive annual general meetings.

The Directors shall convene an extraordinary general meeting whenever they think fit. Extraordinary general meetings shall also been convened on a requisition of the members of the Company as provided for by the Act or, if the Directors fail to convene an extraordinary general meeting within twenty one days from the date of the deposit of the requisition, a meeting may be convened by such requisitionists as provided by the Act.

Twenty one clear days' notice in respect of an annual general meeting and every extraordinary general meeting at which it is proposed to pass a special resolution and fourteen clear days' notice in respect of every other annual or extraordinary general meeting shall be given to all members (other than those who, under the provisions of the Articles or otherwise, are not entitled to receive notices from the Company) and to the Directors and the auditors for the time being of the Company, but the accidental omission to give such notice to, or the non-receipt of such notice by, any member or Director or the auditors shall not invalidate any resolution passed or any proceeding at such meeting.

Every notice shall specify the place, the day and the hour of the meeting and in the case of special business, the nature of such business and shall also state with reasonable prominence that a member entitled to attend and vote at the meeting, may appoint a proxy to attend and vote on a poll thereat instead of him and that the proxy need not also be a member. In the case of a meeting convened for passing a special or extraordinary resolution the notice shall also specify the intention to propose the resolution as a special or extraordinary resolution as the case may be.

For the purpose of determining which persons are entitled to attend and vote at any general meeting and how many votes such persons may cast, the Company may specify in the relevant notice of general meeting a time, not more than forty eight hours before the time fixed for the meeting, by which a person must be entered on the register of members in order to have the right to attend and vote at the meeting.

No business shall be transacted unless the requisite quorum is present when the meeting proceeds to business. Two members present in person or by proxy shall be a quorum for all purposes. If within fifteen minutes (or such longer interval not exceeding one hour as the chairman thinks fit) from the time appointed for the general meeting a quorum is not present, if convened on the requisition of the members the meeting shall be dissolved. In any other case the meeting shall be adjourned to the same day in the next week at the same time and place, or to such other day as the chairman shall determine, being not less than fourteen nor more than twenty eight days thereafter. The Company shall give at least seven clear days notice of any meeting adjourned through lack of quorum. No business shall be transacted at any adjourned meeting other than the business which might have been transacted at the meeting from which the adjournment took place.

3.2.10 *Directors*

Annex I
21.2.2

The business and affairs of the Company shall be managed by the Directors, who may exercise all such powers of the Company as are not by any statute or by the Articles required to be exercised by the Company in general meeting and for such purposes the Directors may establish any local group, divisional board, agency or committee for managing any of the affairs of the Company, either in the United Kingdom or elsewhere, and may appoint any persons to be members of such local group, divisional board, agency or committee or any managers or agents.

Subject to the Articles, the Directors may meet together for the despatch of business, adjourn and otherwise regulate their meetings as they think fit. The quorum necessary for the transaction of the business is two unless otherwise resolved by the Directors. A meeting of the Directors at which a quorum is present shall be competent to exercise all powers and discretions for the time being exercisable by the Directors.

Save as mentioned below, a Director shall not vote in respect of any matter in which he has, directly or indirectly, any material interest (otherwise than by virtue of his interest in shares or debentures or other securities of the Company) or in relation to which he has a duty which conflicts or may conflict with the interests of the Company. A Director shall not be counted in the quorum at any meeting in relation to any resolution in which he is debarred from voting.

Subject to the Act, a Director shall (in the absence some other material interest than is indicated below), be entitled to vote (and be counted in the quorum) in respect of any resolution concerning any of the following matters, namely:

(a)   the giving to him of any guarantee, security or indemnity in respect of money lent or obligation incurred by him at the request of or for the benefit of the Company or any of its subsidiaries;

(b)   giving to a third party any guarantee, security or indemnity in respect of a debt or obligation of the Company or any of its subsidiaries for which he himself has assumed responsibility in whole or in part either alone or jointly with others, under a guarantee or indemnity or by the giving of security;

(c)   where the Company or any of its subsidiaries is offering securities in which offer the director is or may be entitled to participate as the holder of securities or in the underwriting or sub-underwriting in which the Director is to participate;

(d)   relating to another Company in which he and any persons connected with him do not to his knowledge hold an interest in shares (as that term is used in sections 198-211 of the Act) representing one per cent. or more of either any class of the equity share capital, or the voting rights in such company;

(e)   relating to an arrangement for the benefit of the employees of the Company or any of its subsidiaries which does not award him any privilege or benefit not generally awarded to the employees to whom such arrangement relates; or

(f)   concerning insurance which the Company proposes to maintain or purchase for the benefit of Directors of the benefit of persons including Directors.

Unless otherwise determined by the Company by ordinary resolution, there shall be paid to the Directors such sum as the Board may from time to time determine (not exceeding £• per annum or such sum as the Company in general meeting shall from time to time determine) such sum shall be divided among the Directors in such manner and proportion as they may agree or in default of such determination, equally.

Subject to the provisions of the Act every Director, secretary or other officer of the Company (other than an auditor) is entitled to be indemnified against all costs, charges, losses, damages and liabilities incurred by him in the actual purported exercise or discharge of his/her duties or exercise of his/her powers or otherwise in relation to them.

Unless and until otherwise determined by ordinary resolution of the Company, the number of Directors shall be not less than two nor more than •. There is no [age limit nor any] share qualification for Directors.

Annex
III 4.5

[If relevant, include a description of any conversion or redemption provisions in relation to the securities].

Annex I
21.2.3

[If relevant, include a description of the rights, preferences and restrictions attaching to any other class of existing shares.]

Annex I
21.2.6

[If relevant, include a description of any provisions which would have an effect of delaying, deferring or preventing a change of control of the Company.]

3.3   Other relevant laws and regulations

3.3.1   *Disclosure of interests in shares*

Annex I
21.2.7

A shareholder is required pursuant to sections 198 to 210 of the Act to notify the Company when he acquires or disposes of a material interest in shares in the capital of the Company equal to or in excess of three per cent. of the nominal value of that share capital.

Pursuant to Part IV of the Act and the Articles, the Company is empowered by notice in writing to require any person whom the Company knows, or has reasonable cause to believe to be or, at any time during the three years immediately preceding the date on which the notice is issued, within a reasonable time to disclose to the Company particulars of any interests, rights, agreements or arrangements affecting any of the shares held by that person or in which such other person as aforesaid is interested.

3.3.2   *Takeovers*

As a public limited company incorporated and centrally managed Annex III 4.9 and controlled in the UK, the Company is subject to the City Code on Takeovers and Mergers (the "City Code"). The City Code has not, and does not seek to have, the force of law. It has, however, been acknowledged by the government and other regulatory authorities that those who seek to take advantage of the facilities of the securities market in the United Kingdom should conduct themselves in matters relating to takeovers in accordance with high business standards and so according to the City Code.

Under Rule 9 of the City Code, a person who acquires, whether by a single transaction or by a series of transactions over a period of time, shares which (taken with shares held or acquired or acquired by persons acting in concert with him) carry 30 per cent. or more of the voting rights of a company, such person is normally required to make a general offer to all shareholders of that company at not less than the highest price paid by him or them or any persons acting in concert during the offer period and in the 12 months prior to its commencement.

Further, pursuant to sections 428 to 430F of the Act, where the offeror has acquired or contracted to acquire not less than 90 per cent. in value of the shares to which an offer relates, the offeror may give notice, to the holder of any shares to which the offer relates which the offeror has not acquired or contracted to acquire and which he wishes to acquire and is entitled to so acquire, to acquire those shares on the same terms as the general offer.

3.4   [If relevant, include a description of any arrangements known to the Annex I 18.4 Company, the operation of which may at a subsequent date result in a change of control of the Company.]

4.   Share options

[If relevant, provide details of any arrangements for involving the Annex I 17.3 employees in the capital of the Company.]

4.1   The Board has adopted the Share Option Scheme(s), the principal provisions of which are summarised below.

4.2   The Board also adopted an unapproved scheme in • 200[ ] [details].

5. Directors' and other interests

Annex I
17.2 5.1 The interests of the Directors (including the interests of their spouses and infant children and the interests of any persons connected with them within the meaning of Section 346 of the Act), all of which are beneficial, in the issued share capital of the Company which have been notified to the Company pursuant to Sections 324 and 328 of the Act, as at the date of publication of this document and as they are expected to be immediately following completion of the Placing and Admission are as follows:

Name	As at the date of this document		Following the Placing and Admission	
	Ordinary Shares	*per cent.*	*Ordinary Shares*	*per cent.*
•	•	•	•	• •
•	•	•	•	• •

5.2 As at the date of this document, the Directors are also interested in the following unissued Ordinary Shares pursuant to share options granted by the Company under the Share Option Scheme(s):

Name	Date of Grant	No. of Ordinary Shares	Exercise Price	Earliest Exercise Date	Latest Exercise Date
•	• 200[ ]	•	£•	• 200[ ]	• 200[ ]
•	• 200[ ]	•	£•	• 200[ ]	• 200[ ]
•	• 200[ ]	•	£•	• 200[ ]	• 200[ ]

5.3 Save as disclosed in paragraphs 5.1 and 5.2 above, none of the Directors has any interests in the share capital or loan capital of the Company or any of its subsidiaries nor does any person connected with the Directors (within the meaning of Section 346 of the Act) have any such interests, whether beneficial or non-beneficial.

AIM Sch
2(g)(i) and
(ii) 5.4 In addition to their directorships in the Company, the Directors have held the following directorships and/or been a partner in the following partnerships within the five years prior to the date of this document:

(i) [Name]

Current Directorships/Partnerships   *Past Directorships/Partnerships*

[   ]   [   ]

(ii) [Name]
Current Directorships/Partnerships   *Past Directorships/Partnerships*
[   ]   [   ]
(iii)   [Name]
Current Directorships/Partnerships   *Past Directorships/Partnerships*
[   ]   [   ]
(iv) [Name]
Current Directorships/Partnerships   *Past Directorships/Partnerships*
[   ]   [   ]
(v) [Name]
Current Directorships/Partnerships   *Past Directorships/Partnerships*
[   ]   [   ]

5.5   Save as disclosed in paragraph 5.6 below, no Director:

5.5.1   has any unspent convictions in relation to indictable offences; or   AIM Sch 2(g)(iii)

5.5.2   has been bankrupt or the subject of an individual voluntary arrange-   AIM Sch 2(g)(iv) and
ment, or has had a receiver appointed to any asset of such director;   (vii)
or

5.5.3   has been a director of any company which, while he or she was a   AIM Sch 2(g)(v)
director or within 12 months after he or she ceased to be a director,
had a receiver appointed or went into compulsory liquidation, creditors voluntary liquidation, administration or company voluntary
arrangement, or made any composition or arrangement with its
credits generally or with any class of its creditors; or

5.5.4   has been a partner of any partnership which, while he or she was a   AIM Sch 2(g)(vi)
partner or within 12 months after he or she ceased to be a partner,
went into compulsory liquidation, administration or partnership
voluntary arrangement, or had a receiver appointed to any partnership asset; or

5.5.5   has had any public criticism by statutory or regulatory authorities   AIM Sch 2(g)(viii)
(including recognised professional bodies); or

5.5.6   has been disqualified by a court from acting as a director of a   AIM Sch 2(g)(viii)
company or from acting in the management or conduct of the affairs
of any company.

5.6   [Include details of any unspent convictions etc. if relevant.]

5.7   Save as disclosed in paragraph 5.1 above, and as set out below, the Directors are not aware of any person, directly or indirectly, jointly or severally, who exercises or could exercise control over the Company or who is interested in 3 per cent. or more of the issued share capital of the Company as at the date of the publication of this document and immediately following completion of the Placing and Admission:

Name	As at the date of this document		Following the Placing and Admission	
	Ordinary Shares	per cent.	Ordinary Shares	per cent.
•	•	•	•	•
•	•	•	•	•

5.8   [   ] being the Company's major Shareholders, do not have different voting rights from other Shareholders.

5.9   [If relevant include details of any Director, or member of a Director's family, who has a related financial product referred to the Company's AIM securities or securities being admitted, including the date and terms of the related financial product(s) and the detailed nature of the exposure.]

6.   Directors' service agreements and terms of office

6.1   • has entered into a service agreement with the Company as its chief executive dated • 200[   ] for an initial period of • months and thereafter, subject to termination upon 12 months' notice by either party. The agreement provides for an annual salary of £•, the use of a company car, membership of a private medical scheme, permanent health insurance and life assurance cover. Under the service agreement • may elect for part of [his/her] salary to be paid into a personal pension scheme.

6.2   • has entered into a service agreement with the Company as its finance director dated • 200[   ] for an initial period of • months and thereafter, subject to termination upon 12 months' notice by either party. The agreement provides for an annual salary of £•, the use of a company car, membership of a private medical scheme, permanent health insurance and life assurance cover. Under the service agreement • may elect for part of [his/her] salary to be paid into a personal pension scheme.

6.3   The services of • as non-executive director and Chairman and • and • as non-executive directors are provided under the terms of letters of appointment between them and the Company dated • 200[ ] subject to termination upon at least • months' notice, at an initial fee of £• per annum for • and £• per annum for both • and •.

6.4   Save as set out in paragraphs 6.1, 6.2 and 6.3, above, there are no service agreements in existence between any of the Directors and the Company or any of its subsidiaries providing for benefits upon termination of employment. _{Annex I 16.2}

6.5   Details of the length of time in which the Directors [in the financial period of the Company to • or] who are currently in office and the period of their term of office are set out below:

Name	Commencement of period of office	Date of expiration of term of office
•	• 200[ ]	Annual General Meeting to be held in 200[ ]
•	• 200[ ]	Annual General Meeting to be held in 200[ ]
•	• 200[ ]	Annual General Meeting to be held in 200[ ]
•	• 200[ ]	Annual General Meeting to be held in 200[ ]
•	• 200[ ]	Annual General Meeting to be held in 200[ ]

7.   **Material contracts**

The following contracts, not being contracts entered into in the ordinary course of business, have been entered into by the Company and/or its subsidiaries during the two years preceding the date of this document and are or may be material: _{Annex I 22}

7.1   [Share Purchase Agreement relating to •]

7.2   A nominated adviser and broker agreement dated • 200[ ] between the Company (1), [NOMAD] as nominated adviser [and broker] (2) [and [BRO] as broker (3)] pursuant to which the

291

Company has appointed [NOMAD] to act as nominated adviser [and broker] to the Company [and [BRO] to act as broker to the Company] for the purposes of the AIM Rules for a period of • months commencing on the date of the agreement. The Company has agreed to pay to [NOMAD] a fee of £• per annum [and to [BRO] a fee of £• per annum].

7.3   A placing agreement dated • 200[   ] between the Company (1), the Directors (2) [and] [NOMAD] (3) [and the Selling Shareholders (4)] pursuant to which [NOMAD] has agreed to use its reasonable endeavours to arrange for Placees to subscribe for and/or purchase • Placing Shares at the Placing Price [or itself to subscribe for the Placing Shares at the Placing Price]. The agreement is conditional, *inter alia*, upon Admission taking place on or before • 200[   ] or such later date as [NOMAD] and the Company may agree but in any event not later than • 200[   ]. The Company will pay to [NOMAD] a fee of £• and a commission of • per cent. on the aggregate value of the [New Ordinary/Placing] Shares at the Placing Price. [The Selling Shareholders will pay to [NOMAD] a commission of • per cent. on the aggregate value of the Sale Shares at the Placing Price. The Selling Shareholders have also agreed to pay any stamp duty or stamp duty reserve tax arising on the transfer of the Sale Shares.] The agreement provides for the Company to pay all expenses of and incidental to the Placing and the application for Admission, including the fees and costs of other professional advisers, all costs relating to the Placing, including printing, advertising and distribution charges, the fees of the Registrars and the fees payable to the London Stock Exchange.

[The agreement contains warranties and indemnities given by the Company and the Directors in favour of [NOMAD]. [The agreement contains, *inter alia*, undertakings and warranties given by the Company and the Directors in favour of [NOMAD] as to the accuracy of information contained in this document and other matters relating to the Group and its business and an indemnity from the Company in favour of [NOMAD]].

AIM
Sch 2(f)

Under the terms of the agreement the Directors have agreed not to dispose of any interest in their Ordinary Shares for a period of at least 12 months from the date of Admission and thereafter not to dispose of [any interest in/more than 50 per cent. of] their holding until • months from the date of Admission save in the event of an intervening court order, a takeover offer relating to the Company's share capital becoming or being declared to be unconditional, or the death of the Director.

[NOMAD] may terminate the agreement in specified circumstances prior to Admission, principally in the event of a material breach of the agreement or any of the warranties contained in it, or where any event of omission relating to the Group is, or will be in the opinion of [NOMAD], material in the context of the Placing, or where any change of national or international, financial, monetary, economic, political or market conditions is, or will be in the opinion of [NOMAD], materially adverse to the Company or the successful outcome of the Placing.]

8.   **Taxation**

The following information is given in summary form only and is based on tax legislation as it exists at the present time. The information relates to the tax position of holders of Ordinary Shares in the capital of the Company who are resident or ordinarily resident in the United Kingdom for tax purposes. The statements below do not constitute advice to any Shareholder on his or her personal tax position, and may not apply to certain classes of investor (such as persons carrying on a trade in the United Kingdom or United Kingdom insurance companies).

Annex III 4.11

This is only a summary of the tax reliefs available to investors and should not be construed as constituting advice which a potential investor should obtain from his or her own investment or taxation adviser before subscribing for Ordinary Shares.

Inheritance Tax Relief

Provided a Shareholder has owned shares in a qualifying company for at least two years and certain conditions are met at the time of the transfer, 100 per cent. business property relief is available, which reduces the inheritance tax liability on the transfer to nil.

Venture Capital Trusts

[Include if Company meets requirements of VCT legislation]

The Company has applied for advanced assurance from HM Revenue & Customs of the Company's status as a qualifying VCT investment.

Whilst the Company cannot guarantee to conduct its activities in a way to allow it to attain and maintain status as a qualifying VCT investment, the Directors intend, as far as possible, to do so.

EIS Income Tax Relief

[Include if Company meets requirements of EIS legislation]

An investor subscribing for Ordinary Shares will be entitled to claim income tax relief on amounts subscribed up to a maximum of £150,000 for any given year of assessment at the lower rate of income tax. This is currently 20 per cent. providing, on current rates, a maximum tax saving of £30,000. EIS relief is limited to the amount which reduces the investor's liability to nil.

The qualifying period for holding shares as an EIS investment is three years.

EIS Capital Gains Tax Relief

[Include if Company meets requirements of EIS legislation]

If EIS Income Tax Relief is given and is not withdrawn, any gain accruing to an individual on the first disposal, three or more years after the issue of the Ordinary Shares, is not chargeable to capital gains tax. If a disposal of Ordinary Shares on which EIS Income Tax Relief has been given results in a capital loss, the capital loss is allowable. In calculating the loss, the original amount subscribed by the individual is treated as reduced by the amount of the EIS Income Tax Relief given and not withdrawn.

EIS Capital Gains Deferral Relief

[Include if Company meets requirements of EIS legislation]

A UK resident investor can defer the payment of capital gains tax due (on any asset), by reinvesting the gain arising on the sale of that asset into a subscription of Ordinary Shares. The reinvestment must be made during the period between twelve months prior to the date of the disposal of the asset giving rise to the charge and three years after the disposal date.

Income Tax

Under current United Kingdom taxation legislation, no withholding tax will be deducted from dividends paid by the Company.

Individual Shareholders resident for tax purposes in the United Kingdom should generally be entitled to a tax credit in respect of any dividend received. The amount of this tax credit in respect of dividends paid is currently set at $^1/_9$ of the amount of the dividend. Such an individual Shareholder's liability to United Kingdom income tax is calculated on the aggregate of the dividend and the tax credit which will be regarded as the top slice of the individual's income. The tax credit is therefore currently set at 10 per cent. of the combined amount of the dividend and the tax credit. The tax credit will be available to offset such Shareholder's liability (if any) to income tax on the dividend. The tax credit will discharge the income tax liability of an individual Shareholder who is not liable to income tax at a rate greater than the basic rate. A Shareholder who is liable to income tax at the higher rate (currently 40 per cent.) has further income tax to pay at a rate of 22.5 per cent. of the dividend and related tax credit. The tax credit cannot be reclaimed from HM Revenue & Customs.

With certain exceptions for traders in securities, a holder of Ordinary Shares that is a company resident (for taxation purposes) in the United Kingdom and receives a dividend paid by the Company, will not be subject to tax in respect of the dividend.

Stamp Duty and Stamp Duty Reserve Tax

No United Kingdom stamp duty will be payable on the issue by the Company of Ordinary Shares. Transfers of Ordinary Shares for value will give rise to a liability to pay United Kingdom *ad valorem* stamp duty, or stamp duty reserve tax, at the rate in each case of 50p per £100 of the amount or value of the consideration (rounded up in the case of stamp duty to the nearest £5). Transfers under the CREST system for paperless transfers of shares will generally be liable to stamp duty reserve tax.

Any person who is in any doubt as to his or her tax position or who may be subject to tax in any jurisdiction other than the United Kingdom should consult his or her own professional adviser.

9.   **Premises**

9.1   The Group's principal establishments (all of which [are leasehold and] are used for [ ]) are as follows:

Property	Tenure	Lease expiry date	Annual rent (unless otherwise stated)	Approx. square footage
•	[Leasehold/ Freehold]	•	£•	•
•	Freehold]	•	£•	•

Annex I
8.2

9.2 [The Group's property at [address] is affected by [environmental issues] which affect or may affect the Group's utilisation of that property because [provide reasons why issue affects use].]

10. Working capital

AIM Sch
2(c)

In the opinion of the Directors, having made due and careful enquiry, the working capital available to the Company and the Group, taking into account the net proceeds of the Placing and banking and other facilities, will be sufficient for its present requirements, that is for at least twelve months from the date of Admission.

11. Litigation

Annex I
20.8

There are no, and during the 12 month period prior to the date of this document there have not been any, governmental, legal or arbitration proceedings (including any such proceedings which are pending or threatened of which the Company is aware) which may have, or have had in the recent past, significant effects on the Company's or the Group's financial position or profitability.

12. General

Annex I
6.4 12.1 There are no patents or other intellectual property rights, licences or particular contracts which are of fundamental importance to the Company's business, except as set out in Part I.

Annex III
8.1 12.2 The expenses of the Placing and Admission are estimated to be £•, excluding VAT and are payable by the Company.

AIM Sch
2(h) 12.3 Except for fees payable to the professional advisers whose names are set out on page 257 above or payments to trade suppliers, no person has received any fees, securities in the Company or other benefit to a value of £10,000 or more, whether directly or indirectly, from the Company within the 12 months preceding the application for Admission, or has entered into any contractual arrangement to receive from the Company, directly or indirectly, any such fees, securities or other benefit on or after Admission.

12.4 Save as disclosed in this document, there has been no significant _{Annex I} change in the financial or trading position of the Group since • 200[   ], the date to which its most recent audited accounts have been drawn up.

12.5 [With the exception of any arrangements summarised in paragraph _{Annex I} • of Part III no member of the Group is, nor has been, a party to any transactions with related parties which were material to the Group.]

12.6 Where information has been sourced from a third party, the _{Annex I} Company confirms that this information has been accurately repro- _{Annex III} duced and as far as the Company is aware and is able to ascertain from the information published by that third party, no facts have been omitted which would render the reproduced information inaccurate or misleading.

12.7 The financial information set out in this document does not consti- _{Annex I} tute statutory accounts within the meaning of section 240 of the Act. Statutory accounts have been delivered to the registrar of companies for the Company for the periods ended • 200[   ], • 200[   ] and • 200[   ]. Auditors' reports in respect of each statutory accounts have been made under section 235 of the Act and each such report was an unqualified report and did not contain any statement under section 237(2) or (3) of the Act. [The audited accounts for • 200[   ] [have been refused by the statutory auditors because [   ]/are subject to the qualifications and disclosures set out in Part III in full with full reasons for their being made.]]

12.8 [[Previous auditors] prepared the statutory accounts for the financial _{Annex I} [year/period] ended • 200[   ]. [Previous auditors] resigned/were not re-appointed/were removed on • 200[   ] and were replaced by [Auditors] on • 200[   ] because [insert material reasons]].

12.9 [Auditors] has given and has not withdrawn its written consent to _{Annex I} the inclusion in this document of its Accountants' Reports set out in _{Annex III} Part III and Part IV of this document in the form and context in which they appear and has authorised its Accountants' Reports for the purposes of the AIM Rules. Except for this information in the admission document, no other information has been audited or reviewed by statutory auditors.

12.10 [NOMAD] has given and not withdrawn its written consent to the issue of this document and the references to them in the form and context in which such references are included.

Annex I
24 **13.**   **Documents available for inspection**

[Not mandatory – check with NOMAD whether these are required]

Copies of the following documents may be inspected at the registered office of [NOMAD] during normal business hours on any weekday (Saturdays and public holidays excepted) until the date falling one month after the date of Admission.

13.1   the Memorandum and Articles of Association of the Company;

13.2   the Accountants' Report set out in Part III of this document;

13.3   the Pro Forma Statement of Net Assets as set out in Part IV of this document;

13.4   the rules of the Share Option Scheme(s) referred to in paragraph 4 above;

13.5   the service contracts and non-executive directors' letters of appointment referred to in paragraph 6 above;

13.6   the material contracts referred to in paragraph 7 above; and

13.7   the consent letters referred to in paragraph 12 above.

14.   **Availability of document**

AIM
Rule 20 Copies of this document will be available free of charge to the public at the registered office of [NOMAD] during normal business hours on any weekday (Saturdays and public holidays excepted) until the date falling one month after the date of Admission.

Dated • 200[   ].

AIM REQUIREMENTS

AIM Rules	Where in Admission Document	Rule satisfied or N/A	Notes
Rule 7	Part I and Part V para.7.3	✔	
Rule 20	Part V para.14	✔	
Sch 2(c)	Part V para.10	✔	
Sch 2(d)	Part I	✔	
Sch 2(e)	Front cover	✔	
Sch 2(f)	Part V para. 7.3	✔	
Sch 2(g)(i)	Part 1	✔	
Sch 2(g)(ii)	Part V para. 5.4	✔	
Sch 2(g)(iii)	Part V paras. 5.5.1 and 5.6	✔	
Sch 2(g)(iv)	Part V paras. 5.5.2 and 5.6	✔	
Sch 2(g)(v)	Part V paras. 5.5.3 and 5.6	✔	
Sch 2(g)(vi)	Part V paras. 5.5.4 and 5.6	✔	
Sch 2(g)(vii)	Part V paras. 5.5.2, 5.5.4 and 5.6.5	✔	
Sch 2(g)(viii)	Part V paras. 5.5.5 and 5.6	✔	
Sch 2(h)	Part V para. 12.3	✔	
Sch 2(i)	Part V para. 5.9	✔	
Sch 2(j)	Part I	✔	
Sch 2(k)	Part I and throughout	✔	
Annex I, 1.1	Front cover and page 257	✔	
Annex I, 1.2	Front cover, page 269 and page 273	✔	
Annex I, 2.1	Page 257	✔	
Annex I, 2.2	Part V para. 12.8	✔	
Annex I, 4	Part II	✔	
Annex I, 5.1.1	Front cover	✔	
Annex I, 5.1.2	Front cover	✔	
Annex I, 5.1.3	Part V para. 1.1	✔	

AIM Rules	Where in Admission Document	Rule satisfied or N/A	Notes
Annex I, 5.1.4	Part V paras. 1.1, 1.3	✔	
Annex I, 5.1.5	Part I	✔	
Annex I, 5.2.1	Part III	✔	
Annex I, 5.2.2	Part III	✔	
Annex I, 5.2.3	Part III	✔	
Annex I, 6.1.1	Part I	✔	
Annex I, 6.1.2	Part I	✔	
Annex I, 6.4	Part I and Part V para. 12.1	✔	
Annex I, 6.5	Part I	✔	
Annex I, 7.1	Part V para. 1.2	✔	
Annex I, 7.2	Part V para. 1.2	✔	
Annex I, 8.2	Part V para. 9.2	✔	
Annex I, 12.1	Part I	✔	
Annex I, 12.2	Part I	✔	
Annex I, 16.1	Part V para. 6	✔	
Annex I, 16.2	Part V paras. 6.1, 6.2, 6.3 and 6.4	✔	
Annex I, 16.4	Part I	✔	
Annex I, 17.1	Part I	✔	
Annex I, 17.2	Part V para. 5.1	✔	
Annex I, 17.3	Part V para. 4.1 and 4.2	✔	
Annex I, 18.1	Part V paras. 5.1 and 5.7	✔	
Annex I, 18.2	Part V para. 5.8	✔	
Annex I, 18.3	Part V para. 5.7	✔	
Annex I, 18.4	Part V para. 3.4	✔	
Annex I, 19	Part III	✔	
Annex I, 20.1	Part III	✔	
Annex I, 20.1(a)	Part III	✔	
Annex I, 20.1(b)	Part III	✔	

AIM Rules	Where in Admission Document	Rule satisfied or N/A	Notes
Annex I, 20.1(c)	Part III	✔	
Annex I, 20.1(d)	Part III	✔	
Annex I, 20.1(e)	Part III	✔	
Annex I, 20.3	Part III	✔	
Annex I, 20.4.1	Part V para. 12.7	✔	
Annex I, 20.4.2	Part V para. 12.9	✔	
Annex I, 20.4.3	Part III	✔	
Annex I, 20.5.1	Part III	✔	
Annex I, 20.6.1	Part III	✔	
Annex I, 20.6.2	Part III	✔	
Annex I, 20.7	Part I	✔	
Annex I, 20.7.1	Part I and Part III	✔	
Annex I, 20.8	Part V, para. 11	✔	
Annex I, 20.9	Part V para. 12.4	✔	
Annex I, 21.1.1(a)	Part V para. 2.2	✔	
Annex I, 21.1.1(b)	Part V para. 2.2	✔	
Annex I, 21.1.1(c)	Part V para. 2.2	✔	
Annex I, 21.1.1(d)	Part V para. 2.2	✔	
Annex I, 21.1.2	Part V para. 2.6	N/A	
Annex I, 21.1.3	Part V para. 2.7	✔	
Annex I, 21.1.4	Part V para. 2.5	✔	
Annex I, 21.1.5	Part V para. 2.8	N/A	
Annex I, 21.1.6	Part V paras. 2.3 and 5.2	✔	
Annex I, 21.1.7	Part V para. 2.1	✔	
Annex I, 21.2.1	Part V para. 3	✔	
Annex I, 21.2.2	Part V para. 3.2.10	✔	
Annex I, 21.2.3	Part V para. 3.2	✔	
Annex I, 21.2.4	Part V para. 3.2.2	✔	

AIM Rules	Where in Admission Document	Rule satisfied or N/A	Notes
Annex I, 21.2.5	Part V para. 3.2.9	✔	
Annex I, 21.2.6	Part V para. 3.2	N/A	
Annex I, 21.2.7	Part V para. 3.3.1	✔	
Annex I, 21.2.8	Part V para. 3.2.3	N/A	
Annex I, 22	Part V para. 7	✔	
Annex I, 23.1	Part V para. 12.9	✔	
Annex I, 23.2	Part V para. 12.6	N/A	
Annex I, 25.1	Part III	✔	
Annex III, 1.1	Front cover	✔	
Annex III, 1.2	Front cover	✔	
Annex III, 2.1	Part II	✔	
Annex III, 3.4	Part I	✔	
Annex III, 4.1	Front cover and Part V para. 1.3	✔	
Annex III, 4.2	Part V para. 1.1	✔	
Annex III, 4.3	Part I and Page 257	✔	
Annex III, 4.4	Front cover	✔	
Annex III, 4.5 (dividend)	Part V para. 3	✔	
Annex III, 4.5 (vote)	Part V para. 3	✔	
Annex III, 4.6	Part V para. 2.1	✔	
Annex III, 4.7	Part I	✔	
Annex III, 4.8	Part V para. 3.2.4	✔	
Annex III, 4.9	Part V para. 3.3.2	✔	
Annex III, 4.10	Part III para. 2.9	✔	
Annex III, 4.11	Part V para. 8	✔	
Annex III, 7.1	Front cover, page 257 Part V para. 7.2	✔	
Annex III, 7.2	Definitions and Part I	✔	

AIM Rules	Where in Admission Document	Rule satisfied or N/A	Notes
Annex III, 7.3	Part I	✔	
Annex III, 8.1	Part V para. 12.2	✔	
Annex III, 9.1	Placing Statistics	✔	
Annex III, 9.2	Placing Statistics	✔	
Annex III, 10.1	Page 257	✔	
Annex III, 10.2	Part V para. 12.6	✔	
Annex III, 10.3	Part V para. 12.9 and page 257	✔	
Annex III, 10.4	Part V para. 12.6	N/A	

Appendix 2

Specimen AIM Documents List

Specimen AIM Documents List

Abbreviations:

The Company	–	Company
Nominated Adviser	–	Nomad
Company Solicitors	–	CoSols
Solicitors to the Issue	–	IssueSols
Reporting Accountants	–	Rep Accts
AIM Admission Document/Prospectus	–	Admission Document
Registrars	–	Reg
Public Relations	–	PR
Broker	–	Broker
Security Printers	–	Printers

References are to AIM Rules unless otherwise stated

Document	Responsibility
A. Administrative and preliminary documents	
1. List of parties	Nomad
2. Timetable	Nomad
3. List of documents	Nomad
4. Estimate of expenses	Nomad
5. Nominated Adviser and Broker engagement letter	Nomad/ Company/CoSols
6. Solicitor engagement letter	CoSol/IssueSols
7. Accountant engagement letter	Rep Accts/ Nomad/CoSols
8. Printer engagement letter	Printers
9. Directors' declaration forms	Company
10. Memorandum on directors' responsibilities	CoSols
11. Tax clearance	Rep Accts
12. Corporate reorganisation memorandum	CoSols
B. Principal public documents	
13. Admission Document	All parties
14. Share certificate	Company/Reg
15. Documents on display [not required by AIM Rules unless a prospectus]	CoSols – see K below

Document	Responsibility
C. Documents related to the placing	
16. Placing agreement	IssueSols/Broker
17. Placing letters	Broker
18. Presentation slides	Company/Broker
D. Press announcements and publicity	
19. A 10 day announcement to AIM (Rule 2 and Schedule 1)	PR/Nomad
20. Announcement of commencement of dealings	PR/Nomad
E. Due diligence	
21. Legal due diligence report	CoSols
22. 'Long form' – financial due diligence report	Rep Accts
23. Other commercial due diligence report(s)	Company/Expert
F. Supporting documents	
24. Directors' powers of attorney and responsibility letters	CoSols
25. Directors' service contracts/appointment letters	CoSols
26. Share option schemes	CoSols
27. Verification notes (for Admission Document and presentation slides)	CoSols
28. EGM notice and minutes	CoSols
29. Draft 'pathfinder' Admission Document board minutes	CoSols
30. Draft completion board minutes	CoSols
31. Working capital report/memorandum	Company
32. Tax Clearances from Revenue	Rep Accts
33. Registrar's agreement	Reg
34. CREST application form	Company/Broker
35. Terms of reference for audit, remuneration and nomination committees, list of matters specifically reserved for decision of full board and share dealing code	Company/Co Sols
36. Irrevocable undertakings	CoSols
37. Lock-in agreement (Rule 7)	CoSols/Issue Sols
38. Nomad's declaration (Rule 39)	Nomad
G. Supporting correspondence/comfort letters	
39. Comfort letter from the directors to Nomad on compliance with AIM Rules (re Nomad Declaration) (Rule 31, Rule 39 & Schedule 6)	Issue Sols

Document	Responsibility
40. Comfort letter from the directors to Nomad/Broker confirming understanding of their obligations (Rule 31, Rule 39 & Schedule 6)	Issue Sols
41. Comfort letter from the directors to Nomad/Broker confirming working capital statement (Schedule 2 paragraph (c))	Issue Sols
42. Comfort letters from CoSols and Reporting Accountants to Nomad/Broker on compliance with AIM Rules (Rule 39)	CoSols/Rep Accts
43. Comfort letter from Reporting Accountants on working capital report/memorandum	Rep Accts
44. Comfort letter from Reporting Accountants on extraction of financial information	Rep Accts
45. Comfort letter from Reporting Accountants on no material adverse change	Rep Accts
46. Comfort letter from Reporting Accountants giving comfort on status of tax computations/clearances	Rep Accts
47. Comfort letter from Reporting Accountants on taxation information	Rep Accts
48. Comfort letter from Reporting Accountants on pro forma financial information	Rep Accts
49. Comfort letter from Reporting Accountants on any illustrative financial projections in Admission Document	Rep Accts
H. Consent and approvals	
50. AIM to provide letter confirming the shares are admitted (Dealing Notice issued pursuant to Rule 6)	AIM
51. Consent letter re issue of Admission Document from Nomad/Broker	Nomad/Broker
52. Consent letter re issue of Admission Document from the Reporting Accountants	Rep Accts
53. Consent letters from any other Expert or originator of any source material quoted in Admission Document	CoSols
I. Documents to be submitted to Registrar of Companies	
54. Re-registration to PLC/revised constitutional documents and change of name if appropriate	CoSols

Document	Responsibility
J. **Documents to be submitted to AIM (Rule 5 and Guidance Notes to Rule 5)**	
55. Company AIM application form	Nomad
56. Nomad declaration form	Nomad
57. Copy of Company minutes unconditionally allotting any securities issued on Admission	Company
58. Fee	Company
59. Electronic version of the Admission Document	Nomad/Printers
K. **Documents to be on display [Not required by AIM Rules unless Admission Document constitutes a prospectus]**	
60. Memorandum and Articles of Association	CoSols
61. Historical financial information	Rep Accts/ Company
62. Accountants' report and report on pro forma financial information	Rep Accts
63. Expert reports/statements	CoSols
64. Nomad/Broker and accountants consent letters	Nomad/Broker/ Rep Accts
65. Service agreements for directors	CoSols
66. Material contracts	CoSols
67. Rules of share option schemes/long term incentive plans	CoSols
68. Any other document referred to in Admission Document	CoSols

Appendix 3

AIM Admission Timetable

Specimen AIM Flotation Timetable

Abbreviations:

The Company	=	Company
Nominated Adviser	=	Nomad
Company Solicitors	=	CoSols
Solicitors to the Issue	=	IssueSols
Reporting accountants	=	Rep Accts
Registrars	=	Reg
Public Relations	=	PR
Broker	=	Broker
Security Printers	=	Printers

Date	Event	Responsibility
Week 1		
	Initial all parties meeting	All
	Provisional timetable circulated	Nomad
	List of parties circulated	Nomad
	List of documents circulated	CoSols
	Directors' cards circulated to board	CoSols
	Engagement letters with Rep Accts, CoSols, Broker and Nomad circulated in particular agreeing scope of long form report and legal due diligence report	Nomad
Week 2		
	Directors' cards completed and returned to Nomad	Directors
	Draft power of attorney and directors' responsibility statement circulated	CoSols
	Draft memorandum on directors' responsibilities circulated	CoSols
	Long form report and legal due diligence report questionnaires circulated	Rep Accts/ CoSols

Date	Event	Responsibility
	Decide dates for organising EGM for group reorganisation, authority to allot shares and disapply pre-emption rights, share option requirements, adopt new articles (if necessary)	CoSols
	Consult PR on proposed programme of presentations and announcements	Company/ Broker
	Determine tax clearance issues	CoSols/Rep Accts
	Confirm dates for drafts of long form report, working capital memorandum, report on profit forecast, memorandum on financial reporting procedures	Rep Accts/ Company
	Finalise timetable and sign engagement letters	Company
	Commence work on working capital report	Company
	Commence work on long form report	Rep Accts
	Commence work on legal due diligence report	CoSols
	Corporate governance terms of reference and share dealing code circulated	CoSols
	First draft share option schemes circulated	CoSols
	New memorandum and articles of association circulated	CoSols
	Directors' service agreements circulated	CoSols
Week 3		
	EIS/VCT clearance sought	Rep Accts
	Comments on memorandum on directors' responsibilities to CoSols together with comments on power of attorney and directors' responsibility statement	Company/ IssueSols
	First draft Admission Document circulated	Nomad

Date	Event	Responsibility
	First draft placing agreement circulated	IssueSols
	First draft placing letter circulated	Broker
	First draft Nomad/Broker agreements circulated	IssueSols
	First draft "intention to float" announcement circulated	Nomad
	Comments on first draft Admission Document to Nomad	All
	Notice of EGM to shareholders to approve new memorandum and articles, etc.	Company/ CoSols
Week 4		
	Second draft Admission Document circulated including short form report and legal 'statutory and general information'	Nomad
	Audit to date completed	Rep Accts
	First rehearsal of management presentation to institutions and press	Company/ Broker
	Draft estimate of expenses available	Company
	Comments on first draft placing agreement	CoSols
	Comments on second draft Admission Document to Nomad	All
Week 5		
	Circulate directors' pack including draft pathfinder board minutes, final responsibility letters, final powers of attorney, memorandum on directors' responsibilities	CoSols
	Third draft Admission Document circulated	Nomad
	First draft working capital report available	Company/Rep Accts

Date	Event	Responsibility
	First draft long form report circulated	Rep Accts
	First draft legal due diligence report circulated	CoSols
	First draft institutional presentation circulated	Company/ Broker
	First draft verification notes available	CoSols
	Presentation to Broker salesmen	Company/ Broker/PR
	Comments on first draft verification notes	IssueSols
	Progress meeting to include: 1) drafting; 2) verification; 3) final estimate of expenses 4) working capital	All
	First draft consent and comfort letters circulated	CoSols/ IssueSols/Rep Accts
Week 6		
	Fourth draft Admission Document circulated	Nomad
	Second draft placing agreement circulated	IssueSols
	Institutional meetings start to be arranged	Broker
	Comments on consent and comfort letters provided	CoSols/ IssueSols RepAccts
	Printers appointed	Nomad
	Registrars appointed	Company
	Comments on fourth draft Admission Document (drafting meeting as requested/ necessary)	All parties
	Circulate First Printers Proof Admission Document	Printers

Date	Event	Responsibility
	Comments to IssueSols on second draft placing agreement	CoSols
	Verification notes in final form	CoSols
	Second draft long form report available	Rep Accts
	Meeting at Nomad to discuss any final issues on working capital and long form reports	Nomad
Week 7		
	Board meeting to approve pathfinder Admission Document, presentation slides and verification notes and documents in final/near final draft form	All parties
	AIM application forms and supporting letters	Nomad
	Consent letters	Nomad/Rep Accts
	Comfort letters	CoSols/ IssueSols
	CREST application	Broker
	Press release/intention to float announcement	PR
	Nomad/Broker agreement	Nomad
	Placing agreement	IssueSols
	Placing letter	Broker
	Memorandum on directors' responsibilities	CoSols
	Directors' service agreements	CoSols
	Non executives' letter of appointment	CoSols
	Registrars' agreement	Reg
	Draft share certificate	Reg
	Estimate of expenses	Nomad
	Legal due diligence report	CoSols
	Powers of attorney	CoSols

Date	Event	Responsibility
	Directors' responsibility statements	CoSols
	Report on financial reporting procedures	Rep Accts
	Long and short form reports	Rep Accts
	Pro forma financial information	Rep Accts
	Profit forecast (if applicable)	Rep Accts
	Report on working capital	Rep Accts
	Share option scheme	CoSols
	EGM to adopt new memorandum and articles, etc.	Company

Week 8/9

	Institutional marketing commences	Company/ Broker

Week 10

	Institutional marketing completed	Company/ Broker
	Informal pricing meeting to determine price range for discussions with institutions	Company/ Broker
	Any final minor amendments to pathfinder Admission Document	Nomad/ CoSols/Rep Accts
	10 day notice submitted to Stock Exchange	Nomad
	Board meeting to confirm issue price, approve Admission Document as 'P' proof, approve service contracts and letters of appointment, approve verification notes, adopt working capital statement and profit forecast, approve placing agreement and ancilliary documents, approve estimate of expenses, approve press announcement, approve number of shares subject to placing, approve share option scheme(s) and adopt terms of reference and share dealing code	All

Date	Event	Responsibility
	Agree pricing	Company/Broker
	Meeting with Press/Press release	Company/PR
	Bulk print of 'P' proof Admission Document	Printers
	Placing letters despatched to Placees with 'P' proof Admission Document	Broker
	Placing letters received back by Broker	Broker
	10 am completion meeting to approve all documents, sign the placing agreement, provisionally and conditionally allot new shares, appoint a board committee to deal with all matters connected with the admission, including despatch of share certificates to placees as necessary after Admission; all documentation held in escrow overnight	Company/CoSols
	Directors responsibility statement and powers of attorney signed	Company
	Approve announcement of flotation	Company
	Approve and sign off Admission Document	Company
	Bulk print admission document overnight	Printers
	Rep Accts report signed	Rep Accts
	Approve and sign all necessary documentation	All

Week 11

Date	Event	Responsibility
	IMPACT DAY	
	Flotation announcement released	PR
	Placing agreement and other documents released from escrow	Broker
	Documents on display (if applicable)	CoSols
	Three day information submitted to AIM: company application form, nomad's declaration, cheque for exchange fee, electronic copy of Admission Document, and evidence of allotment of new shares	Nomad

Date	Event	Responsibility
Week 12		
	First day of dealings on AIM	Company
	Announcement from Stock Exchange	Stock Exchange
	CREST member accounts credited	Reg
	Company to receive placing monies	Nomad
	Share certificates despatched	Reg

Appendix 4

Specimen AIM Completion Board Minutes

Specimen AIM Completion Board Minutes

CONAME PLC

(the "Company")

Minutes of a meeting of [a Committee of] the Board of Directors of the Company [duly constituted by a meeting of the Board of Directors held on [   ] 200[   ]] held at [   ] on [   ] 200[   ] at [   ] am/pm.

Present: [   ]   (in the Chair)
                    [   ]
                    [   ]
                    [   ]

In Attendance: [   ]
                    [   ]
                    [   ]

---

1. **QUORUM, NOTICE, DECLARATION OF INTERESTS & PREVIOUS MEETING**

    It was noted that due notice had been given of the matters to be proposed at the meeting and that a quorum was present. Mr [   ] took the Chair.

    Pursuant to section 317 of the Companies Act 1985 and the Articles of Association of the Company each of the Directors declared his interest in all matters the subject of the meeting. [Having done so, it was noted that they could each vote on and be counted in the quorum on the business transacted.]

    [The minutes of the meeting of the Board held on [   ] 200[   ] were tabled and IT WAS RESOLVED that they be signed by the Chairman as a true and accurate record of the matters discussed at that meeting.]

2. **PURPOSE OF MEETING**

    The Chairman explained that the meeting had been convened to deal with the final formalities required in connection with the proposed placing ("Placing") of [   ] new ordinary shares of [   ]p each in the capital of the Company ("Ordinary Shares") at [   ]p per share to be made by [Broker Limited] ("Broker") on behalf of the Company [and certain selling shareholders ("Vendors")], and with the admission ("Admission") of the whole of the share capital of the Company, issued and to be issued, to trading on the AIM Market of the London Stock Exchange ("AIM") (all such matters being collectively referred to as the "Proposals"). It was noted that [Nomad Limited] ("Nomad") had agreed to act as the Company's nominated adviser as required by the AIM Rules.

The response to date of the issue of the placing letters to institutional investors ("Placing Letter") with the "P" Proof Admission Document by Broker was reported to the meeting.

3.   **DOCUMENTS TABLED**

In connection with the Proposals the following documents were tabled to the meeting:

3.1.   a final proof (dated [   ] 200[ ]) of the admission document ("Admission Document") as required by the AIM Rules to be published by the Company in connection with the Placing and Admission;

3.2.   verification notes to be signed by the Directors in respect of the contents of the Admission Document ("Verification Notes"), together with the annexures thereto;

3.3.   a legal due diligence report by [   ] ("CoSols");

3.4.   responsibility statements and powers of attorney signed by each of the Directors (respectively "Responsibility Statements" and "Powers of Attorney");

3.5.   a letter addressed to Nomad [and Broker] to be signed by the Directors giving comfort in respect of the contents of the Admission Document ("Responsibility Letter");

3.6.   a letter addressed to Nomad [and Broker] to be signed by the Directors confirming the sufficiency of working capital;

3.7.   the formal application to be signed by the Company for the purposes of Admission ("Application") and the form of declaration to be signed by Nomad required by the London Stock Exchange ("Nomad Declaration");

3.8.   a letter from the Directors to Nomad confirming that they have had their responsibilities as directors of a company admitted to trading on AIM explained to them and that, having made due and careful enquiry, they have established procedures which provide a reasonable basis for them to make proper judgements as to the financial position and prospects of the Company and its subsidiaries ("Nomad Comfort Letter");

3.9.   a memorandum prepared by CoSols concerning the responsibilities of the Directors in connection with the Placing and Admission ("CoSols Memorandum");

3.10.   copy declarations [and supplementary declarations] relating to the Directors previously delivered to Broker and Nomad;

3.11.   letters from [   ] ("Reporting Accountants") to the Company giving comfort in respect of certain statements relating to taxation and certain financial information contained in the Admission Document;

3.12.   a long form financial report prepared by Reporting Accountants relating to the Company and its subsidiaries, together with a letter to Reporting Accountants relating thereto;

3.13.   the short form accountants' report(s) by Reporting Accountants relating to the Company and its subsidiaries the text of which is to be reproduced in the Admission Document and the report on the pro forma financial information also to be reproduced in the Admission Document;

3.14.   [a copy of the illustrative financial projections for the Company for the three financial periods ending [   ] 200[   ] ("Projections"), together with a letter from Reporting Accountants giving comfort in respect of the calculation of the Projections, the text of which is to be reproduced in the Admission Document;]

3.15.   the cash flow projections dated [   ] 200[   ] of the Company and its subsidiaries for the period to [   ] 200[   ] ("Cash Flow Projections"), together with a report thereon prepared by Reporting Accountants and reviewing the working capital statement in the Admission Document ("Working Capital Report");

3.16.   consent letters from Reporting Accountants, Nomad and Broker;

3.17.   letters from CoSols and Reporting Accountants to Nomad and [Broker] concerning the contents of the Admission Document;

3.18.   an engrossment of a placing agreement to be entered into between the Company (1), the Directors (2), Nomad (3) [and] Broker (4) [and the Vendor(s)] ("Placing Agreement");

3.19.   the Placing Letter;

3.20.   engrossments of service agreements to be entered into between the Company and each of Mr [   ] and Mr [   ] ("Service Agreements"), together with letters setting out arrangements as to the payment of bonuses to them;

3.21.   letters of appointment relating to the appointment of each of [   ] and [   ] as non-executive directors of the Company (the "Appointment Letters");

3.22.   [certificates of title prepared by CoSols in respect of the Group's premises at [   ] and [   ] and by Messrs [   ], solicitors, in respect of the Group's premises at [   ]];

3.23.   an agreement to be entered into by the Company and [   ] concerning the provision of services by [   ] as registrars to the Company ("Registrars Agreement");

3.24.   a specimen share certificate;

3.25.   an application prepared by Broker in relation to CREST;

3.26.   draft rules of HM Revenue & Customs Approved Share Option Scheme, the Unapproved Share Option Scheme and the Employee (Savings Related) Share Option Scheme (together the "Share Option Schemes") each proposed to be adopted by the Company;

3.27.   draft terms of reference for proposed remuneration and audit committees, a list of matters specifically reserved for the decision of the full board and a draft code for all directors and employees relating to the proposed rules for dealing in the Ordinary Shares ("Share Dealing Code");

3.28. an engrossment of an option agreement proposed to be entered into by the Company in favour of [   ] ("[   ] Option Agreement");

3.29. copies of letters from the HM Revenue & Customs granting clearance pursuant to section 703 of the Income and Corporation Taxes Act 1988 and section 137 of the Taxation of Capital Gains Act 1992;

3.30. a draft press announcement concerning the Proposals ("Press Announcement"); and

3.31. an estimate of the expenses relating to the Proposals ("Estimate of Expenses").

4. THE PLACING

The Chairman reminded the meeting that the Company was proposing to raise approximately £[   ] million net of expenses under the Placing. The funds raised would be used to [   ], as described in the Admission Document, and also to [   ].

The Placing would comprise [   ] Ordinary Shares at [   ]p per share. It was reported that Broker had agreed to place those shares with institutional and other investors. [The Placing would include [   ] Ordinary Shares being sold by the Vendors, at the placing price of [   ]p per share. As a director and a Vendor, Mr. [   ], in accordance with section 317 of the Companies Act 1985, specifically declared his interest in the business of this meeting to that extent].

The Placing would be conditional upon, inter alia, Admission occurring on or before [   ] 200[   ] (or such later date as Nomad, Broker and the Company agreed, but in any event not later than [   ] 200[   ]).

5. PLACING AGREEMENT

The attention of the meeting was then drawn to the terms of the Placing Agreement and in particular to the following:

5.1. the conditions to which Nomad and Broker's obligations under the terms of the Placing Agreement were subject, including Admission taking place on or before [   ] 200[   ], (or such later date as

Nomad, Broker and the Company may agree) but in any event not later than [   ] 200[   ];

5.2.   the fees and commissions to be paid to Nomad and Broker as set out in clause [   ] of the Placing Agreement;

5.3.   the warranties and undertakings to be given to Nomad and Broker by the Company and the Directors pursuant to clause [   ] of the Placing Agreement;

5.4.   the indemnities to be given by the Company to Nomad and Broker and their respective officers and agents pursuant to clause [   ] of the Placing Agreement;

5.5.   the events which would entitle Nomad and Broker to terminate the Placing Agreement prior to Admission as set out in clause [   ] of the Placing Agreement;

5.6.   the restrictive covenants imposed on the executive Directors by clause [   ] of the Placing Agreement;

5.7.   the Tax Covenant contained in schedule [   ] to the Placing Agreement to be entered into by the executive Directors; and

5.8.   the undertaking from each of the Directors not to, and to procure that none of their connected persons will, dispose of any interest in Ordinary Shares in the Company for a period of [twelve] months after Admission and that no disposals will be made otherwise than through [Broker] (for so long as it remains broker).

6.   SHARE OPTIONS

The rules of the Share Option Schemes were considered, and it was noted that they would be limited to 10 per cent of the Company's issued share capital from time to time. It was noted that the rules of the approved scheme and of the SAYE scheme had previously been submitted to the HM Revenue & Customs for informal approval. It was reported that it was intended to grant options under the Approved Scheme as soon as formal approval had been obtained from the HM Revenue & Customs, and that, subject to the adoption of the Share Option Schemes in general meeting, it was proposed to grant options under the Unapproved Scheme to subscribe for [   ] Ordinary Shares at [   ]p per share and to grant

options under the Approved Scheme for [   ] Ordinary
Shares at [   ] per share.

IT WAS RESOLVED that the Share Option Schemes be and they are
hereby approved for consideration at the Extraordinary General
Meeting referred to in minute 7 below.

IT WAS RESOLVED that, subject to adoption by the Company in
Extraordinary General Meeting of the Unapproved Scheme, the
following options be and they hereby are granted under the
Unapproved Scheme (to take effect in accordance with the
Unapproved Scheme Rules), it being noted that no performance
conditions were attached to those options, and the Directors and
Secretary be and they hereby are instructed to execute and issue the
Option Certificates for those options:

Name and address of Option Holder	Number of Ordinary Shares subject to Option	Price per share	Total Subscription Price payable
[ ]	[ ]	[ ]p	£[ ]
[ ]	[ ]	[ ]p	£[ ]
[ ]	[ ]	[ ]p	£[ ]

The terms of the [   ] Option Agreement were considered
and IT WAS RESOLVED that it be and it is hereby approved and
executed on behalf of the Company, and that the Company hereby
grants to [   ] the option to subscribe for up to [   ]
Ordinary Shares in the capital of the Company at [   ]p per share,
on the terms of the [   ] Option Agreement.

7. EXTRAORDINARY GENERAL MEETING

As part of the arrangements necessary to implement the Proposals it
was explained that it was necessary for the Company to:

7.1.   increase the authorised share capital of the Company from £[   ]
to £[   ] by the creation of [   ] new Ordinary Shares;

7.2.   grant authority to the Directors pursuant to section 80 of the
Companies Act 1985 to allot relevant securities up to an aggregate
nominal amount of £[   ]; and

7.3. empower the Directors to allot equity securities up to an aggregate nominal amount of £[ ] as if section 89 of the Companies Act 1985 did not apply to such allotment.

At the same time, the Chairman reported that it was proposed that the Company adopt the Share Option Schemes, each to be governed by the draft rules tabled to the meeting.

Accordingly, there was tabled to the meeting a notice convening an Extraordinary General Meeting of the Company to pass resolutions necessary to carry into effect the above matters together with a form of consent to the Extraordinary General Meeting being held on short notice to be signed by or on behalf of the holders of all existing issued Ordinary Shares in the Company. Following consideration of the notice IT WAS RESOLVED that the same be approved and dispatched to the members and that, subject to the consent to the Extraordinary General Meeting being held on short notice being duly given, the Extraordinary General Meeting be held forthwith.

The meeting adjourned at [ ] pm.

The meeting resumed at [ ] pm and it was reported that the Extraordinary General Meeting had been duly convened and held (the necessary consents to the Extraordinary General Meeting being held on short notice having been obtained) and the resolutions set out in the notice had been duly passed.

8. APPOINTMENT OF REGISTRARS

IT WAS RESOLVED that [ ] be and they are hereby appointed as Registrars to the Company, upon the terms of the Registrars' Agreement.

9. WORKING CAPITAL

The Cash Flow Projections were carefully considered. It was noted that they had been reviewed by Reporting Accountants and discussed with Nomad and Broker, and the contents of the Working Capital Report were carefully considered. IT WAS RESOLVED that the representation letters to Reporting Accountants in connection with the working capital statement and the letter to Nomad and Broker on working capital be and they are hereby approved and that they be signed by the Managing Director and the Finance Director.

It was noted that the working capital statement is being made in respect of the [   ] month period ending [   ] 200[   ].

IT WAS RESOLVED that the Cash Flow Projections be adopted and that it is the opinion of the Company, having made due and careful enquiry, that, from the time of Admission, the working capital of the Group is sufficient for its present requirements, that is, for at least the next twelve months.

10.   ILLUSTRATIVE FINANCIAL PROJECTIONS

[The Projections were carefully considered, together with the assumptions relating thereto. It was noted that they had been reviewed by Reporting Accountants and discussed with Nomad and Broker, and the contents of the comfort letter by Reporting Accountants upon the Projections was carefully considered. It was noted that the Directors were responsible for the Projections. The Directors confirmed that they had been prepared after due and careful enquiry and that there were no assumptions relevant or material to the Projections which ought to be considered apart from those set out in the Projections and reproduced in the Admission Document. IT WAS RESOLVED that the representation letter to Reporting Accountants in connection with the Projections be and it is hereby approved and that it be signed by the Managing Director and the Finance Director.

IT WAS RESOLVED that the Projections be and they are hereby approved and adopted.]

11.   ACCOUNTANTS REPORTS

The accountants' reports were carefully considered. The Directors confirmed that they had provided all relevant information to Reporting Accountants in the preparation of them and that they were not aware of anything incorrect in, or inconsistent with, such reports. IT WAS RESOLVED that the representation letters to Reporting Accountants in connection with the long form report and the accountants reports be and they are hereby approved and that they be signed by the Managing Director and the Finance Director.

IT WAS RESOLVED that the accountants' reports be and they are hereby approved and adopted.

12. REMUNERATION AND AUDIT COMMITTEES

It was noted that in accordance with the CoSols Memorandum on aspects of corporate governance, which had been circulated to the Board by CoSols, it was appropriate that a remuneration and an audit committee be established under defined terms of reference and that a formal list of matters specifically reserved for the decision of the full Board be adopted. Accordingly, the terms of reference for the remuneration and audit committees and the list of matters specifically reserved for the decision of the full Board were considered and noted. IT WAS RESOLVED that the terms of reference and the list of matters specifically reserved for the decision of the full Board be and they are hereby adopted, and that, pursuant to article [   ] of the Company's Articles of Association, a remuneration committee and an audit committee be established, and that the non-executive Directors be and they are hereby appointed as members of both committees, [   ] to act as chairman of both committees.

13. SHARE DEALING CODE

It was noted that in accordance with the CoSols Memorandum (which dealt with aspects of corporate governance) which had been circulated to the Board by CoSols, it was appropriate that a share dealing code be adopted incorporating the requirements under rules 17 and 21 of the AIM Rules.

The provisions of the Share Dealing Code were considered and noted and IT WAS RESOLVED that the Share Dealing Code be and is hereby adopted. The Company Secretary was instructed to ensure that all staff received a copy of the Share Dealing Code.

14. SERVICE AGREEMENTS AND APPOINTMENT LETTERS

The Directors proceeded to consider the terms of the Service Agreements, Mr [   ] and Mr [   ] each declaring their interests in relation to them. It was noted that each Service Agreement was subject to twelve month's notice of termination (not to be given before [   ] 200[ ] in the case of Mr [   ]). Mr [   ] and Mr [   ] were entitled to annual salaries of respectively £[   ] and £[   ] and were each entitled to the use of a company car, membership of a private medical scheme for the Director and his spouse and dependant children, permanent health insurance, life assurance and critical life cover. In addition, pension contributions are to be payable to Mr [   ] and Mr [   ] of, respectively, £[   ] per month and [   ] per cent. of salary. Each Service Agreement contained restrictive covenants, including post-termination non-competition covenants.

The terms of the bonus arrangement letters were also considered, and it was noted that the bonuses were limited to a maximum of £[   ] for Mr [   ] and £[   ] for Mr [   ], and that they related to the achievement of the Projections set out in the Admission Document].

The Appointment Letters were then considered and it was noted that they were subject to termination upon twelve months written notice from either party. Each would be entitled to an initial annual fee of £[   ] payable [monthly] in arrears.

15.   APPROVAL OF THE ADMISSION DOCUMENT

The Directors were then reminded, in relation to Admission, of the following matters which had been discussed at the meeting of the full board on [   ] 200[   ]:

15.1.   that on the date when it is published, as required by the AIM Rules, the Admission Document will be required to contain all such information as, investors would reasonably require, and reasonably expect to find there, for the purpose of forming a full understanding of the assets and liabilities, financial position, profits and losses and prospects of the Company and its Ordinary Shares and of the rights attaching to those shares and all other matters contained in the Admission Document;

15.2.   that each Director would be responsible for the information contained in the Admission Document and that, if such document did not contain all such information, or if any statement included therein was untrue or misleading on the date on which the Admission Document was published or a significant change affecting any matter required to be included therein occurred or if a significant new matter arose, the inclusion of information in respect of which would have been required if it had arisen when the Admission Document was prepared, each Director may incur liabilities, and may be liable in damages in connection with the information contained in, or omitted from, such document. Written confirmation of all the Directors' responsibilities in the terms of the Responsibility Statements had been obtained. The attention of the meeting was drawn to the fact that an untrue or misleading statement in the Admission Document could lead to civil and/or criminal liability as explained in the CoSols Memorandum which had been circulated to all the Directors and discussed with all the Directors at a meeting held on [   ] 200[   ]. Each of the Directors confirmed that he had read and understood the CoSols Memorandum;

15.3.   it was explained that there was a regulatory requirement to publish a supplementary admission document in respect of any significant change affecting any matter contained in the Admission Document, or any significant new matter, which was capable of affecting the full understanding by an investor as mentioned in minute 15.1 above arising before the Ordinary Shares were admitted to trading on AIM, which was expected to be on [   ] 200[   ]. The attention of the Directors was also drawn to the terms of the Placing Agreement which obliged the Company or the Directors to notify Nomad and Broker if the Company or the Directors became aware at any time before the shares were admitted to trading on AIM that any of the representations and warranties set out in the Placing Agreement was or had become untrue, inaccurate or misleading. Each Director present confirmed that, if, prior to the commencement of dealings, he became aware of any fact or circumstances which would be relevant to any of the foregoing, or if he became aware that there was, or might be, a need to publish a supplementary admission document, then he would take steps immediately to inform Nomad, Broker and his fellow Directors;

15.4.   there would, following Admission, be continuing obligations owed to the London Stock Exchange under the terms of the AIM Rules which, it was explained, would impose obligations on the Company to disclose information on a timely basis to the London Stock Exchange. It was noted that the continuing obligations imposed by the AIM Rules, including the dealing in the Company's securities, were considered in detail in the CoSols Memorandum.

The meeting was then reminded of the detailed consideration of the terms of the Admission Document at the meeting of the board on [   ] 200[   ], which had particularly noted the following sections:

Key Information, including placing statistics:

Part I   –   [   ]
            –   History and development;
            –   [   ]
            –   [   ]
            –   [   ]
            –   Customers;
            –   Competition;
            –   Current trading and prospects;
            –   Dividend policy;
            –   Reasons for the Placing;
            –   The Placing; and
            –   Risk factors;
[Part 2   –   Illustrative financial projections;]
Part 3   –   Accountants' reports;
Part 4   –   Pro forma financial information; and
Part 5   –   Additional information.

A report was then given on the procedures that had been conducted in order to verify the contents of the Admission Document and provide a record of the steps taken to ensure the accuracy of the Admission Document. It was noted that copies of the Verification Notes had been supplied to each of the Directors and had been considered in detail at [two] verification meetings at which all the Directors had been present. These Notes had subsequently been brought up to date and circulated again to the Directors. The completed Notes had been tabled to the meeting and each of the Directors confirmed that he was satisfied with the responses to the Verification Notes which were to the best of their knowledge, information and belief, accurate in all respects.

Having considered the terms of the Admission Document each of the Directors present confirmed that:

15.4.1. the statements as to his interests in the Ordinary Shares of the Company and the other matters relating to him set out in paragraph [5] of Part [5] of the Admission Document are correct, accurate and complete;

15.4.2. to the best of his knowledge, information and belief save as disclosed in paragraph [6] of Part [5] of the Admission Document, there are no contracts to which any member of the Group is a party and which are, and no obligation which is, material for disclosure in the Admission Document;

15.4.3.   to the best of his knowledge, information and belief, save as disclosed in paragraph [9] of Part [5] of the Admission Document, there are no legal or arbitration proceedings, active, pending, or threatened against, or being brought by, the Company or any member of the Group which are having or may have a significant effect on the Company's financial position;

15.4.4.   the Admission Document complies in all respects with the provisions of the AIM Rules published by the London Stock Exchange;

15.4.5.   the Admission Document contains all such other information as the Directors consider necessary to enable investors to form a full understanding of the assets and liabilities, financial position, profits and losses and prospects of the Company and its Ordinary Shares and the rights attaching to the Ordinary Shares and the other matters contained in the Admission Document;

15.4.6.   the statements in the Admission Document could properly be made and he was satisfied that all statements of fact contained in the Admission Document were true and accurate in all material respects and not misleading, that all expressions of opinion, intention and expectation contained therein were fair and honestly held and made after due and careful consideration;

15.4.7.   to the best of his knowledge, information and belief, having taken all reasonable care to ensure that such was the case, there were no other facts relating to the Company not disclosed in the Admission Document the omission of which would make any statement therein misleading or which in the circumstances of the proposed Placing might be material to be disclosed; and

15.4.8.   he accepts responsibility for the Admission Document accordingly.

16.   APPROVAL OF PROPOSALS AND DOCUMENTS

After careful consideration IT WAS RESOLVED that the Placing be approved and IT WAS FURTHER RESOLVED that (subject to the Escrow Condition referred to in minute [17] and such final amendments as may be agreed by the Committee of the Board to be appointed pursuant to minute [18]):

16.1. the Admission Document be approved and Nomad be authorised to arrange for bulk printing;

16.2. the Verification Notes be approved and adopted for the purpose of verifying the contents of the Admission Document;

16.3. the Placing Agreement be approved and any two Directors or one Director and the Secretary be authorised to sign the same on behalf of the Company;

16.4. any Director, the Secretary or CoSols be authorised to initial for the purpose of identification any of the documents referred to in the Placing Agreement as being "in the agreed form";

16.5. the Responsibility Letter and the Nomad Comfort Letter be approved and signed by each of the Directors;

16.6. the Company would comply with the terms of the continuing obligations contained in the AIM Rules of the London Stock Exchange;

16.7. the various reports and letters prepared by Reporting Accountants be noted;

16.8. the various letters prepared by CoSols be noted;

16.9. each of the Service Agreements and bonus arrangement letters and the Letters of Appointment be approved and the Chairman be authorised to sign the same on behalf of the Company;

16.10. the form of the share certificate be and it is hereby approved;

16.11. the Estimate of Expenses be approved and that Nomad or Broker be authorised to arrange the payment of such expenses to the relevant persons out of the proceeds of the Placing, subject to the Company having been informed first of the exact amounts of each invoice;

16.12. the Press Announcement be approved and subject as set out below Nomad is hereby authorised and directed to arrange for its release at or around 7.30am on [   ] 200[ ];

16.13. the Application be approved and Nomad be authorised to deliver the same together with the Nomad Declaration, the AIM fee and an electronic copy of the Admission Document to the London Stock

Exchange and do all such acts and things as Nomad considers necessary in relation thereto in order to facilitate Admission;

but on the basis that all executed documents (apart from the Service Agreements and bonus arrangement letters) are signed but not delivered and held in escrow subject to Nomad having agreed with the Company (which Mr. [   ] or Mr. [   ] is authorised to do on behalf of the Company) that they will release the Press Announcement at or around 7.30 am on [   ] 200[ ] ("Escrow Condition").

17.   PUBLICATION OF THE ADMISSION DOCUMENT

IT WAS RESOLVED that subject to satisfaction of the Escrow Condition, the Admission Document be delivered to the London Stock Exchange and made available publicly, free of charge, at the offices of Nomad for one month from [   ] 200[ ].

18.   APPOINTMENT OF COMMITTEE

IT WAS RESOLVED that a committee ("Committee") comprising any two Directors be established with full authority to take all steps and approve, execute or procure to be executed all such documents, acts and things considered by the Committee to be necessary or desirable to have approved, executed or done for the purpose of implementing the Proposals and all matters ancillary thereto including, without limitation, approving any minor amendments to the Admission Document prior to its publication, and the performance of all the Company's obligations under or arising out of the agreements relating to the Placing and all other documents approved at this meeting, including (but not limited to) the allotment of Ordinary Shares pursuant to the Placing.

19.   ALLOTMENT OF ORDINARY SHARES

19.1.   Broker tabled a final list of placees who had conditionally agreed to subscribe for the new Ordinary Shares being placed by the Company [and to purchase the Ordinary Shares being sold by the Vendors]. IT WAS RESOLVED that [   ] Ordinary Shares be allotted and issued [and, as appropriate, the transfers of [   ] Ordinary Shares being sold by the Vendors be approved] to those persons identified on the final list of placees in those numbers and against those names as set out on such list, subject only to Admission.

19.2.   The Secretary was instructed to liaise in due course with the Company's registrar to arrange for the register of members to be made up, for the issue and despatch to placees of appropriate share certificates or, where applicable, the crediting of CREST accounts, as soon as possible and for the appropriate return of allotments Form 88(2) to be filed with the Registrar of Companies. The Secretary was also instructed to provide to Nomad a copy of these minutes or an extract thereof to the extent required by the London Stock Exchange as proof of allotment of the Ordinary Shares the subject of the Placing.

20.   FILING

The Secretary was instructed to arrange for any necessary forms or returns to be filed with the Registrar of Companies.

There being no further business, the meeting then terminated.

. . . .

CHAIRMAN

Appendix 5

Application to be signed by the Company

London **STOCK EXCHANGE**

Application to be signed by the issuer of the securities

Admission to AIM sought on:

Full legal name of the issuer of the securities:

(the 'Issuer')

Country of incorporation:

The Issuer applies for the securities detailed below to be admitted to AIM

Securities to be admitted to AIM

Amounts and descriptions of securities (e.g. Ordinary Shares of 5p each):

Nature of Admission (e.g. introduction, exercise of options, vendor consideration, placing for cash, block admission):

Are the securities for which the application is now made:

(a) identical in all respects? YES / NO

If NO, how do they differ and when will they become identical?

(b) identical in all respects with an existing class of security (further issues only)? YES / NO

If NO, how do they differ and when will they become identical?

ISIN(s) (new issues only):

Issuer details:

Contact name: _____

Job title: _____

Telephone number: _____

Email address: _____

Registered office address: _____

Issuer's anticipated accounting reference date: _____

Invoicing – Value Added Tax (VAT)

To comply with the EC Invoicing Directive (2001/115/EC) and to ensure that VAT is charged in accordance with EC law please complete the following section

a. Country of Principal Place of Business (PPB): _____
    NB: PPB is usually the head office, headquarters or 'seat' from which the business is run.

b. Is the Issuer registered for VAT in the UK?   YES: [_____]   NO: [_____]

c. Is the Issuer registered for VAT in another EC country?   YES: [_____]   NO: [_____]

d. If YES, please confirm EC VAT registration number: _____
    NB: Where PPB is an EC country (excluding UK) – Failure to provide a valid EC VAT registration number will result in UK VAT being charged in admission and annual fees.

Issuer's declaration

We declare that:

(i)   we have received advice and guidance from a nominated adviser and any other appropriate professional advisers as to the nature of our rights and obligations under the AIM Rules and the Rules of the London Stock Exchange and we understand and accept these rights and obligations;

(ii)   we have taken appropriate advice where necessary and have acted appropriately on any advice given;

(iii) the admission document* complies with the AIM Rules and includes all such information as investors would reasonably expect to find and reasonably require for the purpose of making an informed assessment of the assets, liabilities, financial position, profits, losses, and as to the prospects of the Issuer and the rights attaching to its securities;

(iv)   in our opinion, having made due and careful enquiry, the working capital available to us and our group is sufficient for our present requirements (i.e. for at least twelve months from admission)*;

(v)   any profit forecast, estimate or projection in the admission document* of the Issuer has been made after due and careful enquiry; and

(vi)   procedures have been established which provide a reasonable basis for the directors to make proper judgements as to the financial position and prospects of the Issuer and its group.

*Note: paragraphs (iii) (iv) and (v) above are applicable only if this application relates to an issue of securities requiring the publication of an admission document under the AIM Rules.

Undertaking

We undertake to:

(i)   comply with the AIM Rules and the Rules of the London Stock Exchange as amended from time to time;

(ii)   pay any applicable admission and annual fees; and

(iii) seek advice and guidance from our nominated adviser when appropriate and act appropriately on such advice

AIM – © January 2005   The London Stock Exchange crest and logo and AIM are registered trademarks of London Stock Exchange plc

Appendix 5 – Application to be signed by the Company

Signed by a duly authorised officer (e.g. Director) for and on behalf of:

Full legal name of the Issuer:

Signed:		Print name:	
Job title:		Date:	

Please ensure that all applicable sections on this form have been completed.
Failure to do so may cause delay in admission

Please return this form to:
Issuer Implementation
London Stock Exchange plc
10 Paternoster Square
London EC4M 7LS

Fax: 020 7920 4607
Email: issuerimplementation@londonstockexchange.com

Appendix 6

Declaration by the Nominated Adviser

London **STOCK EXCHANGE**

Declaration by the nominated adviser

Full name of nominated adviser:

Full name of applicant:

Details of the securities to which this declaration applies (e.g. company name, 1,000,000 Ordinary Shares of 5p each):

_____, an officer of the above nominated adviser, duly authorised to give this declaration, hereby confirm that:

SECTION A:

(a)   in relation to this application for admission, to the best of my knowledge and belief, having made due and careful enquiry, this admission document (please delete as appropriate):

    a)   has been drafted in accordance with Schedule 2 of the AIM Rules (effective 1 July 2005) and all relevant requirements of the AIM Rules have been complied with; or

    b)   constitutes a Prospectus complying with the Prospectus Rules having been approved by the Financial Services Authority, and has been drafted in accordance with Schedule 2 of the AIM Rules (effective 1 July 2005) and all relevant requirements of the AIM Rules have been complied with;

Quoted applicants (i.e. applicants from an AIM designated market) only:
(b)   to the best of my knowledge and belief, having made due and careful enquiry the requirements of Schedule One and its supplement (in so far as relevant) have been complied with.

SECTION B:

(b)   the directors of the applicant have received advice and guidance (from this firm or other appropriate professional advisers) as to the nature of their responsibilities and obligations to ensure compliance by the issuer with the AIM Rules and the Rules of the London Stock Exchange as amended from time to time;

(c)   this nominated adviser will be available at all times to advise and guide the directors of the issuer as to their responsibilities and obligations to ensure compliance by the issuer on an ongoing basis with the AIM Rules;

(d)   this nominated adviser will comply with the AIM Admission Rules applicable to it in its role as nominated adviser;

(e)   we are satisfied that the applicant and its securities are appropriate to be admitted to AIM;

f)   this nominated adviser will confirm to the Exchange in writing if it ceases to be the applicant's nominated adviser.

NOTE:

Sections A and B must be completed where securities are being admitted to AIM pursuant to an AIM admission document.

Section A is not applicable where this form is being completed pursuant to a change of nominated adviser only.

Admission to AIM sought on: _____ 20_____

Name of nominated adviser:

Signed: Date:

Administration details

Name(s) of contact(s) at nominated adviser regarding the application.

Please return this form to:

AIM Regulation
London Stock Exchange plc
10 Paternoster Square
London EC4M 7LS

Fax: **020 7920 4787**
Email: **aimregulation@londonstockexchange.com**

Index

All indexing is to paragraph number

ABI (Association of British Insurers)
corporate governance guidelines
9.2.3
accounts
annual, publication 8.4.1
see also **Rule 19 (annual accounts)**
half-yearly 8.4.2
published
eligible company requirements
2.2.1.3
acquisitions and hive-ups
shares issued before 17 March 2004
10.3.12.1
shares issued following 17 March
2004 10.3.12.2
administrative documents
admission procedure 7.4.2
admission
cancellation
at AIM company's request *see*
**cancellation of admission (AIM
company's request)**
eligibility requirements 8.8.8
to CREST
eligibility requirements 13.4.1
further securities 13.4.3
procedures 13.4.2
expedited 1.8
NOMAD, ongoing role following 1.6
pre-admission arrangements,
eligibility requirements 2.2.4
suitability for, eligibility requirements
2.2.2
see also **admission documents; Rule 6
(admission to AIM)**
admission documents
carve-outs 6.5
content requirements 6.5, 7.5.2

additional specific 7.5.5
AIM-PD standard 1.7
disclosure duty, general 7.5.3
display 7.5.7
drafting 5.5.1
filing and publication requirements
6.6
financial information, presentation
4.3
format 6.4
further, and secondary issues 6.8
information to be disclosed in, *see also*
**Schedule 2 (information to be
disclosed on admission
document)**
omissions, *see also* **Rule 4 (omissions
from admission documents)**
Prospectus Directive, equivalent
information to 7.5.4
Prospectus Rules 12.4.2
public nature 7.5.6
requirement for 1.7, 3.1, 7.5.1
responsibility for 6.9
supplementary 6.7
verification
completion 5.5.4
process 5.5.2
relevance 5.5.3
withdrawal rights 6.7
see also **Rule 3 (admission document)**
after-market
trading rules 11.6
agreements
depository 13.6.3
nominated adviser *see* **nominated
adviser agreement**
placing *see* **placing agreement**
service 7.15.4

AIM (Alternative Investment Market)
launching (1995) 1.1
and London Stock Exchange 6.1.1
and Official List 12.2.2
and other markets, companies traded
on 1.8
overseas companies
attracting 12.3
objectives regarding 12.2.1
regulatory status, change of 1.3
smaller growth companies, successful
market for 1.2
statutory framework, implications
6.1.3
AIM companies
cancellation of admission at request
of *see* **cancellation of admission
(AIM company's request)**
and Code of Corporate Governance
non-executive directors,
independent 9.3.2
QCA Guidelines 9.3.1
and CREST
legal relationship 13.5.2
registers of securities 13.5.3,
13.5.4
technical interface 13.5.1
disciplinary action against 2.5.3
further, moratorium on acting for
3.6.14
obligations 2.3.8
and trading rules 11.10
see also **overseas companies**
AIM Designated Markets 12.5.1
AIM Rules
admission process 7.2
AIM-PD standard 1.7
availability 1.7
contents 2.1
see also individual Rules
publication by LSE 2.1
AIM securities
meaning 2.1
AIM-PD standard
admission document, content
requirements 6.5
adoption by LSE 6.1.3

and AIM admission documentation
1.7
announcements
cancellation of admission
contents 2.6.3
requirement for 2.6.1
continuing obligations 8.2
dealing
by directors 11.9.2.1
Substantial Acquisition Rules
(SARs) 11.9.2.3
substantial interests 11.9.2.2
nominated adviser's agreement 3.7.6
Regulatory News Service (RNS)
11.4.1
ten-day 7.17.1
reverse takeovers 8.5.5
three-day 7.17.2
see also **Rule 2 (pre-admission
announcement)**
annual accounts *see* **accounts**: annual
appeals 2.1, 2.5.6
continuing obligations 8.9
by nominated advisers 3.9.3
see also Rules 42–45
applicable employee
defined 2.3.2
application procedure
administrative documents 7.4.2
AIM Rules, admission process 7.2
applications
admission 7.17.3
ten-day announcement 7.17.1
three-day announcement 7.17.2
board 7.13
corporate governance 7.13
costs 7.18
documentation *see* **admission
documents**
due diligence
commercial 7.8.3
financial 7.8.2
general 7.8.1
legal 7.8.4
employee share schemes 7.12
engagement letters 7.4.1
financial public relations 7.16

financial/accounting procedures
forecasts and projections 7.9.3
reporting 7.9.2
working capital 7.9.1
initial steps
administrative documents 7.4.2
engagement letters 7.4.1
legal considerations
directors' responsibility statement
7.6.5
financial promotions 7.6.2
FSMA 2000 7.6.6
general 7.6.1, 7.6.7
general law, liability under 7.6.4
prospectus liability 7.6.3
legal restructuring *see* **restructuring,
legal**
NOMADs, and brokers 7.3
placing agreement 7.14
shareholder resolutions 7.11
timing 7.18
verification 7.7
applications
admission 7.17.3
ten-day announcement 7.17.1
three-day announcement 7.17.2
"approved organisation"
defined 11.9.1.2
assets
business 10.6.1.2
mixed 10.6.1.4
example 10.6.1.7
non-business 10.6.1.3
Association of British Insurers *see* **ABI
(Association of British Insurers)**
audit committee
constitution 9.3.3.1
role 9.3.3.2

bank accounts
separate, taxation regime 10.3.11
board of directors
application procedure 7.13
changes in, disclosure requirements
8.3.5
meetings, directors' documents
7.15.5

broker agreement
solicitors to the company 5.10
brokers
change of, disclosure requirements
8.3.6
eligibility requirements 8.8.3
fees, placing agreements 7.14
nominated advisers
also acting as 3.7.3
and 7.3
retention of, eligibility requirements
2.2.1.6
role 11.4.1
"Bulletin Board"
SEATS Plus system, hit order
mechanism under 11.2
**business asset taper relief (capital
gains tax)**
business assets 10.6.1.2
and deferral relief 10.6.1.5
mixed assets 10.6.1.4
example 10.6.1.7
non-business assets 10.6.1.3
serial investors 10.6.1.6
business property relief
inheritance tax (IHT) 10.6.3.1

Cadbury Committee
corporate governance 9.2.1
**cancellation of admission (AIM
company's request)**
announcement
contents 2.6.3
requirement for 2.6.1
dealing notice 2.6.5
shareholder consent
not required 2.6.4
required 2.6.2
capital
availability of, overseas companies
12.2.3
free market (FMC) 11.3
gross, class tests 8.5.1
see also **working capital**
capital gains tax (CGT)
business asset taper relief
business assets 10.6.1.2

deferral relief and 10.6.1.5
mixed assets 10.6.1.4, 10.6.1.7
non-business assets 10.6.1.3
serial investors 10.6.1.6
gift relief, criteria
companies 10.6.2.2
individuals 10.6.2.1
carve-outs
admission documents 6.5
CDIs (CREST Depository Interests)
overseas securities 13.6.2
**CESR (Committee of European
Regulators)**
and Passport Directive 6.2.1
Prospectus Rules 6.2.3
CGT *see* **capital gains tax (CGT)**
Channel Islands
registers of securities 13.5.4
City Code on Takeovers and Mergers
2.3.2
continuing obligations 8.7
directors' duties and responsibilities
5.9
significant share interests 8.3.3
class tests
transactions 8.5.1
Clayton's Case (Devaynes v Noble)
10.3.8
"close period"
defined 9.1.5
and Rule 21 (deals, restrictions on)
9.1.5
Code of Corporate Governance
9.2.1
audit committee
constitution 9.3.3.1
role 9.3.3.2
non-executive directors 9.3.2
QCA Guidelines 9.3.1
see also **corporate governance**
comfort letters 4.7
**Committee of European Securities
Regulators (CESR)**
and Passport Directive 6.2.1
companies
AIM *see* **AIM companies**
eligible *see* **eligible companies**

investing
corporate venturing scheme (CVS)
10.7.3
definitions 2.2.1.2
eligibility requirements 2.2.1.2
overseas *see* **overseas companies**
Companies Act 1985 (CA 1985)
and "deals" 9.1.4
disclosure of deals 11.9.2.1
and Financial Services Act 1986 6.2.4
and Financial Services and Markets
Act (1985) 6.2.4
legislation 6.2.4
pre-flotation corporate matters 5.4
re-registration as public company
7.10.2
shadow director, defined 2.3.7
significant or substantial interests,
disclosure 8.3.3, 11.9.2.2
Companies House 5.3.2, 7.5.6
**compliance, directors' responsibility
for**
eligibility requirements 8.8.10
see also **Rule 31 (compliance,
directors' responsibility for)**
Confederation of British Industry
and National Association of Pensions
Funds policy 9.2.4
confidentiality
nominated adviser's agreement 3.7.7
conflicts of interest
NOMADS 3.6.5
agreement 3.7.9
consideration
class tests 8.5.1
contact details
eligible companies, basic
requirements 2.2.1.9
continuing obligations
announcements 8.2
appeals 8.9
City Code on Takeovers and Mergers
8.7
disclosure obligations
board changes 8.3.5
directors' dealings 8.3.4
dividend payments 8.3.8

general 8.3.9
material changes 8.3.2
nominated advisers or brokers,
    changes 8.3.6
price-sensitive information 8.3.1
securities in issue, change in
    number 8.3.7
significant share interests 8.3.3
eligibility requirements *see* **eligibility**
    requirements
financial reporting
    annual accounts 8.4.1
    half-yearly reports 8.4.2
overseas companies 12.4.4
sanctions 8.9
share issues, further 8.6
see also **transactions**
control
taxation regime 10.3.9
corporate action timetables *see* **Rules 24**
    and 25 (corporate action
    timetables)
corporate governance
ABI Guidelines 9.2.3
application procedure 7.13
background 9.2.1
Code *see* **Code of Corporate**
    Governance
concept 9.2.1
Modernising Company Law (White
    Paper) 9.2.2.2
National Association of Pension
    Funds policy (NAPF) 9.2.4
UK initiatives
    company law reform 9.2.2.2
    Directors Remuneration
        Regulations 2002 9.2.2.4
    Higgs Report and revised Code
        9.2.2.1
    Smith report 9.2.2.3
corporate transactions, disclosure *see*
    Rules 12–16
corporate venturing scheme (CVS)
companies benefiting 10.7.1
company qualifying criteria 10.7.2
investing company 10.7.3
provisional approval 10.7.4

costs
application procedure 7.18
CREST Depository Interests (CDIs)
overseas securities 13.6.2
CREST settlement system
AIM companies
    legal relationship 13.5.2
    registers of securities 13.5.3, 13.5.4
    technical interface 13.5.1
description/definitions 13.2
domestic securities, admission
    admission procedures 13.4.2
    eligibility requirements 13.4.1
    further securities 13.4.3
eligible companies, basic
    requirements 2.2.1.7
Exchange Rules 11.8
legal framework
    general 13.3.1
    non-UK securities 13.3.2
and market practitioners 11.4
and overseas companies 12.4.1
and overseas securities 13.6.1
shareholder resolutions 7.11
CRESTCo Ltd
application to 13.6.5
Security Application Form 13.4.2
settlement arrangements 2.2.1.7,
    11.8
and USRs 13.3.1
Criminal Justice Act 1993 (CJA 1993)
criminal liability 11.9.1.1
directors' duties and responsibilities
    5.9
directors' share dealings 8.8.4

Data Protection Act 1998 (DPA 1998)
due diligence requirements 5.3.2
de-mergers
legal restructuring 7.10.3
deals
announcements *see* **announcements**:
    dealing
"close period", defined 9.1.5
dealing rules, directors' documents
    7.15.3
definition 9.1.4

disclosure requirements 8.3.4
eligibility requirements (directors)
   8.8.4
lock-ins 9.1.9
notification of 2.3.3, 9.1.7
related parties, defined 9.1.10
restrictions on
   directors and employees 2.3.4
   exemptions 9.1.6
   sanctions for breach 9.1.8
Rule 21
   applicable persons 9.1.3
   applicable securities 9.1.2
   see also **Rule 21 (deals, restrictions
     on)**
Rule 31 9.1
deferral relief
and business asset taper relief
   10.6.1.5
depository agreement
and DI structure 13.6.3
depository interests (DIs), bespoke
   13.6.3
admission to CREST 13.6.5
Designated Markets
listing of 2.2
**Deutsche Börse, closure of Neuer
   Markt (2002)** 12.2.4
directors
board of *see* **board of directors**
changes in 2.3.3
dealings *see* **deals**
disclosure by 2.3.6
documents
   board meetings 7.15.5
   dealing rules 7.15.3
   general 7.15.1
   powers of attorney 7.15.6
   responsibility memorandum and
     statements 7.15.2
   service agreements 7.15.4
eligibility requirements, share
   dealings 8.8.4
flotation, duties and responsibilities
   regarding 5.9
non-executive, Code of Corporate
   Governance 9.3.2

remuneration
   Remuneration Regulations 2002
     9.2.2.4
   see also **remuneration committee**
responsibilities 2.3.5
   responsibility statement
     (application procedure) 7.6.5
role 2.3.1
service contracts 5.7
shadow, defined 2.3.7
DIs *see* **depository interests (DIs),
   bespoke**
disciplinary action
against AIM company 2.5.3
against nominated adviser 2.1, 2.5.4,
   3.9.1
process 2.1, 2.5.5, 3.9.2
*Disciplinary Procedures and Appeals
   Handbook* 8.9
appeals 2.5.6, 3.9.3
dealing restrictions, sanctions for
   breach 9.1.8
disciplinary process 2.5.5, 3.9.2
disciplinary process *see* **Rule 44
   (disciplinary process)**
disclosure requirements
admission documents 7.5.3
board changes 8.3.5
brokers, changes of 8.3.6
corporate transactions, *see also*
     **corporate transactions,
     disclosure**
directors' dealings 8.3.4
dividend payments 8.3.8
Exchange, powers of 2.4.2
fast-track route 12.5.2
general obligations 8.3.9
material changes 8.3.2
miscellaneous information, *see also*
     **Rule 17 (disclosure of
     miscellaneous information)**
nominated advisers, changes of
   8.3.6
price-sensitive information 8.3.1
securities in issue, change in number
   8.3.7
significant share interests 8.3.3

see also **Rule 10 (disclosure principles)** ; **Rule 23 (information disclosure)**
disposals
  fundamental change of business, resulting in 8.5.3
dividend payments
  disclosure requirements 8.3.8
documents
  administrative 7.4.2
  admission *see* **admission documents**
  directors *see* **directors**: documents
  shareholders, sent to 2.1
due diligence
  commercial 7.8.3
  coordinating work of 1.5
  financial 7.8.2
  general issues 7.8.1
  legal 7.8.4
  pre-flotation legal
    examples of actions consequent upon 5.3.3
    information requirements 5.3.2
    questionnaire 5.3.2
    reasons for 5.3.1
    report, draft and final 5.3.4

EIS *see* **Enterprise Investment Scheme (EIS)**
electronic transfer of title (ETT) 13.5.3
eligibility requirements
  brokers 8.8.3
  cancellation of admission 8.8.8
  compliance, directors' responsibility for 8.8.10
  continuing eligibility 8.8.1
  CREST, admission of domestic securities to 13.4.1
  directors
    compliance, responsibility for 8.8.10
    share dealings 8.8.4
  fees 8.8.9
  nominated advisers *see* **nominated advisers (NOMADs), eligibility criteria for approval**
  overseas companies 12.4.1

precautionary suspension 8.8.7
  securities to be admitted 8.8.6
  transferability of shares 8.8.5
  see also **eligible companies; Rule 1 (eligibility for AIM)**
eligible companies
  admission, suitability for 2.2.2
  basic requirements
    broker, retention of 2.2.1.6
    contact details 2.2.1.9
    fees 2.2.1.8
    investing companies 2.2.1.2
    nominated adviser 2.2.1.1
    published accounts 2.2.1.3
    securities to be admitted to trading 2.2.1.5
    settlement arrangements 2.2.1.7
    transferable securities 2.2.1.4
  Official List, trading record requirements 2.2
  ongoing requirements, *see also Rules 32–38*
  pre-admission arrangements, additional 2.2.4
  share structure, reorganisation and rationalisation 2.2.3
employee
  applicable 2.3.2
employee share schemes 5.8
  application procedure 7.12
engagement letters
  application procedure 7.4.1
England and Wales
  registers of securities 13.5.3
Enterprise Investment Scheme (EIS)
  approval
    formal 10.5.1.3
    provisional 10.5.1.1–10.5.1.2
  benefits for investors 10.2.1, 10.2.2
  certificates, issue of 10.5.1.3
  formal approval 10.5.1.3
  HM Revenue and Customs review 10.5.1.5
  investment
    company qualifying criteria 10.2.5
    eligibility for 10.2.2

provisional approval
  requirements 10.5.1.1
  timing 10.5.1.2
qualifying business activities 10.2.6
use of funds test 10.3.2
ESOPs (employee share ownership plans) 5.8
ETT (electronic transfer of title) 13.5.3
European Communities Act (1972)
  and Financial Services and Markets
    Act 2000 (FSMA 2000) 6.2.2

fast-track route
  disclosure requirements 12.5.2
  impact 12.5.5
  key features 12.5.1
  NOMADs, role in 12.5.3
  Prospectus Rules 12.5.4
fees
  admission, three-day announcements
    7.17.2
  brokers, placing agreements 7.14
  eligibility requirements 2.2.1.8, 8.8.9
  licence, taxation regime 10.3.4
  nominated adviser's agreement 3.7.10
*Fees for Companies and Nominated
  Advisers* 2.2.1.8
**Financial Aspects of Corporate
  Governance**
  Cadbury Committee 9.2.1
financial information
  admission document 4.3
  comfort letters 4.7
  long form report 4.2
  pro forma 4.4
  Prospectus Directive requirements
    4.8
  reporting procedures 4.6
  summary 4.9
  working capital 4.5
financial procedures
  forecasts and projections 7.9.3
  reporting 7.9.2
  working capital 7.9.1
financial promotions
  application procedure, legal
    considerations 7.6.2

Financial Services and Markets Act
    2000 (FSMA 2000) 6.2.5, 7.6.2
  statutory framework 6.2.5, 6.11
Financial Reporting Council
  and Combined Code 9.2.2.1
Financial Services Action Plan
  EU Directives 6.1.3
Financial Services Authority *see* **FSA
  (Financial Services Authority)**
**Financial Services and Markets Act
  2000 (FSMA 2000)**
  admission process 7.2
  application procedure, legal
    considerations (s.397) 7.6.6
  civil liability 6.10.2
  and Companies Act (1985) 6.2.4
  criminal liability 6.10.1
  directors' duties and responsibilities
    5.9
  and European Communities Act
    (1972) 6.2.2
  financial promotions 6.2.5, 7.6.2
  half-yearly reports, publication 8.4.2
  insider dealing defences 11.9.1.2
  legislation 6.2.2
  and misleading statements and
    practices 11.9.1.4
  and "offer of transferable securities to
    the public" 6.3.3
  Prospectus Regulations 6.2.2
  Prospectus Rules 6.3.4
  solicitors to issue 5.12
"firm exposure order"
  SEATS Plus system 11.4.1
flotation
  advice by solicitors 5.11
  directors' duties and responsibilities
    5.9
  pre-flotation corporate matters 5.4
  pre-flotation due diligence *see* **due
    diligence**: pre-flotation legal
FMC (free market capital) 11.3
forecasts, financial 7.9.3
FSA (Financial Services Authority)
  announcements 8.2
  Handbook, PD Regulation 8.6
  Prospectus Rules 6.2.3

FSMA 2000 *see* **Financial Services and Markets Act 2000 (FSMA 2000)**
FTSE AIM Index Series (FTSE AIM UK 50 Index and FTSE Aim 100 Index) 1.2
and SETS 11.2
funds use test
taxation regime 10.3.2

GAAP (generally accepted accounting practice)
admission documents, financial information presentation 4.3
annual accounts, publication 8.4.1
fast-track route 12.5.2
and published accounts 2.2.1.3
GDIs (global depository interests), overseas securities 13.6.4
admission to CREST 13.6.5
Glaxo Smith Kline
defeat of (2003) 9.2.2.4
gross assets
class tests 8.5.1
taxation regime 10.3.5
Guernsey
registers of securities 13.5.4
Guidance Notes
admission document, responsibility for 6.9
AIM company, obligations 2.3.8
Exchange, published by 2.1
fast-track route 12.5.2
and Prospectus Rules 12.5.4
lock-ins 2.3.2
Rule 1 2.2.1.1
Rule 34 2.2.1.1

Hampel, Sir Ronald 9.2.2
Higgs Report
corporate governance 9.2.2.1
hit order mechanism
under SEATS Plus system 11.2
"hit order price"
SEATS Plus system 11.4.1
HM Revenue and Customs
Corporate Venturing Scheme, provisional approval 10.7.4

employee share participation 5.8
employee share schemes 7.12
Enterprise Investment Scheme (EIS) 10.5.1.5
provisional approval 10.5.1.1
hive-ups 10.3.12.2
location of trade 10.4
royalties and licence fees 10.3.4
and Small Company Enterprise Centre 10.5.1.1, 10.5.1.2, 10.5.1.3
use of funds test 10.3.2
Venture Capital Schemes Manual 10.2
Venture Capital Trusts (VCTs) 10.5.1.5
provisional approval 10.5.1.1
HSBC Bank plc
base rate 2.2.1.8

ICTA (Income and Corporation Taxes Act) 1988
and loss relief 10.8
timetable/planning 10.3.17
IFRS (International Financial Reporting Standards)
admission documents, financial information 4.3
IHT *see* **inheritance tax (IHT)**
IMAS (Integrated Monitoring and Surveillance System) 11.9.3
indemnities
nominated adviser's agreement 3.7.8
information
on AIM companies 11.10
disclosure *see* **disclosure requirements**
due diligence requirements 5.3.2
financial *see* **financial information**
price-sensitive
disclosure 8.3.1
unpublished 9.1.5
see also **Rule 11 (price-sensitive information, general disclosure)**
pro forma 4.4
provision, requirement for 2.4.1
see also **Rule 22 (information provision)**

trading rules 11.3
see also **RIS (regulatory information service)**
inheritance tax (IHT)
business property relief 10.6.3.1
company qualifying criteria 10.7.2
provisional approval 10.7.4
initial public offering (IPO) 13.4.2
insider dealing
civil liability 11.9.1.3
criminal liability 11.9.1.1
exchange requirements 11.9.1.5
further developments 11.9.1.4
special defences 11.9.1.2
Institute of Chartered Accountants
and pro forma financial information 4.4
Integrated Monitoring and Surveillance System (IMAS) 11.9.3
International Accounting Standards
adoption 6.12
fast-track route 12.5.2
and published accounts 2.2.1.3, 8.4.1
International Financial Reporting Standards (IFRS)
admission documents, financial information 4.3
International Securities Identification Number (ISIN) 11.3
investing companies
corporate venturing scheme (CVS) 10.7.3
definitions 2.2.1.2
eligibility requirements 2.2.1.2
Investment Services Directive
and "offer of transferable securities to the public" 6.3.3
investor protection
sanctions for non-compliance 2.5.2
investor, relations with 11.7
IPO (initial public offering) 13.4.2
Ireland
registers of securities 13.5.4
ISIN (International Securities Identification Number) 11.3
CDIs 13.6.2

Isle of Man
registers of securities 13.5.4

Jersey
registers of securities 13.5.4
joint ventures
taxation regime 10.3.8

language requirements
see also **Rule 30 (language)**
Legal Opinion
CRESTCo, application to 13.6.5
liability
civil 6.10.2
insider dealing 11.9.1.3
criminal 6.10.1
insider dealing 11.9.1.1
licence fees
taxation regime 10.3.4
liquidity
trading rules 11.5
lock-ins
dealings 9.1.9
directors and employees 2.3.2
see also **Rule 7 (lock-ins for new businesses)**
London Stock Exchange (LSE)
and AIM 6.1.1
and AIM-PD 6.1.3
announcements 8.2
disclosure, power to make 2.4.2
Guidance Notes published by 2.1
information to be provided to, *see also* **Schedule 1 (information to be provided to Exchange pursuant to Rule 2)**
insider dealing 11.9.1.5
legal due diligence, reasons for 5.3.1
nominated advisers' responsibilities to 3.2
publication of AIM Rules 2.1
Regulatory News Service Guidelines 8.2
and relevant transactions 3.6.2
Rules 2.1
long form reports 4.2

loss relief
qualifying companies 10.8.1
qualifying investors 10.8.2, 10.8.2.1

market abuse
prevention 11.9.1.4
Market Abuse Directive
application 11.9.1.4
civil liability 6.10.2
future developments 6.12
market maker
defined 11.9.1.2
role 11.4.2
market practitioners, role
brokers 11.4.1
market makers 11.4.2
market regulation *see* **dealing**
announcements; insider dealing
markets
competing, failure of 12.2.4
orderly, maintenance, *see also Rules 40*
and 41
Misrepresentation Act 1967
civil liability 6.10.2
Model Code of Director's Dealings in
Listing Rules 11.9.1.5
Modernising Company Law **(White**
Paper) 9.2.2.2

NAPF *see* **National Association of**
Pension Funds policy (NAPF)
Nasdaq Europe
closure (2003) 12.2.4
National Association of Pension Funds
policy (NAPF)
corporate governance 9.2.4
NOMADs *see* **nominated advisers**
(NOMADs); nominated advisers
(NOMADs), eligibility criteria
for approval
nominated adviser agreement
admission, responsibilities in relation
to 3.7.1
announcements 3.7.6
broker, also acting as 3.7.3
confidentiality 3.7.7
conflicts of interest 3.7.9

corporate client, NOMAD's
relationship with 3.2
fees 3.7.10
indemnities 3.7.8
information provision 3.7.4
law and regulations, compliance with
3.7.5
ongoing responsibilities 3.7.2
and solicitors to the company 5.10
termination 3.7.11
warranties 3.7.12
nominated advisers (NOMADs)
admission document, requirement for
3.1
advice from 2.3.7
agreement *see* **nominated adviser**
agreement
appeals by 2.5.6, 3.9.3
background 1.4
brokers
also acting as 3.7.3
and 7.3
changes in, disclosure requirements
8.3.6
confirmations from, *see also Schedules*
6 and 7
declarations, three-day
announcements 7.17.2
definitions 3.1
disciplinary action against 2.5.4, 3.9.1
eligibility criteria *see* **nominated**
advisers (NOMADs), eligibility
criteria for approval
failure to have 2.5.1
fast-track route, role in 12.5.3
identity 3.4
performance review 3.6.14
Register of 1.4
responsibilities 3.1
admission 3.7.1, 3.9.1
to LSE 3.2
ongoing 3.7.2
retention of 3.5
reviews of 1.4
role 1.4
fast-track route 12.5.3
ongoing following admission 1.6

see also **Rule 39 (nominated advisers)**
nominated advisers (NOMADs),
    eligibility criteria for approval
    1.4, 3.3
  conflicts of interest 3.6.5
  continuing eligibility 8.8.1
  corporate finance, ongoing experience
    3.6.9
  fees, annual 3.6.11
  independence 3.6.4
  moratorium on acting for further
    AIM companies 3.6.14
  nominated advisers, performance
    review 3.6.13
  procedure 3.6.7
  qualified executives 3.6.1
    additional 3.6.12
  record maintenance 3.6.10
  relevant transactions 3.6.2
  staff, adequacy 3.6.8
  see also **nominated advisers'**
    agreement; nominated advisers
    (NOMADs)
Northern Ireland
  registers of securities 13.5.3

"offer of transferable securities to the
  public" 6.3.3
Official List
  admission documents, drafting 5.5.1
  and AIM 12.2.2, 12.5.1
  corporate governance 9.2.1
  as Designated Market 12.5.1
  and market practitioners 11.4
  trading record requirements 2.2
Operating and Financial Review
  admission document, content
    requirements 6.5
  Prospectus Directive requirements
    4.8
Operational Bulletin
  CRESTCo, application to 13.6.5
overseas activities
  taxation regime 10.3.10
overseas companies
  AIM Rules, eligibility requirements
    12.4.1

  AIM objectives 12.2.1
  capital availability 12.2.3
  competing markets, failure of 12.2.4
  continuing obligations 12.4.4
  Prospectus Rules 12.4.2
  regulation, less of 12.2.2
  UK plc, using as new holding
    company 12.4.3
overseas securities
  CREST Depository Interests (CDIs)
    13.6.2
  depository interests (DIs), bespoke
    13.6.3
    admission to CREST 13.6.5
  general 13.6.1
  global depository interests (GDIs)
    13.6.4
    admission to CREST 13.6.5

Panel on Takeovers and Mergers
  lock-ins 2.3.2
  price-sensitive information 8.3.1
  SARs, notification 11.9.2.3
Passport Directive
  single passport concept 6.2.1
PERs (price/earnings ratios) 11.10
placing agreement
  application procedure 7.14
  contents of 5.6.2
  "lock-in" of shares, requirement for
    5.6.4
  negotiation 5.6.3
  parties to 5.6.1
POS Regulations (Public Offer of
  Securities Regulations)
  admission document, content
    requirements 6.5
  fast-track route 12.5.1
  and old regime 6.1.1
  and Prospectus Directive 6.2.2
powers of attorney
  directors' documents 7.15.6
PR (public relations) agency
  admissions 7.16
price-sensitive information
  disclosure
    continuing obligations 8.3.1

see also **Rule 11 (price-sensitive information, general disclosure)**
unpublished 9.1.5
price/earnings ratios (PERs) 11.10
pro forma information 4.4
profits
class tests 8.5.1
projections, financial 7.9.3
Prospectus Regulations
Financial Services and Markets Act 2000 (FSMA 2000) 6.2.2
Prospectus Directive
and admission documents 7.5.4
admission process, AIM Rules 7.2
AIM-PD standard based on 1.7
exemptions applicable 6.3.4
legislation 6.2.1
as "maximum harmonisation" directive 6.2.3
new regime 6.1.2
and POS Regulations (Public Offer of Securities Regulations) 6.2.2
Regulations *see* **Prospectus Regulations**
requirements 4.8
prospectus regime
exemption applicable 6.3.4
liability, application procedure 7.6.3
"professionals only" exemption 6.3.4
prospectus
not required where 6.3.2
"offer of transferable securities to the public" 6.3.3
required where 6.3.1
"qualified investors" 6.3.4
see also **Prospectus Directive; Prospectus Rules**
Prospectus Regulations
admission document, content requirements 6.5
admission documents, drafting 5.5.1
financial information, presentation 4.3
further share issues 8.6

and GDIs 13.6.4
Prospectus Rules
admission document, content requirements 6.5
admission document, responsibility for 6.9
and Committee of European Regulators (CESR) 6.2.3
and dealings 9.1.4
fast-track route 12.5.4
Financial Services and Markets Act 2000 (FSMA 2000) 6.3.4
forecasts and projections 7.9.3
legislation 6.2.3
overseas companies 12.4.2
public company, re-registration as 7.10.2
public relations, financial
application procedure 7.16
purpose and existence test
taxation regime 10.3.1

QCA (Quoted Companies Alliance) 9.3
Corporate Governance Guidelines 9.2.1
qualified executives
nominated advisers (NOMADs), eligibility criteria for approval 3.6.1

records
maintenance of, NOMADS, eligibility criteria 3.6.10
Register of Nominated Advisers 1.4
registers of securities
England and Wales, Scotland and Northern Ireland 13.5.3
Ireland, Channel Isles, and Isle of Man 13.5.4
regulatory information service *see* **RIS (regulatory information service)**
Regulatory News Service Guidelines
London Stock Exchange (LSE) 8.2
regulatory status, change of 1.3
related party transactions 8.5.4
related parties, defined 2.3.2, 9.1.10

remuneration committee
  constitution 9.3.4.1
  role 9.3.4.2
reports
  annual 8.4.1
  application procedures 7.9.2
  due diligence legal, draft and final
    5.3.4
  financial 4.6, 7.9.2
  half-yearly 8.4.2
    see also **Rule 18 (half-yearly**
      reports)
  long form 4.2
residence
  taxation issues 10.3.10
responsibility
    memorandum/statements
  directors' documents 7.15.2
restructuring, legal
  de-merger 7.10.3
  general 7.10.1
  re-registration as public company
    7.10.2
  shareholder agreements 7.10.5
  termination rights and consents
    7.10.4
Revenue and Customs *see* **HM**
    Revenue and Customs
reverse takeovers
  transactions 8.5.5
  see also **Rule 14 (reverse takeovers)**
RIS (regulatory information service)
  announcements 8.2
    block admissions (Schedule 8) 2.1
  price-sensitive information 8.3.1
RNS (Regulatory News Service)
  announcements on 11.4.1
royalties
  taxation regime 10.3.4
Rule 1 (eligibility for AIM) 2.1, 2.2.1.1
Rule 2 (pre-admission announcement)
  applicants 2.1
  fast-track route 12.5.2
  reverse takeovers 8.5.5
Rule 3 (admission document)
  applicants 2.1
  content requirements 7.5.2

fast-track route 12.5.1
  impact 12.5.5
  and Prospectus Rules 12.5.4
  see also **admission documents**
Rule 4 (omissions from admission
    documents)
  applicants 2.1
Rule 5 (application documents)
  applicants 2.1
  fast-track route 12.5.2
Rule 6 (admission to AIM)
  applicants 2.1
  see also **admission**
Rule 7 (lock-ins for new businesses)
    9.1.9
  admission document, content
    requirements 7.5.5
  CREST, eligibility for 13.4.1
  placing agreements 7.14
  related parties 9.1.10
  special conditions for certain
    applicants 2.1, 2.3.1
Rule 8 (conditions) 2.1
  investing companies 2.2.1.2
Rule 9 (conditions) 2.1
Rule 10 (disclosure principles)
    2.1
  overseas companies, continuing
    obligations 12.4.4
  see also **disclosure requirements**
Rule 11 (price-sensitive information,
    general disclosure) 2.1
Rule 12 (disclosure of corporate
    transactions) 2.1
Rule 13 (disclosure of corporate
    transactions) 2.1
  disposals, resulting in fundamental
    change of business 8.5.3
Rule 14 (reverse takeovers) 2.1
  disposals, resulting in fundamental
    change of business 8.5.3
  and fees 2.2.1.8
Rule 15 (disclosure of corporate
    transactions) 2.1
  and investing companies 2.2.1.2
Rule 16 (disclosure of corporate
    transactions) 2.1

Rule 17 (disclosure of miscellaneous information) 2.1
deals, notifying 2.3.3, 11.9.2.1
directors, changes in 2.3.3
and nominated adviser, failure to have (Rule 34) 2.5.1
Rule 18 (half-yearly reports) 2.1
Rule 19 (annual accounts) 2.1, 2.2.1.3
admission document, financial information 4.3
overseas companies, continuing obligations 12.4.4
Rule 20 (publication of documents sent to shareholders) 2.1
Rule 21 (deals, restrictions on) 2.1, 2.3.4
applicable persons 9.1.3
applicable securities 9.1.2
and "close period" 9.1.5
definition of "deals" 9.1.4
Exchange requirements 11.9.1.5
Rule 22 (information provision) 2.1, 2.4.1
Rule 23 (information disclosure) 2.1, 2.4.2
Rules 24 and 25 (corporate action timetables) 2.1
Rule 26 (further issues following admission) 2.1
Rule 28 (further issues following admission) 2.1
Rule 29 (further issues following admission) 2.1
Rule 30 (language) 2.1
overseas companies 12.4.4
Rule 31 (compliance, responsibility for)
AIM company, obligations 2.3.8
dealings by directors 9.1
description 2.1
disclosure by directors 2.3.6
nominated adviser, advice from 2.3.7
responsibilities of directors 2.3.5
Rule 32 (transferability of shares)
ongoing eligibility requirements 2.1, 2.2.1.4
pre-flotation corporate matters 5.4

see also **shares**: transferability
Rule 33 (admission to trading)
ongoing eligibility requirements 2.1, 2.2.1.5
Rule 34 (nominated advisers, retention)
ongoing eligibility requirements 2.1, 2.2.1.1
sanctions for non-compliance 2.5.1
Rule 35 (brokers, retention)
and nominated adviser, failure to have (Rule 34) 2.5.1
ongoing eligibility requirements 2.2.1.6
Rule 36 (settlement arrangements)
ongoing eligibility requirements 2.1, 2.2.1.7
overseas companies 12.4.1
Rule 37 (fees)
ongoing eligibility requirements 2.1
Rule 38 (contact details)
ongoing eligibility requirements 2.1, 2.2.1.9
Rule 39 (nominated advisers, responsibilities)
admission, suitability for 2.2.2
and disciplinary action (Rule 43) 2.5.4
fast-track route 12.5.2
NOMAD, role 12.5.3
nominated adviser and broker agreements 5.10
ongoing eligibility requirements 2.1, 2.2.1
Rule 40 (maintenance of orderly markets) 2.1
sanctions 2.5.2
Rule 41 (maintenance of orderly markets) 2.1
and announcement, requirement for 2.6.1
sanctions 2.5.2
and shareholder consent, requirement for 2.6.2
Rule 42 (disciplinary action against AIM company) 2.1, 2.5.3
and disciplinary process (Rule 44) 2.5.5

Rule 43 (disciplinary action against nominated advisor) 2.1, 2.5.4, 3.9.1
and disciplinary process (Rule 44) 2.5.5
Rule 44 (disciplinary process) 2.1, 2.5.5, 3.9.2
Rule 45 (appeals) 2.1, 2.5.6, 3.9.3
Rules Governing Substantial Acquisitions of Shares *see* **Substantial Acquisition Rules (SARs)**

sanctions
continuing obligations 8.9
dealing restrictions, breach 9.1.8
see also Rules 42–45
Sarbanes-Oxley law (US)
and Higgs Report 9.2.2.1
SARs *see* **Substantial Acquisition Rules (SARs)**
SCEC *see* **Small Company Enterprise Centre**
Schedule 1 (information to be provided to Exchange pursuant to Rule 2) 2.1
fast-track route 12.5.2
NOMAD, role in 12.5.3
Schedule 2 (information to be disclosed on admission document) 2.1
admission process 7.2
board changes 8.3.5
content requirements 6.5, 7.5.2, 7.5.5
due diligence requirements 5.3.2
fast-track route, impact 12.5.5
overseas companies, AIM Rules 12.4.2
Schedule 3 (class tests) 2.1, 8.5.1
Schedule 4 (class tests) 2.1
disposals, resulting in fundamental change of business 8.5.3
Schedule 5 (deals by directors, information on) 2.1
directors' dealings 8.3.4
significant share interests 8.3.3
Schedule 6 (confirmations) 2.1

admission, suitability for 2.2.2
and NOMAD's responsibilities on admission of securities 3.8
Schedule 7 (confirmations) 2.1
admission, suitability for 2.2.2
fast-track route 12.5.2
Schedule 8 (block admissions) 2.1
further share issues 8.6
Schedule 9 (share information, treasury) 2.1
Scotland
registers of securities 13.5.3
SEAQ (Stock Exchange Automated Quotations) 11.2
AIM companies 11.10
market maker, role 11.4.2
typical page 11.2
SEATS Plus
AIM companies 11.10
SEATS Plus system
hit order mechanism under 11.2
market makers, role 11.4.2
order types (AIM securities) 11.4.1
SEATs (Stock Exchange Alternative Trading System) 11.2
securities
admission to trading, eligibility requirements 2.2.1.5
freely transferable, eligibility requirements 2.2.1.4, 8.8.5
further issues following admission, *see also Rules 26, 28 and 29*
Security Application Form
CRESTCo Ltd 13.4.2
application to 13.6.5
SEDOL (Stock Exchange Daily Official List) 11.3
service agreements
directors' documents 7.15.4
service contracts, directors 5.7
SETS (Stock Exchange Electronic Trading Service) 11.2
settlement arrangements
eligible companies, basic requirements 2.2.1.7
"residual settlement", illiquid stocks 11.8

trading rules 11.8
shadow director
defined 2.3.7
directors' dealings (Rule 21) 9.1.3
share structure
reorganisation and rationalisation
2.2.3
shareholders
agreements, legal restructuring 7.10.5
consent, cancellation of admission
2.6.2
not required 2.6.4
publication of documents sent to, *see
also* **Rule 20 (publication of
documents sent to shareholders)**
resolutions 7.11
substantial, definition 2.3.2
shares
acquisitions and hive-ups *see*
acquisitions and hive-ups
issues
costs 10.3.13
further 8.6
"lock-in", requirement for 5.6.4
"qualifying companies" 10.3.14
quoted, becoming 10.3.14
sale of 10.3.15
separate issues, taxation regime
10.3.3
significant interests, disclosure 8.3.3
transferability
eligibility requirements 2.2.1.4,
8.8.5
"offer of transferable securities to
the public" (new prospectus
regime) 6.3.3
see also **Rule 32 (transferability of
shares)**
Shire Pharmaceuticals Group plc
9.2.2.4
single passport concept
Passport Directive 6.2.1
**SIR (Standards for Investment
Reporting)** 4.3
Small Company Enterprise Centre
and HM Revenue and Customs
10.5.1.1, 10.5.1.2, 10.5.1.3

Smith Report
corporate governance 9.2.2.3
solicitors
to the company
admission document *see* **admission
document**
broker agreement 5.10
directors' duties and
responsibilities (flotation) 5.9
employee share participation 5.8
flotation advice 5.11
nominated adviser agreement 5.10
placing agreement *see* **placing
agreement**
pre-flotation corporate matters 5.4
pre-flotation legal due diligence *see*
due diligence: pre-flotation legal
principal functions 5.2.1
service contracts (directors) 5.7
to the issue 5.12
**special conditions for certain
applicants**
see also Rules 7–9
**Standards for Investment Reporting
(SIR)** 4.3
statutory framework
admission document *see* **admission
document**
AIM, implications for 6.1.3
financial promotion 6.11
future developments 6.12
legislation
Companies Act 1985 6.2.4
financial promotions 6.2.5
FSMA 2000 6.2.2
Prospectus Directive, and related
EC measures 6.2.1
Prospectus Rules (FSA) 6.2.3
liability
civil 6.10.2
criminal 6.10.1
new regime 6.1.2
old regime 6.1.1
prospectus regime, new
exemptions applicable 6.3.4
"offer of transferable securities to
the public" 6.3.3

prospectus not required 6.3.2
prospectus required 6.3.1
Stock Exchange
London *see* **London Stock Exchange (LSE)**
Stock Exchange Alternative Trading System (SEATs) 11.2
Stock Exchange Automated Quotations (SEAQ) 11.2
Stock Exchange Daily Official List (SEDOL) 11.3
Stock Exchange Electronic Trading Service (SETS) 11.2
subsidiaries
taxation regime 10.3.6
Substantial Acquisition Rules (SARs)
dealing announcements 11.9.2.3
significant share interests 8.3.3
substantial shareholder
defined 2.3.2
substantial transactions 8.5.2
suspension
precautionary 8.8.7

Taxation of Chargeable Gains Act 1992
timetable/planning 10.3.17
taxation regime
acquisitions and hive-ups
shares issued before 17 March 2004 10.3.12.1
shares issued following 17 March 2004 10.3.12.2
application forms, and placing letters 10.3.18
bank accounts, separate 10.3.11
capital gains tax *see* **capital gains tax (CGT)**
case law 10.3.8
clearance, obtaining
Capital Gains Tax 10.6.1.2–10.6.1.7
EIS and VCTs 10.5.1.1–10.5.1.5
control 10.3.9
corporate venturing scheme *see* **corporate venturing scheme (CVS)**

Enterprise Investment Scheme *see* **Enterprise Investment Scheme (EIS)**
funds use test 10.3.2
gross assets test 10.3.5
holdings
50 per cent 10.3.8
less than 50 per cent 10.3.7
inheritance tax *see* **inheritance tax (IHT)**
joint ventures 10.3.8
licence fees 10.3.4
loss relief
qualifying companies 10.8.1
qualifying investors 10.8.2
placing letters 10.3.18
purpose and existence test 10.3.1
reliefs available 10.1
residence and overseas activities 10.3.10
royalties 10.3.4
share issues, separate 10.3.3
shares
acquisitions and hive-ups 10.3.12.1–10.3.12.2
costs of issue 10.3.13
issue 10.3.16
quoted, becoming 10.3.14
subsidiaries qualifying 10.3.6
timetable and planning 10.3.17
trade, location of 10.4
Venture Capital Trusts (VCTs) *see* **Venture Capital Trusts (VCTs)**
ten-day announcement
applications 7.17.1
reverse takeovers 8.5.5
three-day announcement
applications 7.17.2
trade, location of
taxation regime 10.4
trading rules
after-market 11.6
AIM companies, information about 11.10
dealing announcements *see* **announcements**: dealing
information requirements 11.3

insider dealing *see* **insider dealing**
Integrated Monitoring and
    Surveillance System (IMAS)
    11.9.3
investors, relations with 11.7
liquidity 11.5
market practitioners, role
    brokers 11.4.1
    market makers 11.4.2
reporting 11.8
settlement 11.8
trading system 11.2
transactions
aggregation of 8.5.6
class tests 8.5.1
fundamental change of business,
    disposals resulting in 8.5.3
related party transactions 8.5.4
"relevant", and qualified executives
    3.6.1
reverse takeovers 8.5.5
    see also **Rule 14 (reverse takeovers)**
substantial 8.5.2
see also **continuing obligations**
Transparency Obligations Directive
    6.12
turnover
class tests 8.5.1

UK Listing Authority
admission documents, drafting 5.5.1
corporate governance 9.2.1
further share issues 8.6
Uncertificated Securities Regulations
    see **USRs (Uncertificated**
    Securities Regulations) 1995
underwriting agreement *see* **placing**
    agreement
use of funds test
taxation regime 10.3.2

USRs (Uncertificated Securities
    Regulations) 1995
and CRESTCo 13.3.1
and non-UK securities 13.3.2

Venture Capital Trusts (VCTs)
approval
    formal 10.5.1.4
    provisional 10.5.1.1–10.5.1.2
benefits for investors 10.2.3
formal approval 10.5.1.4
HM Revenue and Customs
    review, ongoing 10.5.1.5
    Venture Capital Schemes Manual
    10.2
investment
    company qualifying criteria
    10.2.5
    relief, eligibility for 10.2.4
provisional approval
    requirements 10.5.1.1
    timing 10.5.1.2
qualifying business activities 10.2.6
Revenue interpretations 10.2
use of funds test 10.3.2
verification
admission documents
    completion 5.5.4
    process 5.5.2
    relevance 5.5.3
application procedure 7.7

warranties
nominated adviser agreement
    3.7.12
working capital
application procedure 7.9.1
financial information 4.5
World Federation of Exchanges
and Designated Markets 12.5.1